# The Practice of Liberal Pluralism

*The Practice of Liberal Pluralism* defends the theory of liberal pluralism, a theory based on three core concepts – value pluralism, political pluralism, and expressive liberty – and explores the implications of this theory for politics.

Liberal pluralism helps clarify some of the complexities of real-world political action and points toward a distinctive conception of public philosophy and public policy. It leads to a vision of a good society in which political institutions are active in a delimited sphere and in which, within broad limits, families, civil associations, and faith communities may organize and conduct themselves in ways that are not congruent with principles that govern the public sphere.

Part I addresses the philosophical foundations of liberal pluralism. Part II extends the analysis of value pluralism to aspects of political behavior and moral motivation. Part III considers the practical aspects of liberal pluralism. Part IV defends liberal pluralism against attacks that it is internally incoherent or that it denies, without justification, key theological premises.

Written in a nontechnical style, this book will appeal to professionals in philosophy, political science, law, and policymaking.

William A. Galston is Saul Stern Professor at the School of Public Policy, University of Maryland.

# The Practice of Liberal Pluralism

WILLIAM A. GALSTON

*University of Maryland*

CAMBRIDGE
UNIVERSITY PRESS

PUBLISHED BY THE PRESS SYNDICATE OF THE UNIVERSITY OF CAMBRIDGE
The Pitt Building, Trumpington Street, Cambridge, United Kingdom

CAMBRIDGE UNIVERSITY PRESS
The Edinburgh Building, Cambridge CB2 2RU, UK
40 West 20th Street, New York, NY 10011-4211, USA
477 Williamstown Road, Port Melbourne, VIC 3207, Australia
Ruiz de Alarcón 13, 28014 Madrid, Spain
Dock House, The Waterfront, Cape Town 8001, South Africa

http://www.cambridge.org

First published 2005

Printed in the United States of America

*Typeface* ITC New Baskerville 10/13 pt.     *System* LATEX $2_\varepsilon$     [TB]

*A catalog record for this book is available from the British Library.*

*Library of Congress Cataloging in Publication Data*

Galston, William A. (William Arthur), 1946–
The practice of liberal pluralism / William A. Galston.
p.  cm.
Includes bibliographical references and index.
ISBN 0-521-84034-1 – ISBN 0-521-54963-9 (pbk.)
1. Liberalism.  2. Pluralism (Social sciences)  I. Title.
JC574.G372  2005
320.51′3–dc22      2004046567

ISBN 0 521 84034 1 hardback
ISBN 0 521 54963 9 paperback

*To Miriam, for more than I have ever said*

Most of the issues that mankind sets out to settle, it never does settle. They are not solved, because . . . they are incapable of solution properly speaking, being concerned with incommensurables.
— Learned Hand

# Contents

*Acknowledgments*                                              *page* ix

1   Introduction                                                      1

PART I   PHILOSOPHICAL FOUNDATIONS OF
LIBERAL PLURALISM

2   Value Pluralism and Its Critics                                  11

3   Political Pluralism and Limits on State Power                    23

4   Expressive Liberty and Constitutional Democracy:
    The Case of Freedom of Conscience                                45

PART II   LIBERAL PLURALISM AND PUBLIC ACTION

5   Value Pluralism and Political Means: Toughness as a
    Political Virtue                                                 75

6   Value Pluralism and Motivational Complexity: The Case
    of Cosmopolitan Altruism                                         95

PART III   POLITICS, MARKETS, AND CIVIC LIFE IN LIBERAL
PLURALIST SOCIETIES

7   The Public and Its Problems                                     117

8   The Effects of Modern Markets on Civic Life                     128

9   The Politics of Reciprocity: The Theory and Practice
    of Mutualism                                                    148

PART IV   DEFENDING LIBERAL PLURALISM

10   Liberal Pluralism and Liberal Egalitarianism                   173

vii

11  Liberal Pluralism Between Monism and Diversity          187
12  Conclusion: Liberal Pluralism at Home and Abroad        197

*Index*                                                     201

# Acknowledgments

This book took shape in part as a response to reactions to my previous book, *Liberal Pluralism* (Cambridge, 2002). In this connection, I want to extend my thanks to Stephen Macedo and Nicholas Wolterstorff for the searching remarks they offered at a panel on *Liberal Pluralism* convened at the Brookings Institution, sponsored by the Pew Forum on Religion and Public Life, and chaired by the indefatigable and multitalented E. J. Dionne, Jr. As well, I thank Dionne, Judge Richard Posner, Alan Ryan, and Robert Pippin for the equally searching (and memorably spirited) remarks they offered at an "author meets critics" panel organized by Peter Berkowitz at the 2002 Annual Meeting of the American Political Science Association.

For providing wonderful forums where previous versions of these materials were presented and discussed, I also want to thank: Nancy Rosenblum and Harvard's political theory colloquium; Robert George and Princeton's James Madison Center; Jacob Levy and the University of Chicago's political science department; Sandy Levinson and the University of Texas Law School; Robert Talisse and Vanderbilt University's philosophy department; and Gerard Bradley, John Finnis, and the University of Notre Dame's philosophy department.

As always, I want to thank my colleagues at the Institute for Philosophy and Public Policy at the University of Maryland for helping to refine my rough thoughts into something more nearly acceptable for public presentation.

Finally, I want to thank the anonymous reviewers for Cambridge University Press, and especially the passionate nay-sayer (you know who you are), for helping make this a much better book than it would otherwise have been. I owe a special debt to the Press's marvelously patient and level-headed Terence Moore, without whom there would have been no book at all.

Chapters 1, 2, 3, 4, 8, 10, 11, and 12 appear here in print for the first time. Earlier versions of the remaining chapters were published, as follows: Chapter 5 as "Toughness as a Political Virtue," *Social Theory and Practice* 17, 2 (1991): 175–97; Chapter 6 as "Cosmopolitan Altruism," *Social Philosophy and Policy* 10, 1 (1993): 118–34; Chapter 7 as "An American Public Philosophy for the Twenty-First Century: The Theory and Practice of Liberal Community," Monograph No. 2, "Toward a New Public Philosophy: A Global Reevaluation of Democracy at Century's End" Series, New York: Carnegie Council on Ethics and International Affairs, 1997; and Chapter 9 as "After Socialism: Mutualism and a Progressive Market Strategy," *Social Philosophy and Policy* 20, 2 (2003): 204–22. I am grateful to *Social Theory and Practice, Social Philosophy and Policy*, and the Carnegie Council for permission to make use of these materials.

# 1

# Introduction

We often use the phrase "liberal democracy," but we don't always think about it very carefully. The noun points to a particular *structure* of politics in which decisions are made, directly or indirectly, by the people as a whole, and more broadly, to an understanding of politics in which all legitimate power flows from the people. The adjective points to a particular understanding of the *scope* of politics, in which the domain of legitimate political decision-making is seen as inherently limited. Liberal governance acknowledges that important spheres of human life are wholly or partly outside the purview of political power. As such, it stands as a barrier against all forms of total power, including the power of democratic majorities.

The question then arises as to how are we to understand the nature and extent of limits on government. The signers of the Declaration of Independence appealed to the self-evidence of certain truths, among them the concept of individuals as bearers of rights that both orient and restrict governmental power. Today, individual rights represent an important (some would say dominant) part of our moral vocabulary. The question is whether they are sufficient to explain and justify the full range of constraints we wish to impose on the exercise of public power – for example, the limits on government's right to intervene in the internal affairs of civil associations and faith-based institutions.

In a recent book, *Liberal Pluralism*,[1] I argued that we must develop a more complex theory of the limits to government. In this endeavor, three key concepts are of special importance. The first is *political pluralism*, an understanding of social life that comprises multiple sources of authority – individuals, parents, civil associations, faith-based institutions, and the state, among others – no one of which is dominant in all spheres, for all purposes, on all occasions.

Political pluralism is a politics of recognition rather than of construction. It respects the diverse spheres of human association; it does not understand itself as creating or constituting those activities. For example, families are shaped by public law, but this does not mean that they are "socially constructed." There are complex relationships between public law and faith communities, but it is preposterous to claim that the public sphere constructs those communities, any more than environmental laws create air and water. Because so many types of human association possess an identity not derived from the state, pluralist politics does not presume that the inner structure and principles of every sphere must mirror those of basic political institutions. For example, in filling positions of religious authority, faith communities may use, without state interference, gender-based norms that would be forbidden in businesses and public accommodations.

The second key concept is *value pluralism*, made prominent by the late British philosopher Isaiah Berlin. This concept offers an account of the moral world we inhabit: While the distinction between good and bad is objective, there are multiple goods that differ qualitatively from one another and that cannot be ranked-ordered. If this is the case, there is no single way of life, based on a singular ordering of values, that is the highest and best for all individuals. This has important implications for politics. While states may legitimately act to prevent the great evils of human existence, they may not seek to force their citizens into one-size-fits-all patterns of desirable human lives. Any public policy that relies on, promotes, or commands a single conception of human good or excellence is presumptively illegitimate.

The third key concept in my account of limited government is *expressive liberty*. Simply put, this is a presumption in favor of individuals and groups leading their lives as they see fit, within the broad range of legitimate variation defined by value pluralism, in accordance with their own understandings of what gives life meaning and value. Expressive liberty may be understood as an extension of the free exercise of religion, generalized to cover comprehensive conceptions of human life that rest on non-religious as well as religious claims.

The concept of expressive liberty yields an understanding of politics as an instrumental rather than ultimate value. Politics is purposive (which is why the critical phrase "in order to" immediately follows "We the People"); we measure the value of political institutions and practices by the extent to which they help us attain the ends for which they were established. In a liberal pluralist regime, a key end is the creation of social space within which individuals and groups can freely pursue their distinctive visions of what gives meaning and worth to human existence. There is a presumption in favor of the free exercise of this kind of purposive activity, and a liberal pluralist state bears, and must discharge, a burden of proof whenever it seeks to restrict expressive liberty.

This standard for state action is demanding, but hardly impossible to meet. While expressive liberty is a very important good, it is not the only good, and it is not unlimited. In the first place, the social space within which differing visions of the good are pursued must be organized and sustained through the exercise of public power; to solve inevitable problems of coordination among divergent individuals and groups, the rules constituting this space will inevitably limit in some respects their ability to act as they see fit. Second, there are some core evils of the human condition that states have the right (indeed the duty) to prevent; to do this, they may rightly restrict the actions of individuals and groups. (According to the U.S. Supreme Court, religious groups have a right to practice animal sacrifice. Does anyone believe that it would be legitimate for them to practice human sacrifice, or that the state would act wrongly if it intervened in the sacrificial practices of a neo-Aztec cult?) Third, the state cannot sustain a free social space if its very existence is jeopardized by internal or external threats, and within limits it may do what is necessary to defend itself against destruction, even if measures clearly essential to self-defense restrict valuable liberties of individuals and groups. A free society is not a suicide pact.

Liberal pluralists, then, endorse the minimum conditions of public order, such as the rule of law and a public authority with the capacity to enforce it. They also endorse what may be called a "minimal universalism" – that is, the moral and practical necessity of organizing public life so as to ward off, to the greatest extent possible, the great evils of the human condition such as tyranny, genocide, cruelty and humiliation, mass starvation, and deadly epidemics. (I call the human condition characterized by the absence of the great evils as one of "basic decency.") This minimal universalism overlaps with contemporary movements for universal human rights and provision of basic needs.

Under modern conditions, a liberal pluralist regime is likely to be "constitutional" in that it will distinguish between ordinary policy and legislation, on the one hand, and basic, more entrenched structures of governance, on the other. A constitution, we may say, represents an authoritative partial ordering of public values. It selects a subset of values within the much broader range of goodness demarcated by value pluralism, and it brings that subset into the foreground. These preferred values then become benchmarks for shaping and assessing legislation, public policy, and much else. All acceptable constitutions must create the preconditions for public order and basic decency. Among the constitutions that satisfy these criteria, there is, within the pluralist understanding, no single ordering that is rationally preferable to all others – certainly not across differences of space, time, and culture, and arguably not even within a given situation.

So understood, liberal pluralist government is both limited and robust. In securing the cultural conditions of its survival and perpetuation, for example, it may legitimately engage in civic education, carefully restricted to the public essentials – the virtues and competences that citizens will need to fulfill diverse roles in a liberal pluralist economy, society, and polity. One thing above all is clear: Because the likely result of liberal pluralist institutions and practices will be a highly diverse society, the virtue of tolerance will be a core attribute of liberal pluralist citizenship. This type of tolerance does not mean wishy-washiness or the propensity to doubt one's own position, the sort of thing Robert Frost had in mind when he defined a liberal as someone who cannot take his own side in an argument. It does not imply, or require, an easy relativism about the human good; indeed, it is compatible with engaged moral criticism of those with whom one differs. Tolerance rightly understood means the principled refusal to use coercive state power to impose one's views on others, and therefore a commitment to moral competition through recruitment and persuasion alone.

Liberal pluralism is (in the terms John Rawls made familiar) a "comprehensive" rather than a "political" theory. It makes sense to connect what one believes to be the best account of public life with comparably persuasive accounts of morality, human psychology, and the natural world. As a practical matter, of course, it makes sense to seek overlapping consensus. Politics as we know it would come to a halt if cooperation required agreement, not only on conclusions, but on premises as well. But philosophical argument, even concerning politics, need not mirror the structure of public life. A political philosopher may assert that X is true, and foundational for a particular understanding of a good, decent, or just society, without demanding that all citizens affirm the truth of X. Indeed, the founders of a political regime may publicly proclaim what they take to be moral, metaphysical, or religious truths as the basis of that regime without insisting that all citizens assent to those truths. In the United States, naturalizing citizens affirm their loyalty to the Constitution, not to the Declaration of Independence, and all citizens pledge allegiance to the republic for which the flag stands, not to Locke or Hutcheson. So I disagree with Martha Nussbaum when she suggests that making public claims about foundational truths somehow signals disrespect for those who dissent.[2] Disrespect requires something more–namely, the use of coercive state power to silence and repress dissenters. Respect requires not parsimony in declaring truth but rather restraint in the exercise of power. By limiting the scope of legitimate public power, liberal pluralism does all that is necessary to secure the theoretical and institutional bases of respect.

These, then, are the basics of the thesis I advanced in *Liberal Pluralism*. Since then, critics have helped me see that in two important respects I failed to take the argument far enough. First, while I appealed to everyday experience to support the principles of political pluralism, value pluralism, and expressive liberty, I did not offer an adequate philosophical justification. Second, I did not sufficiently explore the practical implications of liberal pluralism for key aspects of public action and public life.

This book seeks to fill these gaps. Part I addresses the philosophical foundations of liberal pluralism. Chapters 2, 3, and 4 explore, seriatim, the key concepts of value pluralism, political pluralism, and expressive liberty. In Part II (Chapters 5 and 6), I extend the analysis of value pluralism to aspects of political behavior and moral motivation.

Part III tacks toward practice. Chapter 7 links philosophy and public life via the idea of "public philosophy" rooted in specific cultural and historical circumstances. Chapters 8 and 9 outline the elements of a liberal pluralist public philosophy that responds to these circumstances, focusing on modern markets and economic life.

In Part IV, I assemble and respond to what I consider the most important criticisms to date of *Liberal Pluralism*. To be sure, these are early returns, with many precincts yet to report. Nonetheless, these criticisms convey a vivid and rounded sense of the kinds of qualms that my account of liberal democracy is likely to raise, and replying to them even at this juncture advances the debate. Chapter 10 responds to theorists who have criticized liberal pluralism as insufficiently egalitarian, while Chapter 11 addresses a more diverse set of objections. The concluding Chapter 12 briefly explores the application of liberal pluralism to international laws and regimes.

I conclude this Introduction with four observations on method. First, the materials I use to build my case are heterogeneous, to say the least. Philosophical argument, constitutional law, cultural and economic history, institutional analysis, empirical social science – all of these make more than cameo appearances. Some critics regard this eclecticism as a sign of imprecision, even incoherence. It must be obvious already that I disagree. Methods of inquiry must suit objects of inquiry. I have the highest regard for sustained philosophical reasoning, but often it is not enough to get us where we want to go. For those seeking to craft a three-dimensional account of the basic structures of public life, a diversity of materials is essential.

To pick just one example: To understand what is at stake in the tension between the pursuit of broad public goals and respect for the expressive liberty of individuals and groups, actual cases and controversies are far more illuminating than philosophers' armchair examples. That is why my defense of expressive liberty draws so heavily on U.S. constitutional cases and history.

Second, the adjudication of philosophical disputes often rests on human experience as well as on the logic of argument. So, for example, my defense of value pluralism as the most adequate account of the moral universe we happen to inhabit proceeds, in part, by addressing the best arguments of its critics. If I am right, their objections leave the core of value pluralism unscathed. But the affirmative case for value pluralism flows from our encounter with the world, not with philosophers. As Isaiah Berlin memorably puts it:

[I]f we are not armed with an *a priori* guarantee of the proposition that a total harmony of true values is somewhere to be found...we must fall back on the ordinary resources of empirical observation and ordinary human knowledge. And these certainly give us no warrant for supposing...that all good things, or all bad things for that matter, are reconcilable with each other. The world that we encounter in ordinary experience is one in which we are faced with choices between ends equally ultimate, and claims equally absolute, the realization of some of which must inevitably involve the sacrifice of others.[3]

Readers must decide for themselves whether the world of conflict Berlin describes – not just between good and bad, but also between good and good (in many ways the harder case) – is congruent with their own experience. My point is only that in moral and political matters, human experience is the ultimate benchmark.

I do not mean "raw" experience, of course, and I do not presuppose that all human beings will share the same experiences or draw the same inferences from them. I have concluded, however, that what might be called the "center of gravity" of human experience points to two broad conclusions: First, that as species beings of a certain kind we are structured to experience certain phenomena as great evils to be avoided at virtually all cost; and second, that as free beings endowed with imagination as well as reason, different individuals will pursue a vast diversity of ends, each of which is rightly regarded as legitimate in itself, but which are not compossible in the aggregate. It is the burden of this book to suggest that these propositions are not devoid of implications for public life.

Third, the road from the general premises of political philosophy to concrete conclusions about regimes and institutions is paved with more than logical deductions. In constructing this road, political philosophy necessarily makes use of materials quarried from multiple sources of knowledge – for example, a psychology that helps define the extent to which stable political arrangements can require devotion to the common good at the expense of self-interest. So I make no apology for drawing from psychological studies (among many others) to frame conclusions about institutions and policies that give life to the theory of liberal pluralism. If I am right about how political philosophy must proceed, then I am simply being explicit about the debts that every venture into this discipline implicitly or avowedly incurs.

This brings me to my concluding point. I have devoted much of my scholarly life to political philosophy, but I am not, and would never claim to be, a professional moral philosopher. While the inner logic of the questions that most concern me in political philosophy from time to time leads me across the border into moral philosophy, I am always a tourist, at best.

Nonetheless, because critics have raised questions about the relationship between positions I espouse and some central questions of modern moral philosophy, it may clarify matters to state that value pluralism as I understand it commits me to what Brad Hooker labels "Rossian generalism" and John Rawls calls "intuitionism" rather to the full-blown thesis of moral particularism. There are certain considerations whose moral valence is invariant – that always count as reasons for or against a course of action – but there are no fully general rules for weighting or rank-ordering the multiple considerations that bear on the choice-worthiness of that option.[4] My position is Rossian in the additional sense that some considerations establish strong presumptions in favor of particular choices (Ross calls them *prima facie* duties) such that only powerful reasons, outside the normal course of events, will suffice to rebut these presumptions.

Ordinary morality is not a set of universal rules, valid in all circumstances, but it is better to begin by assuming that we need to make a special effort to justify departures from what is ordinarily, and for the most part, the good or right thing to do. Within the political sphere, this moral orientation leaves space for the kinds of unpleasant actions that the exigencies of emergencies sometimes require – without placing political leaders outside the realm of normal moral restraints.

## Notes

1.  William A. Galston, *Liberal Pluralism: The Implications of Value Pluralism for Political Theory and Practice* (New York: Cambridge University Press, 2002).
2.  Martha Nussbaum, "Political Objectivity," *New Literary History* 32, 4 (2001): 883–906.
3.  Isaiah Berlin, *Four Essays on Liberty* (Oxford: Oxford University Press, 1969), pp. 170–1.
4.  See Brad Hooker, "Moral Particularism: Wrong and Bad," in *Moral Particularism*, Brad Hooker and Margaret Olivia Little, eds. (Oxford: Clarendon, 2000), pp. 1–6. The entire volume should be consulted for its relentlessly exhaustive (and exhausting) exploration of these issues.

PART I

# PHILOSOPHICAL FOUNDATIONS OF LIBERAL PLURALISM

# 2

# Value Pluralism and Its Critics

In *Liberal Pluralism*, taking Isaiah Berlin as my point of departure, I offered an extensive description of value pluralism but a parsimonious defense. I suggested that ordinary moral experience is consistent with value pluralism and that proposed alternatives to pluralism encounter serious difficulties. I argued that utilitarianism (the most prominent form of modern monism) is insensitive, not only to the separateness of persons, but also to the heterogeneity of goods. In this chapter, I reverse the emphasis of *Liberal Pluralism*. I provide a summary description of value pluralism and then defend it at some length by considering a range of philosophically significant objections that have been raised in recent years.

## 1 VALUE PLURALISM: A SUMMARY DESCRIPTION

Following Charles Larmore and others, I distinguish value pluralism from various forms of nonpluralist accounts of morality. A theory is nonpluralist, I say, if it either (a) reduces goods to a single measure of value or (b) creates a comprehensive hierarchy or ordering among goods. (Theories that do [a] are usually called monistic.) A moral theory is pluralistic if it does neither (a) nor (b).

Value pluralism is not relativism. The distinction between good and bad, or between good and evil, is objective and rationally defensible.

According to value pluralism, objective goods cannot be fully rank-ordered. There is no common measure of value for all goods, which are qualitatively heterogeneous. There is no *summum bonum* that is the chief good for all individuals. There are no comprehensive "lexical orderings" among types of goods. And there is no "first virtue of social institutions," but, rather, a range of public values the relative importance of which will depend on particular circumstances.

Some objective goods are basic in the sense that they form part of any choiceworthy conception of a human life. To be deprived of such goods is to be forced to endure the great evils of human existence. All decent regimes endeavor to minimize the frequency and scope of such deprivations.

Beyond this (parsimonious) list of basic goods, there is a wide range of legitimate diversity – of individual conceptions of good lives, and also of public cultures and purposes. This wide range of legitimate variation defines the zone of individual liberty, and also of deliberation and decision-making. Where necessity (natural or moral) ends, choice begins.

Observe that in the account just offered, nonpluralism and pluralism are rival forms of moral realism. Both presuppose the existence of moral realm that is in some sense "there," apart from our emotional projections and cultural constructions. Each purports to describe the actual structure of that realm. It is therefore correct to argue, as Glen Newey does, that the debate between pluralism and nonpluralism does not reach the broader disputes between realism and its critics. It is also correct to argue that the "rational interminability" of many disputes over value does not provide convincing evidence in favor of pluralism, because interminability could also result from, for example, a Humean understanding of moral propositions as not allowing truth-like modes of assessment.[1]

## 2   ISSUE ONE: COMPARISONS AND COMPARABILITY

The core idea of value pluralism – heterogeneous goods without a common measure of value – has sparked a complex technical debate. It is now conventional to distinguish between two possible interpretations of the core idea – *incommensurability* and *incomparability*. Incommensurability means the absence of any single scale of units of value along which items can be precisely measured. It rules out cardinal rankings among items as well as their straightforward aggregation, and therefore forms of valuation (cost/benefit analysis, utilitarianism, and consequentialist maximizing) that rely on cardinal measures. Incomparability is a broader notion that rules out ordinal rankings as well. Options A and B are incomparable if we cannot say that A is better than B, worse than B, or just as valuable as B (on whatever interpretation of value is at work). Incommensurability does not imply incomparability. Ordinal rankings may well be possible even when cardinal measures do not exist.[2] Incommensurability need not create obstacles to deliberation and choice; incomparability may well do so.

Ruth Chang argues that all comparisons (and therefore all judgments of comparability and incomparability) must proceed with respect to a "covering value." Some values – kindness, cruelty, courage, endurance – are specific enough to serve as covering values. By contrast, "generic relationships" (better than, worse than, as good or valuable as) require some further specification: A is better than B with respect to V. These structures suggest than comparisons can fail in two different ways. (1) While a covering value V' that applies to both A and B may exist, it is not possible to say that A is better than, worse than, or as good as B with respect to V'. In cases of this sort, A and B are said to be incomparable. (2) Given A and B, it is not possible to identify a covering value that (i) captures what is at stake in the comparison in a manner that does not distort A or B, and (ii) passes the specificity test. In cases of this sort, A and B are said to be noncomparable.[3]

Chang and others may be right to question the possibility, or coherence, of assertions of incomparability. But when pluralists talk about the heterogeneity of values, what they mostly have in mind is the second kind of case – namely, noncomparability. We are, pluralists believe, often called upon to deliberate and choose in circumstances in which it is not possible to specify a covering value that meets the appropriate conditions.

This failure can occur in three different ways. First, the proposed covering value may admit of varying specifications, and no specification can be judged preferable to the others. This sort of impasse often arises during efforts to fill job openings. While all members of the hiring committee are broadly committed to finding a first-rate grants administrator (or moral philosopher), they may disagree as to the appropriate specification of that general covering value. Even when they can agree on the list of specific virtues and skills that constitute excellence within a given domain, they may continue to disagree as to their relative weight and priority. And there may be no neutral way of resolving the dispute. The choice among the candidates for position X is equivalent to the choice among competing specifications of the good X, and vice versa.

Second, the proposed covering value may on its face fail the specificity test. For example, Donald Regan argues against value pluralism on the grounds that there is one and only one value that ultimately matters to practical reason – namely, G. E. Moore's unanalyzable, nonnatural "good." A belief in Moorean good, he argues, "is the only view that really allows us to make sense of deliberation and choice."[4] But it is hard to see how good, so understand, offers any practical guidance for deliberation. Regan's own argument makes this clear: Insofar as goodness guides choice, he concludes, it consists in "to-be-promotedness."[5] But this seems like a summary judgment of the outcome of deliberation rather than a guide to its conduct. If our task is to choose between A and B, it hardly helps to be told that we are to determine which comports better with to-be-promotedness. We already knew that; we want to know what we ought to promote, what are the features of the alternatives that rank higher than others.

Third, there may be an unresolvable dispute as to the nature of the covering value. Chang asserts that "every choice situation is governed by some value," a "choice value" that establishes what matters in the particular situation.[6] But many practical disputes resolve around competing accounts of what matters, or matters most, and there is no guarantee that there is a neutral standpoint from which the dispute can be adjudicated. To be sure, deliberation may help us discard some accounts as clearly dominated by others, but when deliberation hits a wall, we may still be left with multiple possibilities. (Decision-procedures such as voting rules are designed in part to address this kind of impasse.)

Chang suggests that the appearance of unresolvable disputes among proposed covering values may be illusory. She asks us to consider a case involving the best use of a Christmas bonus: either donate the money to feed starving children or invest the funds in your retirement account. The donation has great moral merit, and the investment option has great prudential merit. We can say which option is better with respect to morality and which to prudence, but there doesn't seem to be any way to say which is better with respect to both, considered together; that is, there seems to be no covering value that comprises both. And yet we can often reach what seem to be compelling practical judgments in such compound cases, as when we act to save a drowning child at minimal risk and inconvenience to ourselves. Such cases, Chang concludes, prove that there must be a (nameless) covering value in terms of which such comparisons proceed, one that has both other-regarding and self-regarding values as components.[7]

Perhaps so. But choice situations with this structure admit of a different interpretation. Consider a stylized but not wholly unrealistic case. A small town in Oregon is home to a sawmill employing 500 residents. The mill is the economic and social hub of the community. (Indeed, if the mill were to go out of business, the town might well disappear.)

The town is also home to a rare species of bird (found nowhere else) whose existence the continued operation of the mill places in serious jeopardy.

No doubt there are some individuals who are indifferent to the continued existence of the birds, and others who cannot see the good of a mode of production that they believe inflicts unacceptable damage on the environment. For the purposes of this argument, however, let us stipulate that both the livelihood of the townspeople and the existence of the birds are genuine goods and that it is hard to specify a common unit of value that captures without undue distortion the distinctive good of each. Most individuals who accept both of these goods as genuine would agree that the quantitative trade-offs between them matter. It's one thing if the birds could be saved at the cost of a handful of jobs, quite another if saving the birds means reducing employment at the mill by (say) 90 percent. (This is not to say that everyone would agree to the same trade-off curve.) We are intuitively comparing overall states of affairs comprising heterogeneous goods, and we are rendering an all-things-considered judgment.

Does this mean, as Chang argues, that there must be some single underlying covering value in light of which this comparison proceeds? Not necessarily. I would argue that when we agree that X and Y are qualitatively distinct but genuine goods, we also agree that each defines a dimension that varies quantitatively in respect of the particular good. Based on shared human experience, we make qualitative judgments regarding the various quantitative measures in particular choice situations. So, for example, we judge a gain or loss of value along a particular dimension as significant, moderate, or trivial. When we are comparing qualitatively different goods, no one of which enjoys lexical priority or imperative force relative to the rest, we employ rough-and-ready decision rules as presumptions. A significant gain along dimension X presumptively outweighs a trivial loss along Y, unless we can adduce a compelling consideration to the contrary. As we move down dimension X and up Y, the choice becomes more and more difficult. At some point, it may become indeterminate. But at no point do we invoke, or presuppose, a nameless compound covering value that constitutes a single dimension of variation.

Regan raises an objection in much the same spirit as Chang's. "It seems to be widely acknowledged," he states, that we can "often compare great values of one type against relatively slight values of another type." But the concession that intertype comparisons are sometimes possible "seems . . . to give away a great deal, and indeed to make it unclear why they should ever not be possible."[8]

I confess that I do not see why this is so. If I am asked whether Socrates or Michelangelo was the greater human being, I will not know what to say. But surely I can say that Socrates was greater than some obscure watercolorist. I may not be able to discern which of two peaks shrouded in clouds towers above the other, but I can distinguish a mountain from a molehill. These are the kinds of judgments human beings make every day without a homogeneous scale of values to guide them. And if a theory says that we cannot make such judgments . . . so much the worse for the theory. One does not have to be a dyed-in-the-wool Aristotelian to believe that there is, in moral matters anyway, a presumption in favor of "saving the phenomena."

### 3 ISSUE TWO: CONFLICTS AMONG VALUES

Let me now address the issue, central to Berlinian value pluralism, of conflicts among values. It is fair to say that everyone experiences what on the surface appear to be conflicts among goods we cherish and pursue. For example, most choices we regard as difficult seem to present such conflicts. The question is whether the most plausible description of these conflicts will sustain our first impression, or rather offer a better account of what was only a misleading appearance.

Newey argues that the challenge for the pluralist "is to show that a monistic explanation of the conflict cannot be right."[9] I disagree. Moral monism is not the default position, and pluralists should not bear an asymmetrical burden of proof. Rather, we should begin with moral experience, and look for the best available account of this experience. I very much doubt that pluralists will ever be able to show that monists "cannot" be right, or vice versa. A lower standard – locating the preponderance of evidence and argument – is the most that either side can hope to meet.

I follow Berlin's account of pluralism in asserting that values are not only heterogeneous but also inharmonious. Both personal and political life regularly confront us with situations in which every option entails a sacrifice of genuine good. Ronald Dworkin challenges this view. While he does not go so far as to reduce all goods to a single measure of value, he questions the nonharmony thesis. There is no moral problem if good and bad conflict. The purported difficulty stems from the conflict among goods. Even if X, abstractly conceived, is a good, more X may not be better than less X. In particular, Dworkin insists, liberty and equality do not conflict in the manner that Berlin suggests, because more liberty (understood as the capacity to act without external impediments) is not necessarily preferable to less liberty, so understood. When we move from this understanding of liberty to a more plausible conception that preserves its standing as an affirmative value, we observe that liberty shouldn't be understood as the freedom to do whatever we want, but rather the freedom to act as long as we respect the rights, properly understood, of others. While it is clear that equality conflicts with Berlin's conception of negative liberty, it is not evident that it conflicts with Dworkin's conception.[10]

Dworkin makes a strong case for two propositions: First, as a general matter, values must pass a goodness test; Berlinian value-conflict cannot arise unless the competing dimensions of value are all instances of the good. And second, Berlin's account of liberty does not pass that test. But to grant these propositions is not to clinch a general case against value pluralism. While it may make sense, as Dworkin suggests, to work toward "integrity" among key moral concepts, and therefore to prefer conceptions of our values that do not conflict, there is no guarantee that the nonconflicting conceptions will match our considered judgments concerning the goods at stake. If not, as Dworkin says, "we would have to concede conflict."[11]

Dworkin stacks the deck, however, by characterizing political conflict in a way that seems designed to minimize value conflict. Consider Abraham on Mount Moriah, caught between what he regarded is the indubitable command of the sovereign God and the patent immorality of the sacrifice God required. If these competing demands are independent of one another and authoritative, then Abraham could not avoid a tragic choice with an awful consequence. But Dworkin insists that politics is not like that. In disputes over, for example, codes prohibiting racist speech, "we are not beholden to two independent sovereign powers... On the contrary, we are drawn to each of the rival positions through arguments that, if we were finally to accept them as authoritative, would release us from the appeal of the other one."[12]

This begs the question. As Charles Taylor points out, Berlin's nonharmony thesis supposes that I do in fact see the competing goods "as in some way imposing themselves, as binding on me, or making a claim on me. Otherwise the conflict could be easily set aside."[13] The question is whether moral experience and reflection support this supposition. I think they do. The dispute over hate-speech codes involves multiple considerations that reflect different dimensions of value. Even if we reach an all-things-considered judgment that endorses one side of the argument, it may well be the case that we will set aside something of genuine value. Simply put, the rightness of the right answer (assuming there is one) offers no guarantee that all the goods at stake are located within that answer, and our ordinary experience suggests the contrary. When questions are "hard," it is because we cannot find a solution that combines all the values at stake in a single course of action. In these circumstances, which are not rare, we are not "released" from the appeal of the other side. Indeed, I would suggest, it is a sign of moral awareness and maturity to keep the genuine worth of the options we have rejected firmly in view. The alternative is an oversimplified view that breeds moral hubris.

Regret is a moral emotion that attends the experience of moral conflict. Michael Stocker discusses a category of conflicts arising from situations in which it is tolerably clear what must be done, but doing it nonetheless requires us to reject an alternative that is in key respects preferable. In *Nicomachean Ethics* III.1, for example, Aristotle brings up the case of a man's having to do something ignoble to save his family from a tyrant. If he rescues his family, he gives up his honor; if he saves his honor, he sacrifices his family. Even if he "clearly sees that he must save his family, . . . he can regret the loss of his honor." Indeed, this loss is regrettable "even if losing it is entirely justified, perhaps obligatory."[14] Elsewhere, Stocker suggests that regret is irrational if the conflict simply involves different quantities of a single homogeneous good. If the issue is more or less, we are to choose the greater; full stop.[15]

It is open to the monist, of course, to argue that the apparently heterogeneous phenomena can, after all, be reduced to a common measure. He then bears the burden of proposing and defending a single dimension of value that can do the job. Assume *arguendo* that he does so. The monist then faces a choice. He may argue that the existence of the single dimension means that regret is irrational, based on an illusion, to be set aside as far as is psychologically possible. Alternatively, he may argue that monism is consistent with rational regret. In this vein, Newey suggests that monists can save the phenomena of practical conflict.[16] I confess that I do not see how. The more straightforward view seems more plausible: If regret is a rational moral emotion, it is because the clash of plural values evokes it. Conversely, if monism is correct, regret is unreasonable. The need to erase rather than save the phenomenon of regret increases the monist's (already substantial) burden of proof, and adds weight to the case for pluralism.

### 4 ISSUE THREE: CONSTITUTIVE NORMS

A leading pluralist, Joseph Raz, argues that the nature of certain goods, rightly understood, offers an important argument in favor of the radical heterogeneity among goods. Consider friendship, undoubtedly an important human good. As Ruth Chang summarizes Raz's thesis, "It is a conceptual truth that friends judge that friendships are incomparable with cash. Judging that they are incomparable is part of what it is to be a friend."[17]

Chang regards this as a "curious argument." Suppose I am faced with a choice between friendship and a dollar: "If I judge that the friendship is worth more than a dollar,"she wonders, "have I thereby lost all my friends?"[18] This rhetorical question trades on the ambiguity of "worth more." On one construal of the phrase, the problem is that the bid isn't high enough: If someone had offered me a million dollars, I would have sacrificed the friendship for material gain. It does not seem at all curious to conclude, as Raz does, that one's willingness to sacrifice a friend for any amount of money is incompatible with the relationship of friendship, rightly understood. To be a friend is to believe that money and friendship do not occupy the same scale of values. Likewise, to be a loyal citizen is to reject the possibility that one could betray one's country for money, however large the bribe. These examples remind us of the famous story of George Bernard Shaw at the dinner party. Seated next to a rather stuffy woman, he turned toward her and asked, "Madam, will you sleep with me for a million pounds?" Reportedly she colored prettily and replied, "Why yes, Mr. Shaw." After a pregnant pause Shaw then asked her, "Will you sleep with me for fifty pounds?" She drew herself up and responded, huffily, "Mr. Shaw, what do you take me for?" To which Shaw responded: "We've already established that, madam. Now we're just haggling about the price."

In another sense of the phrase "worth more," however, Chang is quite right. The point is not only that preferring some amount of money to one's friend is incompatible with friendship; it is also a moral error, because it is to mistake what is in fact the inferior good for the greater. So it is wrong to suggest that friendship and money are somehow incomparable. In fact, an "asymmetry in merit" divides them. Chang traces this asymmetry, plausibly enough, to the fact that friendship is mainly an intrinsic good and money, an instrumental good. In some sense, we judge the intrinsic good to be more valuable or of a higher status than the instrumental good. Trading an intrinsic good for any amount of an instrumental good sullies the former (though not the latter).[19]

To some extent, this is a story about moral motivation, not just moral goods. To see this, add a layer of complexity to the story. Suppose you are a dissident in a repressive regime. Knowing that you need money to purchase lifesaving drugs for your desperately ill child, the authorities offer you a substantial bribe to betray your friend, a fellow dissident. It is one thing to seek the money out of greed, quite another to accept it in the name of saving one's child. In the latter case, we are faced with a clash between two high-level intrinsic goods. It is not clear that the willingness to betray one's friend to save one's child is incompatible with the generic capacity for friendship, or even with that particular relation of friendship. (It is a more difficult question as to whether the willingness to sacrifice one's child to keep faith with a friendship is compatible with the constitutive norms of parenthood.)

## 5 ISSUE FOUR: DECIDING AMONG PLURALIST ALTERNATIVES

The pluralist account of morality draws a broad-brush line between good and bad but often leaves a number of goods among which there are no clear and compelling grounds to choose. As Raz puts it, "In typical situations, reason does not determine what is to be done. Rather, it sets a range of options before agents . . . [It is then] our will [that] leads us to do one thing rather than another . . . will plays a role in human agency separate from that of reason."[20]

Raz's concept of the will is somewhat mysterious (some have called it quasi-existentialist) because it is not clear on his account what determines the direction of the will. Raz denies that wants are reasons for action: "Rather, our wants become relevant when reasons have run their course."[21] On this point, at least, the antipluralist Don Regan seems to have a more plausible case. He argues that (to take Raz's own example) if I am offered a pear or a banana, and choose the banana because I would enjoy it more, then the prospect of an more enjoyable experience would be "a reason, in the fullest sense" for choosing the banana.[22] So while we cannot say that want-satisfaction is a reason for action *simpliciter*, it can be a reason for action when there are no compelling moral objections to the action that ranks higher along the dimension of want-satisfaction. More broadly: Pluralism gives us agent-neutral reasons for discarding certain options, and then allows agent-relative reasons (including want-satisfaction) to influence the choice among the options that remain.

Put another way, pluralism helps define the set of generically eligible values, and in particular situations, the set of options consistent with these values. An eligible value becomes a value for me when I endorse it as my own. My endorsement may reflect facts about me that I did not choose and cannot alter – features of my distinctive perceptual apparatus, psychology, or sensorium, for example. Or the endorsement may reflect features of my distinctive social and cultural context. A political culture, we may say, represents a distinctive selection among, or weighting of, eligible public values. Growing up as a member of a particular community, I am led (perhaps insensibly) to take these values on as aspects of my own personality and to draw on them in decision-making situations where they are relevant.

In interpersonal choice situations, an endorsed eligible option has greater weight than a nonendorsed eligible option. The bare fact that someone might have endorsed C rather than A or B is trumped by the fact that no decision-making agent has in fact done so. Endorsement winnows down the eligible set to options that are "live" in that specific context.

## 6 CONCLUSION

During the past generation, moral philosophers have added precision to the theory of value pluralism that Isaiah Berlin advanced with such passion and panache, and they have raised a number of objections that have forced the proponents of value pluralism to sharpen their defense. In this chapter, I have reviewed and responded to the criticisms that seem to cut deepest. My conclusion is that none of them forces the value pluralist to surrender his post. It is always possible, of course, that someone will produce a better (even fatal) criticism. For the most part, moral philosophy is a matter of establishing plausibility rather than offering proof. As Aristotle famously reminds us in *Nicomachean Ethics* I.3, the same precision is not to be expected of every sector of inquiry or discourse: "It is equally unreasonable to accept merely probably conclusions from a mathematician and to demand strict demonstration from an orator."

Notes

1. Glen Newey, "Value-Pluralism in Contemporary Liberalism," *Dialogue* XXXVII (1998): 498–9.
2. Ruth Chang, "Introduction," *Incommensurability, Incomparability, and Practical Reason* in Chang, ed. (Cambridge, MA: Harvard University Press, 1997), pp. 1–2.
3. Chang, "Introduction," pp. 5–6, 27–9.
4. Donald Regan, "Value, Comparability, and Choice," in *Incommensurability, Incomparability, and Practical Reason*, Chang ed. (Cambridge, MA: Harvard University Press, 1997), pp. 129, 131.
5. Regan, "Value, Comparability, and Choice," p. 142.
6. Chang, "Introduction," p. 7.
7. Chang, "Introduction," pp. 32–3.
8. Regan, "Value, Comparability, and Choice," p. 135.
9. Newey, "Contemporary Liberalism," p. 502.
10. Ronald Dworkin, "Do Liberal Values Conflict?" *The Legacy of Isaiah Berlin*, in Mark Lilla, Ronald Dworkin, and Robert Silvers, eds. (New York: New York Review of Books, 2001), pp. 73–90.
11. Dworkin, "Do Liberal Values Conflict?" p. 127.
12. Dworkin, "Do Liberal Values Conflict?" p. 82.
13. Charles Taylor, "Plurality of Goods," in *The Legacy of Isaiah Berlin* in Lilla, Dworkin, and Silvers, eds. (New York: New York Review of Books, 2001), p. 113.
14. Michael Stocker, "Abstract and Concrete Value: Plurality, Conflict, and Maximization," in *Incommensurability, Incomparability, and Practical Reason*, Chang, ed., (Cambridge, MA: Harvard University Press, 1997), pp. 198–200.
15. Discussed in Newey, "Contemporary Liberalism," pp. 501, 503.
16. Newey, "Contemporary Liberalism," p. 504.
17. Chang, "Introduction," p. 19.
18. Chang, "Introduction," p. 19.
19. Chang, "Introduction," p. 19–20.
20. Raz, "Incommensurability and Agency," in *Incommensurability, Incomparability, and Practical Reason*, Chang, ed. (Cambridge, MA: Harvard University Press, 1997), p. 127.
21. Raz, "Incommensurability and Agency," p. 125.
22. Regan, "Value, Comparability, and Choice," p. 145.

# 3

## Political Pluralism and Limits on State Power

### 1 LIBERAL DEMOCRACY AND CIVIL ASSOCIATION

A liberal democracy is (among other things) an invitation to struggle over the control of civil associations. State/society debates have recurred over the past century of U.S. history, frequently generating landmark Supreme Court cases. While the specific issues vary, the general form is the same. On one side are general public principles that the state seeks to enforce; on the other are specific beliefs and practices that the association seeks to protect. *Boy Scouts of America v. Dale*[1] is the latest chapter in what will no doubt be a continuing saga.

Within the U.S. constitutional context, these issues are often debated in terms such as free exercise of religion, freedom of association, or the individual liberty broadly protected under the Fourteenth Amendment to the U.S. Constitution. Rich and illuminating as it is, this constitutional discourse does not go deep enough. It is necessary to reconsider the understanding of politics that pervades much contemporary discussion, especially among political theorists, an understanding that tacitly views public institutions as plenipotentiary and civil society as a political construction possessing only those liberties that the polity chooses to grant and modify or revoke at will. This understanding of politics makes it all but impossible to give serious weight to the "liberal" dimension of liberal democracy.

The most useful point of departure for the reconsideration of politics I am urging is found in the writings of the British political pluralists and thinkers working in the Calvinist tradition.[2] This pluralist movement began to take shape in the nineteenth century as a reaction to the growing tendency to see state institutions as plenipotentiary. This tendency took various practical forms in different countries: French anticlerical republicanism; British parliamentary supremacy; the drive for national unification in Germany and Italy against subordinate political and social powers. Following Stephen Macedo (though disagreeing with him in other respects), I shall call this idea of the plenipotentiary state "civic totalism."[3]

Historically, one can discern at least three distinct secular–theoretical arguments for civic totalism. (Theological arguments, which raise a different set of issues, are beyond the scope of these comments.) The first is the idea, traced back to Aristotle, that politics enjoys general authority over subordinate activities and institutions because it aims at the highest and most comprehensive good for human beings. The *Politics* virtually begins with the proposition that "all partnerships aim at some good, and . . . the partnership that is most authoritative of all and embraces all the others does so particularly, and aims at the most authoritative good of all. That is what is called . . . the political partnership" (*Politics* I.1. 1252a3–6). (For our present purposes, whether this statement is an adequate representation of Aristotle's full view is a matter we may set aside.)

Hobbes offered a second kind of justification for civic totalism: Any less robust form of politics would in practice countenance divided sovereignty – the dreaded *imperium in imperio,* an open invitation to civic conflict and war. Sovereignty cannot be divided, even between civil and spiritual authorities (*Leviathan,* "Of Commonwealth," ch. 29). In Hobbes's view, undivided sovereign authority has unlimited power to decide whether, and under what conditions, individuals and associations would enjoy liberty of action. No entity, individual or collective, can assert rights against the public authority. Indeed, civil law may rightfully prohibit even the teaching of truth, if it is contrary to the requirements of civil peace (*Leviathan,* "Of the Kingdom of Darkness," ch. 46; cf. "Of Commonwealth," ch. 17).

A third argument for civic totalism was inspired by Rousseau: Civic health and morality cannot be achieved without citizens' wholehearted devotion to the common good. Loyalties divided between the republic and other ties, whether to civil associations or to revealed religious truth, are bound to dilute civic spirit. And the liberal appeal to private life as against public life will only legitimate selfishness at the expense of the spirit of contribution and sacrifice without which the polity cannot endure. Representing this tradition, Emile Combes, a premier in the French Third Republic, declared that "There are, there can be no rights except the right of the State, and there [is], and there can be no other authority than the authority of the Republic."[4]

I do not wish to suggest that these three traditions converge on precisely the same account of civic totalism. A chasm divides Hobbes and Rousseau from Aristotle. To oversimplify drastically: Greek religion was civil, offering support for the institutions of the polis. The postclassical rise of revealed religion – especially Christianity – ruptured the unity of the political order. Much Renaissance and early modern theory sought to overcome this diremption and restore the unity of public authority. Hobbes and Rousseau wrote in this "theological–political" tradition and tried in different ways to subordinate religious claims to the sovereignty of politics.

For this reason, among others, Hobbes and Rousseau were less willing than was Aristotle to acknowledge the independent and legitimate existence of intermediate associations. They were drawn instead to a doctrine, originating in Roman law and transmitted to modernity through Jean Bodin among others, according to which intermediate associations existed solely as revocable "concessions" of power from the sovereign political authority. Individuals possessed no inherent right of association, and associations enjoyed no rights other than those politically defined and granted. In short, intermediate associations were political constructions, to be tolerated only to the extent that they served the interests of the state. This Roman-law stance may be contrasted with the view of early Calvinists that a civil association required no special fiat from the state for its existence. As Frederick Carney puts it, "Its own purposes, both natural and volitional, constitute its *raison d'etre*, not its convenience to the state."[5]

These three traditions may seem far removed from the mainstream of contemporary views. Doesn't the liberal strand of "liberal democracy" qualify and limit the legitimate power of the state? Isn't this the entering wedge for a set of fundamental freedoms that can stand against the claims of state power?

The standard history of liberalism lends support to this view. The rise of revealed religion created a diremption of authority and challenged the comprehensive primary of politics. The early modern wars of religion sparked new understandings of the relationship between religion and politics, between individual conscience and public order, between unity and diversity. As politics came to be understood as limited rather than total, the possibility emerged that the principles constituting individual lives and civil associations might not be congruent with the principles constituting public institutions. The point of liberal constitutionalism, and of liberal statesmanship, was not to abolish these differences but rather, as far as possible, to help them serve the cause of ordered liberty.

## 2 THE TOTALIST TEMPTATION

Despite this history, many contemporary theorists, including some who think of themselves as working within the liberal tradition, embrace propositions that draw them away from the idea of limited government and toward civic totalism, perhaps against their intention. There are three principal variants of the totalist temptation. Some thinkers argue that if state power is exercised properly – that is, democratically – it need not be limited by any considerations other than those required by democratic processes themselves. Others believe that a healthy and sustainable democracy requires congruence, enforced by law if necessary, between regime-level political principles and the structure of associations, faith communities, and even families. Still others contend that political considerations systematically outweigh claims stemming from other sources. Let me examine each of these positions.

### 2.1  Only Democracy can Limit Democracy

Jürgen Habermas offers the clearest example of this tendency. He insists that once obsolete metaphysical doctrines are set aside, "there is no longer any fixed point outside the democratic procedure itself." But this is no cause for worry or regret: whatever is normatively defensible in liberal rights is contained in the discourse-rights of "sovereign [democratic] citizens."[6] The residual rights not so contained constitute, not bulwarks against oppression, but rather the illegitimate insulation of "private" practices from public scrutiny.

An eminent American democratic theorist, Robert Dahl, is tempted by Habermas's stance. He characterizes as "reasonable" and "attractive" the view that members of political communities have no fundamental interests, rights, or claims other than those integral to the democratic process or needed for its preservation. The only limits to the legitimate scope of democratic power are the requisites of democracy itself. Put simply: A demos that observes the norms of democratic decision-making may do what it wants.[7]

Unlike Habermas, Dahl is not entirely comfortable with restricting the domain of rights to the conditions of democracy. He concedes that this proposal raises a "disturbing" question: what about interests, rights, and claims that cannot be adequately understood as aspects of the democratic process but that nonetheless seem important and defensible? What about fair trials, or freedom of religion and conscience? Without definitively answering this question, Dahl examines the various ways in which the defense of rights may be institutionalized, concluding that those whose would temper democratic majorities with "guardian" structures such as courts bear a heavy burden of proof that they rarely, if ever, discharge successfully. The most reliable cure for the ills of democracy is more democracy; the resort to nonmajoritarian protections risks undermining the people's capacity to govern itself.[8]

My objection to this line of thinking has nothing to do with reservations against majoritarian decision making as such. Like Jeremy Waldron, I endorse the "dignity of legislation."[9] The theory of liberal pluralism defines a very wide range of questions that must be resolved politically rather than philosophically. Especially in the context of cultural heterogeneity, value pluralism renders unanimity virtually unattainable. No matter how long we deliberate, some parts of the political community will almost certainly continue to disagree. In normal circumstances, some form of majoritarian politics is the default position for democracies.

My objection is farther back, at the threshold: I deny that all aspects of human life are equally collective, equally subject to public decision of whatever form. Among the most valuable immunities from public authority are those that are not embedded in or derived from democratic governance. To say that the content of these liberties can only be determined democratically is to beg the question or, worse, to answer it by fiat. My counterproposal is that we reflect instead on the substance of valued liberties and place them within the most plausible context of justification we can find.

## 2.2 Democracy Requires Top-to-Bottom Congruence

For an example of this variant of totalism, consider the argument Stephen Macedo lays out in his 2000 book, *Diversity and Distrust.*[10] Throughout this book, Macedo stresses the "positive ambitions" of liberal constitutionalism and the "transformative project" required to realize them. Liberals, he insists, must hold fast to the "full measure of our civic ambitions."[11] For example, liberalism's transformative project requires public policy to "shape or constitute all forms of diversity so that people are *satisfied* leading lives of bounded freedom [and to] mold *people* in a manner that ensures that liberal freedom is what they want."[12] The health of our regime, he believes, depends on its "ability to turn people's deepest convictions – including their religious beliefs – in directions that are congruent with the ways of a liberal republic."[13]

Macedo's repeated use of the term "regime" is instructive. In the Greek conception of the regime, to which he tacitly appeals, politics is architectonic, and other aspects of human existence – economic, social, aesthetic – are subordinate. Even religion is understood as civil rather than autonomous, let alone as a source of reservations against state authority. This is more than a question of power. For a regime to be healthy, runs the argument, it must be a unity, and its political principles must therefore ramify through the rest of its citizens' lives. All matters are potentially public matters.

While acknowledging that the lives of liberal citizens are "in a [formal] sense" divided between public and private, Macedo insists that this division is "superficial" because liberal institutions and practices legitimately shape all of our deepest commitments so as to make them supportive of the liberal regime. Faith-based commitments are not exempt; he unflinchingly asserts that "we have a shared account of basic civic values that impose limits on what can be true in the religious sphere."[14]

Macedo is aware that his approach, undertaken in the name of liberalism, may seem "deeply illiberal."[15] His elaboration of his view does little to dispel this impression. Consider the following claim: Liberal citizens should be "alert to the possibility that religious imperatives, or even inherited notions of what it means to be a good parent, spouse, or lover, might in fact run afoul of guarantees of equal freedom." Confronted with such conflicts, liberal citizens should be "committed to honoring the public demands of liberal justice in all departments of their lives."[16] The reason is the primacy of the political: "A liberal democratic polity [rests] on shared political commitments weighty enough to override competing values."[17] Even when we acknowledge the diverse spheres of human and the diversity of legitimate values at work within them, he concludes, "Nothing about reasonable pluralism should shake our confidence in the overriding weight of shared public principles."[18]

Despite his firm endorsement of the primacy of the political, Macedo criticizes what he characterizes as John Dewey's civic totalism. Here, at least, we are in agreement. Throughout his life, which he began as a devout Congregationalist, Dewey was moved by a craving for wholeness. Early on, he was drawn to Hegelian idealism as an alternative to Kantian dualism and to the cold world of modern natural science in which human beings have no secure place. The ethical humanism he developed in the 1890s sought to break down the wall between religion, philosophy, and politics by emphasizing what he called "the religious meaning of democracy." Dewey's mature vision of the fully deliberative community was intended to transgress the boundaries, rooted in Kant's three critiques, between science, ethics, and aesthetics. He never ceased to pursue a Hegel-inspired "expressivism" in which norms such as "self-unification, harmony, wholeness, plenitude" remained central.

Dewey saw political participation as the vehicle for self-realization, understood in the Idealist manner as positive freedom. But he never succeeded in defining self-realization, which remained vague in its successive idealist, naturalist, and esthetic formulations. Nor did he persuasively defend positive freedom, however understood, against fears of paternalism and loss of privacy raised by those devoted to a more negative conception of liberty. And even if self-realization were granted as the abstract universal *telos*, it hardly follows that all individuals would find it in any single activity – including political participation.

Dewey's politics inclined excessively toward harmony. In opposition to William James (as well as to later figures such as Isaiah Berlin), Dewey long refused to admit that worthy values could conflict, or, as James characteristically put it, that "some part of the ideal must be butchered" in the quest for wholeness. As a result, his understanding of social conflict was superficial at best. He hoped that even deep differences could be resolved through the application of "socialized intelligence"; he failed to appreciate either the application of power or the recognition of diversity as serious alternatives to the achievement of rational consensus.

In a classic article, George Kateb argues for the moral distinctiveness and moral superiority of representative democracy: Political authority is chastened, diversity acknowledged, privacy respected, individuality encouraged, coercion minimized. By contrast, Kateb contends, the moral costs of direct democracy are prohibitive: the overriding of differences in the name of "community"; the effacement of boundaries and separations, with everything subjected to the publicly political imperative; the relentless disparagement of nonpublic life. The core of direct democracy, be concludes, is the life of citizenship, "public and continuous and all-absorbing, and laid as an obligation on all, not freely chosen by a random few. But the life of citizenship is procrustean ... The politics of direct democracy and its social conditions and consequences are the death of autonomy."[19]

Dewey's religion of democracy illustrates these risks. In the name of expanding public power to address public problems, Dewey systematically downplayed significant reservations against his venture – in particular, fear of public tyranny and concern for privacy and individuality. Such qualms, he believed, were rooted in an outdated philosophical commitment to atomistic individualism and in a covert effort to defend a rapacious capitalist system against public regulation. He was not entirely wrong, of course. But in reducing so much of the liberal impulse to selfishness and error, he overlooked its deeper roots in American history and culture, and in the philosophy of pluralism.[20]

Roberto Unger's thought exemplifies, even more dramatically than Dewey's, the human costs of the craving for wholeness translated into political doctrine. For Unger, the essence of human personality is that it is "infinite." It has the capacity to transcend all contexts: traits of character, moral rules, political institutions, cognitive structures, and so on. No one context is hospitable to the full range of practical, passionate, political, or philosophical projects that personality can imagine. This infinity is not just an abstract capability, but – in the old language of teleology – an immanent impulse as well. The health of each individual personality is incompatible with its acceptance of the constraints inherent in specific contexts. Indeed, Unger argues, vice, psychological illness, and simple unhappiness are all consequences of the failure to relieve the tension between personal desire and contextual constraint. Modernist visionaries identified and struggled with this tension. Their struggle may have taken the form of an artistic fringe in conflict with bourgeois society. But its inner meaning is a universal truth about the human condition.

Unger's account of personality rests on a sharp distinction between "character" and "self." Character is the set of routinized habits and dispositions that channel individual behavior into fixed patterns. Self, on the other hand, is the dual capacity to reject routine patterns of conduct and to imagine and act on alternatives to them.

Even if we grant Unger's distinction between routinized character and fluid self, it does not follow that the latter is to be given normative preference. The mere fact that we are able to upset settled patterns in favor of new experiences does not mean that we should do so. The fact that the imagination can counterpose itself to moral rules does not mean that these rules should be transgressed.

This point may be broadened. Unger articulates a deep hostility to the "vast spiritual sloth" and "overwhelming apathy" that allegedly characterize ordinary human experience. Rejecting the solace most human beings find in ordered existence, he insists that to understand deeply "is always to see the settled from the angle of the unsettled." He even finds in the forcible destruction of everyday patterns a fount of moral insight:

> [T]he growth of the transforming and ennobling passions ... and the ability of these passions to penetrate the crust of everyday perception and habit seem to depend upon loss and sacrifice ... [T]he primary form of loss and sacrifice is the sacrifice and the loss of your settled place in a settled world. This is the event that allows you to distinguish the gold from the tinsel: the opportunities of human connection from the forms of established society, and the disclosures of incongruous insight or disobedient desire from the distraction and the narcosis of habit.

So steelworkers are ennobled by unemployment? Husbands and wives are ennobled by shattering divorces? Parents are ennobled by the death of children? Citizens are ennobled by brutal civil war? The most charitable response to Unger's proposition is that disaster strengthens some of these unfortunate human beings but destroys the others. A franker response is that his proposition is a classic example of theoretical deduction swamping experiential truth.

The preference for the unsettled over the settled, the impulse to imagine and to act out context-smashing transgressions, is indeed characteristic of modernist artists, authors, and revolutionaries. Unger's error is to assume that the motives and satisfactions of a tiny elite somehow constitute the (hidden) essence and desire of all human beings. A world restructured to accommodate the iconoclastic cravings of modernist visionaries is a world from which others would recoil in dread. Most human beings find satisfaction within settled contexts and experience the disruption of those contexts not as empowerment, but rather as deprivation. The everyday life that Unger holds in such contempt is not the imposition of the few on the many. It retains its customary form precisely because it is the mode of existence that the overwhelming majority of the human race prefers.

To the extent that modernism craves transformative efficacy, therefore, it is driven toward "revolution "from above" – that is, toward coercion. It is no accident that in its rage against the stolid persistence of bourgeois society, modernism flirted with fascism and bolshevism throughout the twentieth century. Nor is it an accident that Unger's political modernism, ostensibly justified in the name of the greatest possible openness to individual expression, culminates in the forcible destruction of traditional ways of life. Unger is admirably – if chillingly – candid on this point:

[P]eople have . . . always put their sense of basic security in the maintenance of particular social roles, jobs, and ways of life. Any attempt to indulge this conception of security would prove incompatible with the institutions of the empowered democracy and with the personal and social ideals that inspire them . . . [P]eople can and should wean themselves away from a restrictive, rigidifying view of where they should place their sense of protection.

They (and, if not they, their children) will discover that the security that matters does not require the maintenance of a narrowly defined mode of life. They reach this conclusion in part . . . by awakening to a conception of the personality as both dependent upon context and strengthened through context smashing.

To summarize this strand of Unger's argument: Modernist social theory rests on a normative conception of personality that is valid for, and binding upon, everyone. Today, some of us accept this conception while others stubbornly resist it. Within suitably constructed institutions, we all will (eventually) come to experience the correctness of the modernist vision. And in the interim, while our generation has not yet been re-educated (or replaced by suitably socialized children), we will certainly not be "indulged." Instead, we will be shaken out of our narcoleptic trance and purged of stubborn habits. We will be forced to be free.

Unger anticipates a certain resistance to this proposal on the part of the "classical liberal," who recognizes that modernist social theory culminates in totalitarian interventions in areas that even traditional despots are content to leave alone. Unger concedes the factual accuracy of this accusation, but seeks to transmute its moral meaning:

[T]he classical liberal is wrong to think . . . that an institutional order can . . . draw a watertight distinction between the public institutions of a people and the forms of close association or intimate experience to which the people are drawn . . . . The authority of the radical project lies in its vision of the individual and collective empowerment we may achieve by cumulatively loosening the grip of rigid roles, hierarchies, and conventions . . . But it does not claim to be indifferent to the choice among alternative styles of association.

Roberto Unger's thought is a cautionary tale of how moral monism (a unitary and universal conception of the good life for human beings) can lead to a dangerous political monism that denies the independence of all nonpolitical activities and associations.[21]

A gulf of tone and temper separates Unger's modernist fantasy from the sober and careful account of deliberative democracy developed by

Amy Gutmann and Dennis Thompson. Nonetheless, their thesis raises some similar concerns about the relation between public and nonpublic life. For liberal democrats, I have argued, there are two critical questions about democracy: the *nature* of democratic decision-making and the *scope* of legitimate democratic authority. It seems to me that Gutmann and Thompson deal far more adequately with the first question than with the second. One comes away from *Democracy and Disagreement*[22] with a very clear (albeit contestable) sense of how democratic deliberation should be conducted, but with (at best) a general conception of the limits of state power. To be sure, there is a guiding concept – the preservation of "personal integrity."[23] But in nearly all cases, the movement from general concept to specific conception is mediated by democratic deliberation – not the most secure and comforting basis for the maintenance of liberty: "In keeping with the spirit of a deliberative constitution, we argue that citizens and public officials are responsible for setting limits to . . . liberty . . . through a deliberative process."[24] By contrast, liberal constitutionalism both specifies basic liberties and tries to keep them outside the normal processes of democratic revision.

To be fair, Gutmann and Thompson do identify a few core violations of personal integrity. Unless individuals have the right to resist "certain kinds of constraints on their personal beliefs (for example, on their religious or moral convictions, their mental integrity is in jeopardy."[25] The question I want to raise is whether their conception of democratic deliberation proves in the end to be compatible with this account of individual liberty. I will focus on what I take to be the linchpin of deliberation for Gutmann and Thompson – the principle of reciprocity – and on their application of this principle to conscientious religious dissenters. I argue that reciprocity, so understood, requires an intolerable sacrifice of personal integrity, but that a more generous and defensible conception of reciprocity does not.

The essentials of Gutmann and Thompson's account of reciprocity are by now well-known. Building on the work of Rawls and Scanlon, they say that the "foundation of reciprocity is the capacity to seek fair terms of social cooperation for their own sake . . . From a deliberative perspective, a citizen offers reasons that can be accepted by others who are similarly motivated to find reasons that can be accepted by others . . . [Thus,] a deliberative perspective does not address people who reject the aim of finding fair terms for social cooperation; it cannot reach those who refuse to press their public claims in terms accessible to their fellow citizens."[26]

This understanding of reciprocity raises some deep questions (for example, about the nature of moral motivation), but I won't pursue them here. Instead, staying within the bounds of Gutmann and Thompson's account, I want to offer three caveats. First, the phrase "social cooperation" suggests a common course of action that all citizens (must) pursue. But there are other equally legitimate forms of cooperation, including agreements to disagree, to go our various ways without hindrance or cavil, to "live and let live."

Second, there are different kinds of "public claims." Individuals may argue that the political community as a whole ought to pursue a particular course of action. (This is, I think, the core case that Gutmann and Thompson have in mind.) But they may also argue that the question at hand should not be treated as a public matter in the first place; or that even if it is a legitimate public matter, some individuals and groups may (or must) be exempted from the constraints of otherwise general decisions. Some public claims are "offensive" – you (all) should do what I say – while others are "defensive" – I need not do what you say, even if you speak in the voice of the entire political community. The kinds of reasons offered in support of defensive claims may rightly differ from those for offensive claims.

Third, the requirement that the terms of public argument should be "accessible" to one's fellow citizens turns out to be highly restrictive: "Any claim fails to respect reciprocity if it imposes a requirement on other citizens to adopt one's sectarian way of life as a condition of gaining access to the moral understanding that is essential to judging the validity of one's moral claims."[27] Over the past two decades, a substantial debate has developed over the nature of what Rawls calls "public reason," a debate that Gutmann and Thompson seem to resolve by definitional fiat. Without wading into this philosophical swamp, let me simply say that we should be very cautious about interpreting the norm of reciprocity so as to screen out the kinds of foundational beliefs that give meaning and purpose to many lives. In the pluralist approach I am advocating, the presumption is in favor of inclusion.

An inclusive understanding of public reason is especially appropriate in the context of what I have called defensive public claims. It is one thing to take the offensive – for example, by claiming that the United States should be a "Christian nation" and should restore official Christian prayer to public schools. That was the situation that existed in the grade schools of my youth when I (a Jew) was compelled to recite the Lord's Prayer. I do not see how such a regime could possibly be defended through legitimate public reasons. It is quite a different thing to seek, on conscientious grounds, defensive exemption from general public policies that may be legitimate and acceptable to a majority of citizens.

The historical experience of moral and religious conflict suggests that a policy of living peacefully with continuing differences may often be the best we can do. In the end, Gutmann and Thompson recognize this: Even after clearly unacceptable positions have been weeded out, competing proposals with genuine moral standing may well remain. In one of the most compelling sections of their book, they spell out their strategy for moral accommodation – "a kind of excellence of character that permits a democracy to flourish in the face of fundamental moral disagreement."[28] It has two components: *Civic integrity* requires consistency – in speech, between speech and action, and in accepting all (not just convenient) consequences of one's preferred principles. *Civic magnanimity* requires the respectful acknowledgment of the moral status of opposing positions, open-mindedness, and the "economy of moral disagreement" – defending one's own position on grounds that minimize the portion of opposing positions that must be rejected. This, it seems to me, is the substantive heart of the civility so often called for and so poorly understood. Whether or not deliberation can reach closure or reduce moral conflict, the serious practice of moral accommodation is an essential virtue in a liberal pluralist society.

Ian Shapiro has criticized both Unger's "vanguardist" proposals for destroying hierarchies from above and the Gutmann/Thompson account of deliberation as the core of democratic decision-making. His own democratic theorizing, however, offers another version of what I have called the "totalist temptation."

At first glance, this charge seems implausible. Shapiro begins, as I do, by examining the contours of the social realm, concluding that "civil society is made up of activities that differ qualitatively from one another." Different modes and rules of decision-making, he suggests, are appropriate to these different activities.[29] Moreover, he affirms a version of value pluralism, in which democracy is neither the only human good, nor the highest good, nor the dominant constitutive good of the social realm.[30]

Nonetheless, Shapiro ends up in a position that is hard to distinguish from Dewey's brand of democratic totalism. Notwithstanding Shapiro's apparent affirmation of political pluralism, he insists that democracy is a "foundational" good in that it appropriately conditions every social sphere; our concern is "with democratizing the power relations that structure social life."[31] He reaches this conclusion because in the end, his political pluralism doesn't go very deep. On the contrary: Social spheres are homogeneous in the sense that "no realm of social life is immune to relations of power and conflict."[32] For this reason, politics is ubiquitous, and "no social practice can be declared to be beyond politics and therefore beyond the possibility of political regulation."[33]

This argument seems to me to move from tautology to non sequitur. If we define politics as the realm of power and conflict, and if all social relationships bear the marks of power and conflict, then all of society is "political" by definition. But it hardly follows that the special kind of politics in which the people as a whole make collective decisions appropriately regulates every social sphere. I agree with Shapiro that democracy requires the people "to be sovereign over their collective activities."[34] But that formulation evades the critical question of which activities are rightly regarded as "collective."

Shapiro offers two arguments against the "liberal" effort to place some matters beyond the bounds of collective determination. First, he claims, liberals wrongly suppose that governmental tyranny is the only form of oppression that should worry us. I don't know of many minimally sentient liberals who believe anything of the sort. Their point is rather that the coercive power of the state, membership in which citizens usually do not choose and from which they cannot easily exit, presents special problems; and, conversely, a civil society characterized by wide choice and relative ease of exit can help resist not only *associational* but also *governmental* oppression. The assertion that liberals cannot square their principles with (for example), public laws against spousal abuse is just wrong. The physical safety of all citizens is a quintessentially public matter.

Second, Shapiro criticizes liberals for believing that "whether or not our lives should be governed by collective institutions is an intelligible question about politics." This is wrongheaded because putatively "private" institutions are in fact public creations.[35] The problem is that Shapiro's claim in many cases is controversial, and in some is just wrong. To pick the most obvious example: Many contemporary religious institutions antedate the modern state, which cannot therefore be said to have "created" them. The fact that such institutions are subject to some forms of state regulation hardly suffices to establish the claim that they are creatures of the state and wholly subordinate to its power. It is closer to the truth to say that the authority of both governmental and religious institutions is limited, and indeed that they are mutually and reciprocally limiting.

Nor is it true that public authority necessarily comes into play when civil institutions act in ways that affect the lives of non-members as well as members. We need not accept Shapiro's principle that the right to participate flows from causal links between the actions of others and one's own interests.[36] An example will clarify why we need not. Suppose that the Catholic Church in the United States decided that it could no longer afford to operate its system of parochial schools, and abruptly closed them. Millions of students would flow into the public schools, forcing state and local governments to spend billions more each year. The interests of the citizenry as a whole would surely be affected. Does it follow that non-Catholics should have a right to participate in the Church's decision about its educational mission?

Let us grant that relationships within religious denominations are political in Shapiro's sense. It doesn't follow that their brand of politics is subordinate to the political decisions of the people as a whole. And it certainly doesn't follow that the democratic norms and rules that (arguably) enjoy a preferred position within the arena of collective decision-making necessarily enjoy even the presumption of priority in other spheres.

The organization of religious authority often reflects a particular conception of Divine will or law, as well as historical and analogical accounts of the ways in which ecclesiastical legitimacy is constituted and transmitted. I do not deny that religious and secular claims can clash and that there are often compelling reasons to give secular claims pride of place. But it does not follow that the structures of power that enjoy legitimacy in the secular sphere somehow constitute norms against which religious institutions and practices should be measured. If you believe that the Bishop of Rome is the Vicar of Christ, then you will reject any general presumption (even if rebuttable) that hierarchy is intrinsically illegitimate.

Shapiro suggests that in large measure, democracy is about "opposition to the arbitrary exercise of power."[37] That raises the question of when power is arbitrary. Shapiro's answer: hierarchies for which the governed could see "no rationale or justification."[38] But members of communities have often seen reasons for hierarchical and undemocratic modes of organizations, and they are not always wrong. Indeed, Shapiro acknowledges that some hierarchies can rebut the presumption of illegitimacy.[39] Not all undemocratic power is arbitrary. If so, democracy cannot be foundational in the sense that it is a strictly necessary condition for justice within a given social sphere.[40]

I would observe, finally, that there is a tension between two basic features of Shapiro's conception of democracy – that it is both foundational and subordinate to the ends of the activities in which we engage. If, as he acknowledges, there is sometimes a flat-out contradiction between the goals of social life and the democratic organization of social life, it is by no means clear why the goals should be compromised in the name of democracy.[41] It may just be a fact of human life that military organizations can be democratic or effective but not both. As long as military institutions acknowledge due subordination to external public control, it is not clear why their hierarchical internal organization should be regarded as morally troubling. All of this is to say that although Shapiro has made a case that doing things democratically has intrinsic value, he has not made the case that *only* democratic modes of social action have intrinsic value, let alone that the intrinsic value of democracy trumps other goods in cases of conflict.

## 2.3  The Claims of Democratic Politics Enjoy Primacy

Let me now turn to the most complex case of the phenomenon I call the totalist temptation. John Rawls asserts that "the values of the special domain of the political . . . normally outweigh whatever values may conflict with them."[42] Why is this the case? Rawls offers two reasons. First, political values are very important; they determine social life and make fair cooperation possible. Second, conflict between political and nonpolitical values can usually be avoided, so long as political values are appropriately understood.[43]

Rawls famously maintains that justice is the preeminent political value – the "first virtue of social institutions" – and that "laws and institutions no matter how efficient and well-arranged must be reformed or abolished if they are unjust."[44] Nonetheless, he asserts, consistent with the liberal tradition, that the principles of justice do not directly regulate institutions and associations – such as churches and families – within society.[45] (Principles of justice do affect these institutions indirectly, via the influence of just background institutions.)

The difficulty is to explain why, within the structure of Rawls's theory, the principles regulating the basic structure of society should not be applied directly to institutions such as churches and the family. Taken literally, many of these background principles would seem to warrant such interventions. For example, imbalances in parenting responsibilities can affect women's "fair equality of opportunity." Does this mean, as Rawls seems to suggest, that "special provisions of family law" should prevent or rectify this imbalance?[46] If the family is part of the basic structure of society, as Rawls now claims, why does he judge it "hardly sensible" that parents be required to treat their children in accordance with the principles directly governing the basic structure?[47]

The ambiguous status of the family reflects a deeper structural problem in Rawls's account. At one point, he offers a formulation that seems promising: We distinguish between the point of view of citizens and of members of associations. As citizens, we endorse the constraints of principles of justice; as association members, we want to limit those constraints so that the inner life of associations can flourish. This generates a "division of labor" that treats the basic structure and civil association as being, so to speak, on a par with one another.[48]

But on closer inspection, it turns out that there's a hierarchical relationship after all, with the principles of justice serving as trumps. Otherwise put, the basic structure constitutes the end, and the various associations are in part means to that end. So, for example, "the treatment of children must be such as to support the family's role in upholding a constitutional regime."[49] But what if (say) religious free exercise includes teachings and practices that don't do this? (Imagine a religious group that has no intention of altering the public structure of equal political rights for women, but teaches its own members that women shouldn't participate in public life.)

Rawls is certain (quite sensibly in my view) that "We wouldn't want political principles of justice to apply directly to the internal life of the family."[50] The reasoning appears to be that various associations have inner lives that differ qualitatively from that of the political realm, so that political principles would be "out of place." This then raises a question: Why aren't political and nonpolitical associations understood as related horizontally rather than vertically? Why can't nonpolitical associations be seen as limiting the scope of politics at the same time that the basic structure of politics constrains associations?

Rawls's apparent answer runs as follows: The sphere or domain of the nonpolitical has no independent existence or definition, but is simply the result (or residuum) of how the principles of justice are applied directly and indirectly. In particular, the principle of equal citizenship applies everywhere.

In one sense, this is clearly true. If an association uses coercion to prevent some of its members from exercising their equal political rights, the state must step in to enforce those rights. But the more usual case is one in which the association organizes itself according to norms (of membership or activity) that are inconsistent with principles of equal citizenship. What is the state's legitimate power in the face of these dissenting practices? Is it so obvious that the legitimate activities of non-political associations should be defined relative not to the inner life of those associations but rather to the principles of the public sphere? Can't we say something important about the distinctive natures of individual conscience, friendship, families, communities of faith or inquiry, and shouldn't those primary features of our social life have an effect on the scope of political principles, not just vice versa? Even if justice is the first virtue of public institutions and enjoys lexical priority over other goods of the public realm (a debatable proposition), it does not follow that the public realm enjoys comprehensive lexical priority over the other forms of human activity and association.

### 3 THE PLURALIST ALTERNATIVE

It is in the context of questions such as these that political pluralism emerges as an alternative to all forms of civic totalism. Political pluralism, to begin, rejects efforts to understand individuals, families, and associations simply as parts within and of a political whole. Relatedly, pluralism rejects the instrumental/teleological argument that individuals, families, and associations are adequately understood as existing "for the sake of" some political purpose. For example, religion is not (only) civil, and in some circumstances may be in tension with civil requirements. This is *not* to say that political communities must be understand as without common purposes. The political order is not simply a framework within which individuals, families, and associations may pursue their own purposes. But civic purposes are not comprehensive and do not necessarily trump the purposes of individuals and groups.

Political pluralism understands human life as consisting of a multiplicity of spheres, some overlapping, with distinct natures and inner norms. Each sphere enjoys a limited, but real, autonomy. Political pluralism rejects any account of political community that creates a unidimensional hierarchical ordering among these spheres of life. Rather, different forms of association and activity are complexly interrelated. There may be local or partial hierarchies among subsets of spheres in specific context, but there are no comprehensive lexical orderings among categories of human life.

For these reasons, among others, political pluralism does not seek to overcome, but rather endorses, the postpagan diremption of human loyalty and political authority created by the rise of revealed religion. That this creates problems of practical governance cannot be denied. But pluralists refuse to resolve these problems by allowing public authorities to determine the substance and scope of allowable belief (Hobbes) or by reducing faith to civil religion and elevating devotion to the common civic good as the highest human value (Rousseau). Fundamental tensions rooted in the deep structure of human existence cannot be abolished in a stroke, but must rather be acknowledged, negotiated, and adjudicated with due regard to the contours of specific cases and controversies.

Pluralist politics is a politics of recognition rather than of construction. It respects the diverse spheres of human activity; it does not understand itself as creating or constituting those activities. Families are shaped by public law, but that does not mean that they are socially constructed. There are complex relationships of mutual impact between public law and faith communities, but it is hardly the case that the public sphere creates these communities. Many types of human association possess an existence that is not derived from the state. Accordingly, pluralist politics does not presume that the inner structure and principles of every sphere must (for either instrumental or moral reasons) mirror the structure and principles of basic political institutions.

A pluralist politics is, however, responsible for coordinating other spheres of activity, and especially for adjudicating the inevitable overlaps and disputes among them. This form of politics evidently requires the mutual limitation of some freedoms, individual and associational. It monopolizes the legitimate use of force, except in cases of self-defense when the polity cannot or does not protect us. It understands that group tyranny is possible, and therefore protects individuals against some associational abuses. But pluralist politics presumes that the enforcement of basic rights of citizenship and of exit rights, suitably understood, will usually suffice. Associational integrity requires a broad though not unlimited right of groups to define their own membership, to exclude as well as include, and a pluralist polity will respect that right.

A pluralist polity is not a neutral framework (assuming such a thing is even possible) but rather pursues a distinctive ensemble of public purposes. As David Nicholls, a leading scholar of political pluralism, argues, it presupposes a limited body of shared belief: in civil peace, in toleration for different ways of life, in some machinery for resolving disputes, and (notably) in the ongoing right of individuals and groups to resist conscientiously any exercise of public power they regard as illegitimate.[51] So understood, political pluralism serves as a barrier against the greatest preventable evils of human life, but it pursues, at most, a partial rather than comprehensive good. As Nicholls puts it:

[B]y limiting power we limit the ability to do good, but we also limit the chance of doing evil. Pluralists would, on the whole, have concentrated on avoiding the worst in politics rather than trying to achieve the best. They [reject] the Hobbist notion that anarchy is the only great threat to society, and that absolute power must be put into the hands of the rulers, in order to avert this danger; the preservation of life at any cost was not for them the sole end of politics.[52]

## 4 CONCLUSION: THE PHILOSOPHICAL STATUS OF POLITICAL PLURALISM

I will conclude this inquiry with a Rawlsian question: Is political plural-ism along the lines I've just sketched a "comprehensive" account of these matters or rather a "political" account that can be assessed independent of controversial moral or metaphysical doctrines? I believe that Nicholls is on the right track when he argues that political pluralism is not a fully freestanding doctrine: "Political pluralism may well be compatible with many ethical theories, but it is surely the case that it is incompatible with some ethical theories."[53] He goes on to observe, plausibly enough, that "It is likely that a monist in [moral or metaphysical] philosophy would reject political pluralism and would hope that the unity which is char-acteristic of the whole universe might become concrete in institutional form."[54]

Put this affirmatively: Political pluralism and Berlinian moral pluralism fit together in theory and in practice. Taken together, they offer the firmest basis for an account of liberal democracy that does justice to its "liberal" dimension, to its understanding of legitimate public power as important but inherently limited, and to the specific judgments (legal, legislative, and socio-cultural) that those thinking and acting in a liberal spirit should reach.

## Notes

1.  530 U.S. 640 (2000).
2.  For the British tradition, see *The Pluralist Theory of the State: Selected Writings of G. D. H. Cole, J. N. Figgis, and H. J. Laski*, Paul Q. Hirst, ed. (London: Routledge, 1989). For the Calvinist tradition, see *Political Order and the Plural Structure of Society*, James W. Skillen and Rockne M. McCarthy, eds. (Atlanta: Scholars Press, 1991).

3. For the full account of our agreement and (mainly) disagreement, see my review of Macedo's latest book, *Diversity and Distrust: Civic Education in a Multicultural Society* (Cambridge, MA: Harvard University Press, 2000), published in *Ethics* 112(2) (January 2002): 386–91.

4. Quoted by J. N. Figgis in Hirst, *Pluralist Theory*, p. 112.

5. Carney, "Associational Thought in Early Calvinism," in *Voluntary Associations: A Study of Groups in Free Societies*, D. B. Robertson ed. (Richmond, VA: John Knox Press, 1966), p. 46.

6. Quoted and discussed in John Rawls, *Political Liberalism* (New York: Columbia University Press, 1996), p. 379.

7. Robert Dahl, *Democracy and Its Critics* (New Haven: Yale University Press, 1989), pp. 182, 183.

8. Dahl, *Democracy and Its Critics*, pp. 183–92.

9. Jeremy Waldron, *The Dignity of Legislation* (Cambridge: Cambridge University Press), 1999.

10. Stephen Macedo, *Diversity and Distrust: Civic Education in a Multicultural Democracy* (Cambridge, MA: Harvard, 2000).

11. Macedo, *Diversity and Distrust*, pp. 229–30.

12. Macedo, *Diversity and Distrust*, p. 15; Macedo's emphasis.

13. Macedo, *Diversity and Distrust*, p. 43.

14. Macedo, *Diversity and Distrust*, p. 37.

15. Macedo, *Diversity and Distrust*, p. 137.

16. Macedo, *Diversity and Distrust*, p. 239.

17. Macedo, *Diversity and Distrust*, p. 134.

18. Macedo, *Diversity and Distrust*, p. 197.

19. George Kateb, "The Moral Distinctiveness of Representative Democracy," in *The Inner Ocean: Individualism and Democratic Culture* (Ithaca, NY: Cornell University Press, 1992) p. 55.

20. These remarks on Dewey are drawn from my "John Dewey and the Religion of Democracy," *Raritan* 12(3) (1993): 144–54.

21. The preceding remarks on Unger are drawn in part from my "False Universality: Infinite Personality and Finite Existence in Unger's *Politics*," in Robin W. Lovin and Michael J. Perry, *Critique and Construction: A Symposium on Unger's Politics* (Cambridge: Cambridge University Press, 1990), pp. 14–28.

22. Amy Gutmann and Dennis Thompson, *Democracy and Disagreement* (Cambridge, MA: Harvard University Press, 1996).

23. Gutmann and Thompson, *Democracy and Disagreement*, p. 204.

24. Gutmann and Thompson, *Democracy and Disagreement*, pp. 200–1.

25. Gutmann and Thompson, *Democracy and Disagreement*, p. 204.

26. Gutmann and Thompson, *Democracy and Disagreement*, pp. 52–3, 55.

27. Gutmann and Thompson, *Democracy and Disagreement*, p. 57.

28. Gutmann and Thompson, *Democracy and Disagreement*, p. 79.

29. Ian Shapiro, *Democratic Justice* (New Haven: Yale, 1999), p. 32.

30. Ian Shapiro, *Democracy's Place* (Ithaca, NY: Cornell, 1996), p. 112.

31. Shapiro, *Democratic Justice*, p. 27.

32. Shapiro, *Democracy's Place*, p. 116.

33. Shapiro, *Democracy's Place*, p. 115.
34. Shapiro, *Democratic Justice*, p. 31.
35. Shapiro, *Democracy's Place*, pp. 226–7.
36. Shapiro, *Democratic Justice*, p. 233.
37. Shapiro, *Democratic Justice*, p. 30.
38. Ibid.
39. Shapiro, *Democratic Justice*, p. 42.
40. This is perhaps why Shapiro moves from the 1996 formulation that "democracy is essential to ordering social relations justly" (Shapiro, *Democracy's Place*, p. 112) to the more nuanced 1999 position that "although democracy is not sufficient for social justice, *usually* it is necessary (Shapiro, *Democratic Justice*, p. 21; emphasis mine).
41. Shapiro, *Democratic Justice*, pp. 42–3.
42. Rawls, *Political Liberalism*, pp. 139, 157.
43. Rawls, *Political Liberalism*, pp. 139–40.
44. John Rawls, *A Theory of Justice* (Cambridge, MA: Harvard University Press, 1971), p. 3.
45. John Rawls, *Justice as Fairness: A Restatement*, Erin Kelly, ed. (Cambridge, MA: Harvard University Press, 2001), p. 10.
46. Rawls, *Justice as Fairness*, p. 11.
47. Rawls, *Justice as Fairness*, p. 165. To complicate matters further, on one and the same page (10), Rawls seems to characterize the family both as part of the basic structure of society and as an institution within the basic structure. I don't see how it can be both, and it makes a huge difference which it is.
48. Rawls, *Justice as Fairness*, p. 165.
49. Ibid.
50. Ibid.
51. David Nicholls, *The Pluralist State* (London: Macmillan, 1975), p. 123.
52. Nicholls, *The Pluralist State*, p. 29.
53. Nicholls, *The Pluralist State*, p. 105.
54. Nicholls, *The Pluralist State*, p. 113.

# 4

# Expressive Liberty and Constitutional Democracy

## *The Case of Freedom of Conscience*

### 1 INTRODUCTION

A key concept in my account of limited government is *expressive liberty*. Simply put, this is the normatively privileged and institutionally defended ability of individuals and groups to lead their lives as they see fit, within the broad range of legitimate variation defined by value pluralism, in accordance with their own understanding of what gives meaning and worth to human existence. In a liberal pluralist regime, a key end is the creation of social space within which expressive liberty may be exercised.

Is expressive liberty (or liberty however understood) anything more than a political construction, subject to alteration through normal political processes? I doubt that theoretical argumentation alone can resolve such questions. So I want to take a different tack – an appeal to moral intuitions and experiences encoded in the U.S. tradition of constitutional adjudication. Specifically, I want to ask how claims based on freedom of conscience are most plausibly understood.

### 2 FREEDOM OF CONSCIENCE: TWO CASES

To frame this inquiry, I begin by recalling an important but largely forgotten episode in U.S. constitutional history: a rapid and almost unprecedented turnabout by the Supreme Court on a matter of fundamental importance. I begin my tale in the late 1930s.

Acting under the authority of the state government, the school board of Minersville, Pennsylvania, had required both students and teachers to participate in a daily pledge of allegiance to the flag. In the 1940 case of *Minersville v. Gobitis*,[1] the Supreme Court decided against a handful of Jehovah's Witnesses who sought to have their children exempted on the grounds that this exercise amounted to a form of idolatry strictly forbidden by their faith. With but a single dissenting vote, the Court ruled that it was permissible for a school board to make participation in saluting the American flag a condition for attending public school, regardless of the conscientious objections of parents and students. Relying on this holding, and quoting liberally from the majority's decision, the West Virginia State Board of Education issued a regulation making the flag salute mandatory statewide. When a challenge to this action arose barely three years after *Gobitis*, the Court reversed itself in *West Virginia v. Barnette* by a vote of 6 to 3.[2] To be sure, during the brief interval separating these cases, the lone dissenter in *Gobitis* had been elevated to Chief Justice and two new voices, both favoring reversal, had joined the court, while two supporters of the original decision had departed. But of the seven justices who heard both cases, three saw fit to reverse themselves and to set forth their reasons for the change.

This kind of abrupt, explicit reversal is very rare in the annals of the Court, and it calls for some explanation. A clue is to be found, I believe, in the deservedly well-known peroration of Justice Jackson's majority decision overturning compulsory flag salutes:

If there is any fixed star in our constitutional constellation, it is that no official, high or petty, can prescribe what shall be orthodox in politics, nationalism, religion, or other matters of opinion or force citizens to confess by word or act their faith therein. If there are any circumstances which permit an exception, they do not now occur to us. We think the action of the local authorities in compelling the flag salute and pledge transcends constitutional limitation on their power and invades the sphere of intellect and spirit which it is the purpose of the First Amendment to our Constitution to reserve from all official control.[3]

I want to suggest that the protected "sphere of intellect and spirit" and the antipathy to forced professions of faith to which Jackson refers enjoy a central place in the development of American political thought and in liberal political theory more generally. Expounded under the rubric of "conscience," not least by James Madison, it provides one of the clearest examples of expressive liberty, and of limits to legitimate state power understood as inherent rather than constructed. It is to Madison's exposition of this concept that I now turn.

### 3 FREEDOM OF CONSCIENCE: MADISON'S VIEW

Consider, first, the language that Madison drafted for inclusion in the Virginia Declaration of Rights (1776), asserting:

> That religion, or the duty which we owe our CREATOR, and the manner of discharging it, can be directed only by reason and conviction, not by force or violence; and therefore, that all men are equally entitled to enjoy the free exercise of religion, according to the dictates of conscience, [unpunished and unrestrained by the magistrate, Unless the preservation of equal liberty and the existence of the State are manifestly endangered]; And that it is the mutual duty of all to practice Christian forbearance, love, and charity towards each other. (Madison's proposal for the Virginia Declaration of Rights, June 1776; brackets indicate words deleted in the final version adopted)

Note that by removing reservations against rights of conscience based on the good order of society, the Virginia Convention's revision of Madison's proposal had the effect of making those rights even stronger, less contingent on circumstances, than Madison had suggested. Still, through most of American history, some version of Madison's caveat has prevailed. In a line of cases extending back to 1878, the Supreme Court has distinguished between religious belief, which enjoys total immunity from state action, and religious practices, which may be regulated or even prohibited if they run afoul of basic individual or social interests that government has a duty to protect.

In *Cantwell v. Connecticut*,[4] the Court expounded this distinction with exceptional clarity. The religion clause of the First Amendment

> embraces two concepts – freedom to believe and freedom to act. The first is absolute but, in the nature of things, the second cannot be. Conduct remains subject to regulation for the protection of society. The freedom to act must have appropriate definition to preserve the enforcement of that protection. In every case the power to regulate must be so exercised as not, in attaining a permissible end, unduly to infringe the protected freedom.[5]

In subsequent cases, the Court refined this doctrine: The state interests in the name of which basic liberties are restricted must be "compelling" (vital and urgent), and the means must be narrowly drawn so as to minimize the intrusion on liberty.[6]

To return to the development of Madison's thought: In his famous "Memorial and Remonstrance" (1785), coauthored with Thomas Jefferson and directed against a Virginia proposal to publicly fund teachers of Christianity, Madison further explained the basis of his stance on freedom of conscience:

We remonstrate against the said Bill,

1. Because we hold it for a fundamental and undeniable truth, "that Religion or the duty which we owe to our Creator and the manner of discharging it, can be directed only by reason and conviction, not by force or violence." The Religion then of every man must be left to the conviction and conscience of every man; and it is the right of every man to exercise it as these may dictate. This right is in its nature an unalienable right. It is unalienable, because the opinions of men, depending only on the evidence contemplated by their own minds cannot follow the dictates of other men: It is unalienable also, because what is here a right toward men, is a duty toward the Creator. It is the duty of every man to render to the Creator such homage and such only as he believes to be acceptable to him. This duty is precedent, both in order of time and degree of obligation, to the claims of Civil Society. Before any man can be considered as a member of Civil Society, he must be considered as a subject of the Governour of the Universe: And if a member of Civil Society, who enters into any subordinate Association, must always do it with a reservation of his duty to the General authority; much more must every man who becomes a member of any particular Civil Society, do it with a saving of his allegiance to the Universal Sovereign. We maintain therefore that in matters of Religion, no mans right is abridged by the institution of Civil Society and that Religion is wholly exempt from its cognizance. True it is, that no other rule exists, by which any question which may divide a Society, can be ultimately determined, but the will of the majority; but it is also true that the majority may trespass on the rights of the minority.[7]

Madison's efforts continued at the national level during the early Constitutional period. Indeed, two of the amendments that Madison drafted for inclusion in the Bill of Rights, one of which would have been binding on the states, made explicit reference to "rights of conscience."

The civil rights of none shall be abridged on account of religious belief or worship, nor shall any national religion be established; nor shall the full and equal rights of conscience be in any manner, or in any pretext, infringed. (Amendment to the Constitution drafted by Madison for inclusion in the Bill of Rights, June 8, 1789)

No state shall violate the equal rights of conscience, or the freedom of the press, or the trial by jury in criminal cases. (Amendment to the Constitution drafted by Madison for inclusion in the Bill of Rights, June 8, 1789)

In presenting these two amendments to the House of Representatives on June 8, 1789, Madison commented: "I cannot see any reason against obtaining even a double security on these points...because the State Governments are as liable to attack these invaluable privileges as the General Government is." In the subsequent floor debate on the draft Bill of Rights, Madison characterized the proposed restriction on the states as "the most valuable amendment in the whole list"(August 17 1789).[8]

Although the House of Representatives accepted Madison's proposal to make guarantees of basic rights binding on the states, the Senate refused to go along. It took nearly 150 years for the Supreme Court to decide that the Fourteenth Amendment had provided the vehicle for enforcing these rights vis-à-vis state governments as well as the federal government. In *Cantwell*, the Supreme Court ruled that a state statute severely restricting religious solicitation represented a deprivation of liberty without due process of law in contravention of the Fourteenth Amendment. "The fundamental concept of liberty embodied in that Amendment," the Court stated, "embraces the liberties guaranteed by the First Amendment. The First Amendment declares that Congress shall make no law respecting an establishment of religion or prohibiting the free exercise thereof. The Fourteenth Amendment has rendered the legislatures of the states as incompetent as the Congress to enact such laws."[9]

## 4 SUBSTANTIVE DUE PROCESS, FUNDAMENTAL LIBERTIES, AND FREEDOM OF CONSCIENCE

Over the nineteenth century, the Supreme Court played, at most, a minor role in protecting what we now understand as the basic civil rights of individuals. During the decades after the Civil War, the Court increasingly deployed a broad construction of individual property rights against the states while typically leaving political and civil liberties under the aegis of state power – a jurisprudential strategy that reached its peak in the famous (for some, infamous) 1905 decision of *Lochner v. New York.*[10] Legal commentators and dissenting justices began asking how these two tendencies could be reconciled.

In 1920, the case of *Gilbert v. Minnesota* came before the Supreme Court.[11] Gilbert, a pacifist, had criticized American participation in World War I. He was convicted under a state statute prohibiting advocacy or teaching that interfered with or discouraged enlistment in the military. While the Court's majority declined to extend Fourteenth Amendment liberty guarantees to Gilbert, Justice Brandeis dissented, writing:

I have difficulty believing that the liberty guaranteed by the Constitution, which has been held to protect [a wide property right], does not include liberty to teach, either in the privacy of the home or publicly, the doctrine of pacifism ... I cannot believe that the liberty guaranteed by the 14th Amendment includes only liberty to acquire and to enjoy property.[12]

Over time, the Court's unwillingness to abandon its doctrine of broad economic rights helped create the basis for a broader understanding of constitutionally protected and enforceable liberties. Two important cases decided in the 1920s spearheaded this expansion and helped lay the foundation for nationally recognized rights of conscience. The first stemmed from a Nebraska law that, reflecting the nativist passions stirred by World War I, prohibited instruction in any modern language other than English. Acting under this statute, a trial court convicted a teacher in a Lutheran parochial school for teaching a Bible class in German. In *Meyer v. Nebraska*,[13] the Supreme Court struck down this law as a violation of the Fourteenth Amendment's liberty guarantee. Writing for a seven-member majority, Justice McReynolds declared:

That the State may do much, go very far, indeed, in order to improve the quality of its citizens, physically, mentally, and morally, is clear; but the individual has certain fundamental rights which must be respected. A desirable end cannot be promoted by prohibited means.[14]

Two years later, the Supreme Court handed down a second key ruling. The background to the case was this: Through a ballot initiative, the people of Oregon enacted a law requiring all parents and legal guardians to send children between the ages of eight and sixteen to public schools. This amounted to outlawing most nonpublic schools. The Society of Sisters, an Oregon corporation that maintained a system of Catholic schools, sued on the grounds that this laws was inconsistent with the Fourteenth Amendment. In *Pierce v. Society of Sisters*,[15] decided in 1925, the Court agreed. Justice McReynolds, this time writing for a unanimous court, declared:

The fundamental theory of liberty upon which all governments in this Union repose excludes any general power of the State to standardize its children by forcing them to accept instruction from public teachers only. The child is not the mere creature of the State . . . [16]

I now jump forward six years, to 1931. In that year, the Supreme Court handed down its decision in the case of *U.S. v. Macintosh*.[17] The facts were as follows: Douglas Clyde Macintosh was born in Canada, came to the United States as a graduate student at the University of Chicago, and was ordained as a Baptist minister in 1907. He began teaching at Yale in 1909, and in short order became a member of the faculty of the Divinity school, Chaplain of the Yale Graduate School, and Dwight Professor of Theology. When World War I broke out, he returned to his native Canada and volunteered for service on the front as a military chaplain. He reentered the United States in 1916 and applied for naturalization in 1925. When asked whether he would bear arms on behalf of his country, he said he would not give a blanket undertaking in advance without knowing the cause for which his country was asking him to fight or believing that the war was just, declaring that "his first allegiance was to the will of God." After he was denied naturalization, he went to court.

The government argued that naturalization was a privilege, not a right, that the government has the right to impose any conditions it sees fit on that privilege, that the exemption of native-born citizens from military service on grounds of conscience was a statutory grant, not a Constitutional right, and that the Congress had not provided such statutory exemption for individuals seeking naturalization. The lawyers for Macintosh argued that our history makes it clear that conscientious exemption from military service was an integral element of the rights of conscience, guaranteed by the First Amendment, that inhere in individuals, and that in any event this was one of the rights reserved to the people by the Ninth Amendment.

By a vote of 5 to 4, a deeply divided Court decided in favor of the government. The case turned both on matters of statutory construction and on broader considerations. Writing for the majority, Justice Sutherland said:

When [Macintosh] speaks of putting his allegiance to the will of God above his allegiance to the government, it is evident, in light of his entire statement, that he means to make *his own interpretation* of the will of God the decisive test which shall conclude the government and stay its hand. We are a Christian people . . . , according to one another the equal right of religious freedom, and acknowledging with reverence the duty of obedience to the will of God. But, also, we are a Nation with the duty to survive; a Nation whose Constitution contemplates war as well as peace; whose government must go forward upon the assumption, and safely can proceed upon no other, that qualified obedience to the Nation and submission and obedience to the laws of the land, as well those made for war as those made for peace, are not inconsistent with the will of God.[18]

Writing for the four dissenters, Chief Justice Hughes began by offering an argument based on statutory construction, but like Sutherland, he did not end there. Hughes framed the broader argument this way:

Much has been said of the paramount duty to the State, a duty to be recognized, it is urged, even though it conflicts with convictions of duty to God. Undoubtedly that duty to the State exists within the domain of power, for government may enforce obedience to laws regardless of scruples. When one's belief collides with the power of the State, the latter is supreme within its sphere and submission or punishment follows. But, in the forum of conscience, duty to a moral power higher than the State has always been maintained. The reservation of that supreme obligation, as a matter of principle, would undoubtedly be made by many of our conscientious and law-abiding citizens. The essence of religion is belief in a relation to God involving duties superior to those arising from any human relation ... One cannot speak of religious liberty, with proper appreciation of its essential and historic significance, without assuming the existence of a belief in supreme allegiance to the will of God.... [F]reedom of conscience itself implies respect for an innate conviction of paramount duty. The battle for religious liberty has been fought and won with respect to religious beliefs and practices, which are not in conflict with good order, upon the very ground of the supremacy of conscience within its proper field. What that field is, under our system of government, presents in part a question of constitutional law and also, in part, one of legislative policy in avoiding unnecessary clashes with the dictates of conscience. There is abundant room for enforcing the requisite authority of law as it is enacted and requires obedience, and for maintaining the conception of the supremacy of law as essential to orderly government, without demanding that either citizens or applicants for citizenship shall assume by oath an obligation to regard allegiance to God as subordinate to allegiance to civil power.[19]

## 5 FROM *GOBITIS* TO *BARNETTE*: THE RISE AND FALL OF FELIX FRANKFURTER

This brings me back to the dueling court decisions with which I began. As we will see, *Gobitis* and *Barnette* bring into play a number of issues much debated among students of jurisprudence and political theory during the past decade: the clash between history-based and principle-based interpretations of constitutional norms; the roles of courts and legislatures in a constitutional democracy; the competition between parents and the state for control of education; the appropriate contents and limits of civic education. The deepest issue is the relative weight to be given to claims based on individual liberties and those based on social order and cohesion. Legal doctrines of presumption, burden of proof, and tests ("rational basis," "compelling state interests," "clear and present danger") serve as proxies for competing moral intuitions and judgments.

Writing for the majority in the Pennsylvania case (*Gobitis*), Justice Frankfurter offered an argument in favor of a democratic state whose legitimate powers include the power to prescribe civic exercises such as the flag salute. He began by locating the controversy in a complex field of plural and competing claims: liberty of individual conscience versus the state's authority to safeguard the nation's civic unity. The task is to "reconcile" these competing claims, which means "prevent[ing] either from destroying the other." Because liberty of conscience is so fundamental, "every possible leeway" should be given to the claims of religious faith. Still, Frankfurter reasoned, the "very plurality of principles" prevents us from establishing the "freedom to *follow* conscience" as absolute.[20]

The next issue concerns the meaning of these clashing principles. Frankfurter suggested that in considering the judicial enforcement of religious freedom, we are dealing with a "*historic* concept."[21] That is, we should not look at its underlying logic or principles, but rather and only at the way this concept has been applied in the past. We may well wonder whether this constitutes an adequate account of constitutional interpretation. ("cruel and unusual"?) But even if it were, it would not necessarily support Frankfurter's conclusion. He insisted that "conscientious scruples have not, in the course of the long struggle for religious toleration, relieved the individual from obedience to a general law not aimed at the promotion or restriction of religious belief."[22] But (as a number of commentators quickly pointed out) the *Cantwell* decision handed down just two weeks before *Gobitis* had done precisely that: It exempted individuals (in fact, Jehovah's Witnesses) engaged in religious activities from regulations not facially aimed at restricting free exercise, but rather at preventing fraud.

Still, Frankfurter insisted, "The mere possession of religious convictions which contradict the relevant concerns of a political society does not relieve the citizen from the discharge of political responsibilities."[23] On its face, this premise is fair enough, but it raises the question of what must be added to "mere possession" to create a valid claim against the state. When (if ever) does the Constitution require some individuals to be exempted from doing what society thinks is necessary to promote the common good? Conversely, what are the kinds of collective claims that rightly trump individual reservations?

Frankfurter offers a specific answer to the latter, as follows: Social order and tranquility provide the basis for enjoying all civil rights – including rights of conscience and exercise. Indeed, all specific activities and advantages of government "presuppose the existence of an organized political society." Laws that impede religious exercise are valid when the legislature deems them essential to secure civic order and tranquility. National unity is the basis of national security – a highest–order public value (as we would now say, a "compelling state interest"). National unity is secured by the "binding tie of cohesive sentiment," which is the "ultimate foundation of a free society." This sentiment, in turn, is fostered by "all those agencies of the mind and spirit which may serve to gather up the traditions of a people, transmit them from generation to generation, and thereby create that continuity of a treasured common life which constitutes a civilization."[24]

If the cultivation of unifying sentiment is a valid end of government action, Frankfurter concluded, then courts should not interfere with legislative determinations of appropriate means. We do not know what works and what does not; we cannot say for sure that flag salutes are ineffective. In judging the legislature, we may use only the weakest of tests: Is there any basis for the means the legislature has chosen to adopt? If there is, the courts must stay out.[25] But if satisfying the weakest test is enough, then the countervailing claims cannot be that important after all. So religious free exercise, which at the beginning of the opinion is characterized as "so subtle and so dear" as to require every possible deference, is reduced to a near-nullity by the end.

Frankfurter was aware that the thrust of his argument stood in tension with the Court's holding in *Pierce*. To square the circle, he offered a tendentious reinterpretation of that decision as defending diverse opinions about how to socialize children.[26] But, as we have seen, the *Pierce* court cited not the fact of diversity but rather a fundamental theory of liberty as the basis for its decision, precisely the kind of general claim against the state that Frankfurter was anxious to sidestep. It is hardly surprisingly to learn that while still a law professor, Frankfurter inveighed against *Pierce* when the decision was first handed down on the grounds that a Court that deployed fundamental principles of liberty against state regulation of education could deploy comparable principles against state regulation of the economy. If you like *Pierce*, his reasoning went, you must accept *Lochner*. And that is a cost that outweighs the gains.[27] It is perhaps understandable that Frankfurter could not foresee the emergence of a new jurisprudence that would reorder the relationship between religious and economic regulation. But that is no excuse for deliberately understating the evident force of conscience-based claims.

Toward the conclusion of his opinion, Frankfurter touched on an issue that figures centrally in our current debates – the right of public authorities "to awaken in the child's mind considerations . . . contrary to those implanted by the parent."[28] He is right to suggest that the bare fact of a clash with parents does not suffice to render a state's action illegitimate. But who seriously thinks that parental claims are always trumps? The thesis is rather that there are certain classes of claims that parents can interpose against state authority, especially when the state employs particularly intrusive means in pursuit of public purposes. Recall that what was at stake in *Gobitis* was not just the right of the state to require civic education, but rather the state's power to compel students to engage in affirmations contrary to conscientious belief. It is not unreasonable to suggest that compelling the performance of speech and deeds contrary to faith is a step even graver than prohibiting activities required by faith, and places the state under an even heavier burden to justify the necessity of its coercion.

Frankfurter endorsed no such principle. Quite the reverse: To foster social order and unity, he asserted, the state "may in self-protection utilize the educational process for inculcating those almost unconscious feelings which bind men together."[29] And if the state gets it wrong? Frankfurter answered this question, and concluded his opinion, with a profession of faith in the democratic process: It is better to use legislative processes to protect liberty and rectify error rather than transferring the contest to the judicial arena. As long as the political liberties needed for effective political contestation are left unaffected, "education in the abandonment of foolish legislation is itself a training in liberty [and] serves to vindicate the self-confidence of a free people."[30] There is clearly some wisdom in this position, which is enjoying a modest resurgence today. What it overlooks is the cost, especially to the most affected individuals and groups, of waiting for a democratic majority to recognize its mistake.

In the course of this exposition of Frankfurter's opinion, I have offered a running critique, which some may regard as unreasonable. Have I not presupposed political and jurisprudential developments that Frankfurter had no way of anticipating? Given the cards he was dealt, didn't he play his hand reasonably? To be sure, Justice (soon to be Chief Justice) Stone had forcefully dissented. The law in dispute, he argued, did more than suppress and prohibit the free exercise of religion; it sought to coerce individuals to perform acts to which they are conscientiously opposed. Civil liberties, he argued, are "guarantees of freedom of the human mind and spirit and of reasonable freedom and opportunity to express them . . . If these guaranties are to have any meaning they must, I think, be deemed to withhold from the state any authority to compel belief or the expression of it where that expression violates religious convictions, whatever may be the legislative view of the desirability of such compulsion."[31]

Stone acknowledged that liberty guarantees are not absolute; the state has the right to do what it needs to do to survive and to protect basic interests, such as public order and health. These considerations suffice to justify measures such as the draft and mandatory vaccinations. But the very existence of protected civil liberties implies a restriction of government powers, an accommodation of public policy to the liberties in question. A valid end does not imply that all means in its pursuit are permitted. In the case of conflicts, there should, whenever possible, be a "reasonable accommodation between them so as to preserve the essentials of both." Even if national unity is an important interest of the state, Stone argued, "there are other ways to teach loyalty and patriotism which are the sources of national unity, than by compelling the pupil to affirm that which he does not believe and by commanding a form of affirmance which violates his religious convictions."[32]

There was no basis, Stone continued, for saying that the protection of civil rights should be left to legislatures; this was "no less than the surrender of the constitutional protection of the liberty of small minorities to the popular will." The Constitution is liberal as well as democratic. It "expresses more than the conviction of the people that democratic processes must be preserved at all costs. It is also an expression of faith and a command that freedom of mind and spirit must be preserved, which government must obey, if it is to adhere to that justice and moderation without which no free government can exist."[33]

Despite his eloquence, Stone persuaded none of his brethren to follow him. Might he not be regarded as a noble but idiosyncratic voice, without resonance either on the Court or in the country? On the contrary: Frankfurter's opinion raised a storm of controversy the moment it was handed down,[34] and many of the criticisms leveled against it at that time anticipated the kind of jurisprudence that emerged only a few years later and flowered in the following decades. Let me offer a few examples of these critiques, drawn from a far longer list.

William Fennell, a prominent member of the New York Bar, distinguished between the "liberal democrat" who "puts complete trust in the majority popular will to correct foolish legislation which violates . . . constitutional liberties" and the "liberal constitutionalist" who recognizes the important role of the Supreme Court in scrutinizing legislation that touches on the rights of minorities. The liberal democrat will use judicial review to safeguard individual rights "of speech, press, assembly, the franchise" needed to ensure the integrity of the democratic process. But only democratic majorities have the right to correct mistakes flowing from the exercise of procedural democracy.[35] Arguing against Frankfurter's endorsement of the liberal democratic position, Fennell asked his readers to consider its consequences for previous decisions such as *Pierce*: Wouldn't Frankfurter's jurisprudence have left every

Catholic in the state of Oregon vulnerable to the anti-Catholic majority's repressive folly?

If the 'reconstructed court' (to use Frankfurter's own phrase in another case) continues to adhere in cases involving religious liberty to the doctrine of the majority in the *Gobitis* case, the scope of the state police power will be immeasurably enhanced and religious liberty will be at the mercy of shifting political majorities. It is to the lasting credit of the new Chief Justice [Stone] that he comprehended that the Constitution expresses more than the conviction that democratic processes must be preserved at all costs: it is also an expression of faith and a command *which government itself must obey* that freedom of mind and spirit must be preserved. This is the very 'genius' of American constitutional democracy.[36]

Writing in the *Michigan Law Review*, William F. Anderson noted that the *Gobitis* majority was of the opinion "that in questionable cases personal freedom could best be maintained by the democratic process as long as the remedial channels of that process functioned, . . . thereby distinguishing liberty of exercise of religion from liberty of speech, press, and assemblage in that the latter are indispensable to the remedial channels of the democratic process . . . " Anderson worried that this process-based argument did not go far enough, either in theory or in practice: "If individual liberties are something more than the by-product of a democratic process, if in fact they have an intrinsic value worthy of protection, it is difficult to justify a decision which subordinates a fundamental liberty to a legislative program of questionable worth."[37]

Reviewing the 1939–1940 term of the Supreme Court in the *American Political Science Review*, the redoubtable Robert E. Cushman declared that "All of the eloquence by which the majority extol the ceremony of flag saluting as a free expression of patriotism turns sour when used to describe the brutal compulsion which requires a sensitive and conscientious child to stultify himself in public."[38]

What may well be regarded as the *coup de grace* was delivered by Thomas Reed Powell, Joseph Story professor of Law at Harvard, a pioneering legal realist, and no softy. He was a liberal, but no one could accuse him of lacking spine. His article entitled "Conscience and the Constitution" is published in a book with the title *Democracy and National Unity* (no merely theoretical topic in 1940) and drips with scorn for the plaintiff Jehovah's Witnesses. Powell termed them "ignorant communicants of peculiar sects," "unreflecting, dogmatic, indoctrinated," "simple-minded and unintelligent." He even compared them to "mental defectives" and spoke approvingly of an education that weans the children away from the "nonsense of their parents."[39]

And yet... Powell could not bring himself to accept Frankfurter's opinion. Three stumbling blocks proved insurmountable. First: As a matter of legal fact, he could not agree with Frankfurter's assertion that freedom of religion cannot be deployed against general legislation not specifically directed against religion. The *Cantwell* decision, handed down a mere two weeks before *Gobitis*, held just the reverse.[40] Second: As a practical matter, the effort to coerce children to salute the flag insincerely and contrary to conscience "seems... likely to be self-defeating" when measured against its goal of fostering patriotism and national unity.[41] But finally, the case presented more than a question of practical policy. The issue of religious liberty was squarely on the table, in tension with the inculcation of national unity. By the logic of Frankfurter's own argument, if important constitutional values are in competition, then they must be weighed against one another. The majority failed to do this: "After general obeisance to religious freedom, almost no further weight is accorded to it in the opinion of the Court."[42] In a serious weighing of competing values, Powell insisted, the Court must address quantitative as well as qualitative issues: How important is it to the nation to compel children to join in a patriotic ceremony, which for them is idolatry? To what extent would exempting them impair the power of the state to preserve itself? Is the public interest slight or major? The Court must make a substantive choice, and that choice must rest on a judgment of relative significance. The majority's own language tacitly concedes this, citing the paramount importance of national unity, but it fails to discharge its responsibility to assess what rests on the other side of the scale.[43]

Judgments based on quantitative variations along clashing dimensions of value provide the basis for reasonable distinctions. If we decide that it is wrong to compel school children to salute the flag against conscience, does that mean that we must find in favor of conscientious objectors to military service? No, said Powell: "No sensible person... can think it necessary. The differences of degree [in the state interests at stake] are too great."[44]

This is not to suggest that conscientious scruples can stand against all compulsion to do positive acts. Quite the contrary. The question is one of degree. I should think that it requires more justification to compel a man or child to commit what he regards as a sin than to restrict him in the areas in which he can practice what he regards as a command of the Lord.... The public need for coerced and insincere saluting of the flag by little children seems to me to be trivial...[45]

The effects of these criticisms became apparent by 1942, when the Court decided the case of *Jones v. Opelika*.[46] The facts were these: Jehovah's Witnesses had been going door-to-door selling religious books. Various municipalities enacted statutes requiring all booksellers to take out licenses and pay substantial fees in order to distribute books legally. The Jehovah's Witnesses refused to do so, citing free exercise claims as well as other arguments.

Writing for a five-man majority, Justice Reed began with the standard distinction between religious conscience and religious acts. He argued that, granting the presumption in favor of First Amendment freedoms, public determinations of time, place, and manner were rightly viewed as consistent with those freedoms. When proponents of religious views use "ordinary commercial methods" to propagate their view, fees and other regulations represent a "natural and proper exercise of the power of the State"[47]:

Nothing more is asked from one group than from another which uses similar methods of propagation. We see nothing in the collection of a non-discriminatory licensing fee, ... from those selling books or papers, which abridges the freedoms of worship, speech, or press.[48]

Led by Chief Justice Stone, four member of the Court dissented. In his opinion, Stone made two principal points. First, it is essential to examine the extent of the burden the law places on religious free exercise, which the majority blithely refused to do. The power to tax may well amount to the power to censor or suppress. Second, it does not suffice to say that the tax on speech and religion is "non-discriminatory." The First Amendment is not confined to safeguarding freedom of speech and freedom of religion against discriminatory attempts to wipe them out. On the contrary, the Constitution, by virtue of the First and the Fourteenth Amendments, has put those freedoms in a preferred position."[49]

Justice Murphy's dissent addressed Stone's questions and amplified his argument. The burden, Murphy insisted, was significant, and that fact was significant in resolving the case. To be sure, it was necessary to distinguish between burdens on thought and those on action. But this distinction should not be taken so far as to become unrealistic: "[E]ven an aggressive mind is of no missionary value unless there is freedom of action, freedom to communicate its message to others by speech and writing."[50] Moreover, the defendants had failed to specify the harms to be avoided through the licensing system or to show that the statutes were drawn narrowly and precisely to address those evils. Nor, finally, would it do to argue that the statutes were for the purpose of raising general revenues rather than averting specific harms, because the "exercise, without commercial motives, of freedom of speech, freedom of the press, or freedom of worship are not proper sources of taxation for general revenue purposes."[51]

> The mind rebels at the thought that a minister of any of the old established churches could be made to pay fees to the community before entering the pulpit. These taxes on petitioners' efforts to preach the 'news of the Kingdom' should be struck down because they burden petitioners' right to worship the Deity in their own fashion and to spread the gospel as they understand it.[52]

Even more significant than these two individual dissents was a brief dissenting statement jointly authored by three justices (Murphy, Black, and Douglas) who had formed part of the *Gobitis* majority. They wrote:

> The opinion of the Court sanctions a device which in our opinion suppresses or tends to suppress the free exercise of a religion practiced by a minority group. This is but another step in the direction which *Minersville School District v. Gobitis* took against the same religious minority and is a logical extension of the principles upon which that decision rested. Since we joined in the opinion in the *Gobitis* case, we think this is an appropriate decision to state that we now believe that it was also wrongly decided.[53]

In the course of a comprehensive survey of the development of liberties protected under the Fourteenth Amendment, John Raeburn Green commented that while there was nothing good to be said about the majority decision, "[n]evertheless *Jones v. Opelika*... in the long run will mark an advance for [religious] liberty, because of the dissenting opinions."[54] He was right, and sooner than he thought. In the very next year (1943), the replacement of Justice Byrnes, one of the *Opelika* majority, led to its reversal by a vote of 5 to 4 in the case of *Murdock v. Pennsylvania*.[55] More remarkably, *Gobitis* was overruled by a stunning 6 to 3, in *West Virginia v. Barnette*. I turn now to Justice Jackson's majority opinion in that case, a highlight of which we have already encountered.

Jackson did not question the state's right to educate for patriotism and civic unity. But what was at stake, in his view, was not education, rightly understood, but something quite different: "Here ... we are dealing with a compulsion of students to declare a belief."[56]

> [C]ensorship or suppression of expression of opinion is tolerated by our Constitution only when the expression presents a clear and present danger of action of a kind the State is empowered to prevent and punish. It would seem that involuntary affirmation could be commanded only on even more immediate and urgent

grounds than silence. But here the power of compulsion is invoked without any allegation that remaining passive during a flag salute ritual creates a clear and present danger that would justify an effort even to muffle expression. To sustain the compulsory flag salute we are required to say that a Bill of Rights which guards the individual's right to speak his own mind, left it open to public authorities to compel him to utter what is not in his mind.[57]

The issue, Jackson asserted, is not one of policy – that is, of effectiveness of means in pursuit of a legitimate end such as national unity. The prior question is whether the state possesses the rightful power to promote this end through compulsion contrary to conscience, a power the *Gobitis* majority assumed to inhere in our constitutional government. If it does not, then the issue is not exempting dissenters from otherwise valid policies, but rather reining in a state that is transgressing the bounds of legitimate action.[58]

Jackson insisted that limited government is not weak government. Assuring individual rights strengthens government by bolstering support for it. In the long run, individual freedom of mind is more sustainable and powerful than is "officially disciplined uniformity."[59] "To believe that patriotism will not flourish if patriotic ceremonies are voluntary and spontaneous instead of a compulsory routine is to make an unflattering estimate of the appeal of our institutions to free minds."[60]

Limited government is not simply a wise policy, Jackson argued; it is also a matter of constitutional principle:

The very purpose of a Bill of Rights was to withdraw certain subjects from the vicissitudes of political controversy, to place them beyond the reach of majorities and officials and to establish them as legal principles to be applied by the courts. One's right to life, liberty, and property, to free speech, a free press, freedom of worship and assembly, and other fundamental rights may not be submitted to vote; they depend on the outcome of no elections.[61]

Limitations on government affect means as well as ends. There is no question that government officials and institutions may seek to promote national unity through persuasion and example. "The problem is whether under our Constitution compulsion as here employed is a permissible means for its achievement."[62] It is in this context that Jackson penned his famous words about the fixed star in our constitutional constellation, the sphere of intellect and spirit that our laws protect from all official interference.

The three repentant justices who had issued promissory notes in their *Opelika* dissent redeemed them by joining the *Barnette* majority. Black and Douglas began their concurrence by noting that "[S]ince we originally joined with the Court in the *Gobitis* case, it is appropriate that we make a brief statement of reasons for our change of view." They offered three such reasons. First: As a constitutional matter, while the state can impose reasonable regulations on the time, place, or manner of religious activity, it can suppress religious liberty only to ward off "grave and pressingly immediate dangers." But the state was far from discharging its burden in this case; the danger was remote at best, and the policy only speculatively connected to its professed end. Second, the state's burden is especially heavy because the nature of the means employed – "the statutory exaction of specific words" – constitutes a form of "test oath" that has always been especially abhorrent in the United States. And even if this policy were constitutionally acceptable, it would be self-defeating: "Words uttered under coercion are proof of nothing but loyalty to self-interest. Love of country must spring from willing hearts and free minds, inspired by a fair administration of wise laws enacted by the people's elected representatives within the bounds of express constitutional prohibitions."[63]

The third penitent, Justice Murphy, also concurred. Freedom of thought and religion, he contended, implies the right both to speak and to remain silent, except when compulsion is required for the preservation of an ordered society – as in the case of compulsion to testify in court. The compelled flag salute did not come close to meeting that test: Its benefits were too indefinite and intangible to justify the restriction on freedom and invasion of privacy.[64]

Justice Frankfurter, the author of the majority opinion in *Gobitis*, penned a lengthy dissent, a personal apologia whose tone of injured dignity was set by its opening sentence: "One who belongs to the most vilified and persecuted minority in history is not likely to be insensible to the freedoms guaranteed by our Constitution."[65] But he declared that what was at stake was not a constitutional question but rather a policy judgment. In this arena, courts should override legislatures only if reasonable legislators could not have chosen to employ the contested means in furtherance of legitimate ends. As a general proposition, there is a presumption in favor of legislatures, and legislation must be considered valid if there exists some rational basis for connecting it to a valid public purpose.[66]

Exceptions to this presumption arise when the state employs constitutionally prohibited means. But the mandatory flag salute was not of this character. The state action at issue, Frankfurter asserted, was not intended to promote or discourage religion, which was clearly forbidden. Rather, it was "a general non-discriminatory civil regulation [that] in fact [but not as a matter of intended effect] touches conscientious scruples or religious beliefs of an individual or a group."[67] In such cases, it is the legislature's role to make accommodations, not the court's.

Jefferson and those who followed him wrote guarantees of religious freedom into our constitutions. Religious minorities as well as religious majorities were to be equal in the eyes of the political state. But Jefferson and the others also knew that minorities may disrupt society. It never would have occurred to them to write into the Constitution the subordination of the general civil authority of the state to sectarian scruples... The constitutional protection of religious freedom terminated disabilities, it did not create new privileges. It gave religious equality, not civil immunity. Its essence is freedom from conformity to religious dogma, not freedom from conformity to law because of religious dogma... The essence of the religious freedom guaranteed by our Constitution is this: no religion shall either receive the state's support or incur its hostility. Religion is outside the sphere of political government. This does not mean that all matters on which religious organizations or beliefs may pronounce are outside the sphere of government.[68]

Many other laws (for example, compulsory medical measures) have employed compulsion against religious scruples, but courts have not struck them down:

Law is concerned with external behavior and not with the inner life of man. It rests in large measure upon compulsion... The consent on which free government rests in the consent that comes from sharing in the process of making and unmaking laws. The state is not shut out from a domain because the individual conscience may deny the state's claim.[69]

Indeed, Frankfurter asserted, it was wrong to describe the mandatory flag salute as compelled belief:

Compelling belief implies denial of opportunity to combat it and to assert dissident views. Such compulsion is one thing. Quite another matter is submission to conformity of action while denying its wisdom or virtue with ample opportunity for seeking its change or abrogation.[70]

In an oddly prophetic passage, Frankfurter contended that the majority's decision led to a *reductio ad absurdum*:

Consider the controversial issue of compulsory Bible-reading in public schools... Is this Court to... [deny] states the right to entertain such convictions in regard to their school systems, because of a belief that the King James version is in fact a sectarian text to which parents of the Catholic and Jewish faiths and some Protestant persuasions may rightly object to having their children exposed?... Is it really a fair construction of such a fundamental concept as the right freely to exercise one's religion that a state cannot choose to require all children who attend public school to make the same gesture of allegiance to the symbol of our national life because it may offend the conscience of some children, but that it may compel all children [who] attend public school to listen to the King James version although it may offend the consciences of their parents?[71]

Frankfurter concluded his dissent with a profession of political faith. Liberal democracy is more a matter of active, self-governing citizens than of protective or tutelary courts:

> Of course patriotism cannot be enforced by the flag salute. But neither can the liberal spirit be enforced by judicial invalidation of illiberal legislation ... Only a persistent positive translation of the faith of a free society into the convictions and habits and actions of a community is the ultimate reliance against unabated temptations to fetter the human spirit.[72]

## 6 CONCLUSION: JURISPRUDENCE, MORAL INTUITION, AND POLITICAL THEORY

I am not a legal historian. I have told this tale, not for its own sake, but with moral intent. I want to use these materials as a basis for testing our judgments about two questions. First: Looking at the judicial bottom-line – the "holding" – are we more inclined to favor the outcome in *Gobitis* or in *Barnette*? Second: What kinds of broader principles underlie our judgment concerning these specific cases?

It is easy to sympathize with Frankfurter's dismay at the deployment of judicial review to immunize concentrated economic power against public scrutiny; with his belief that democratic majorities should enjoy wide latitude to pursue the common good as they see it; with his assertion that the requirements of social order and unity may sometimes override the claims, however worthy, of individuals, parents, civil associations, and religious faith; and with his conviction that the systematic substitution of judicial review for democratic self-correction can end by weakening citizenship itself. Nonetheless, I believe (and I am far from alone), that Frankfurter's reasoning in *Gobitis* was unsound, and his holding unacceptable. There are certain goods and liberties that enjoy a preferred position in our order and are supposed to be lifted above everyday policy debate. If liberty of conscience is a fundamental good, as Frankfurter acknowledges, then it follows that state action interfering with it bears a substantial burden of proof. A distant harm, loosely linked to the contested policy, is not enough to meet that burden. The harm must be a real threat; it must be causally linked to the policy in question; and the proposed remedy must do the least possible damage to the fundamental

liberty, consistent with the abatement of the threat. The state's mandatory pledge of allegiance failed all three of these tests. *Gobitis* was wrongly
decided; the ensuing uproar was a public indication that the Court had
gone astray; and the quick reversal in *Barnette*, with fully half the justices
in the new six-member majority switching sides, was a clear indication of
the moral force of the objections.

We now reach my second question: Is our judgment on these cases a
particularized moral intuition, or does it reflect some broader principles?
The latter, I think. What Justice Jackson termed the "sphere of intellect
and spirit" is at or near the heart of what makes us human. The protection of that sphere against unwarranted intrusion represents the most
fundamental of all human liberties. There is a strong presumption against
state policies that prevent individuals from the free exercise of intellect
and spirit. There is an even stronger presumption against compelling
individuals to make affirmations contrary to their convictions. (These
presumptions drove Madison's understanding of freedom of conscience,
discussed earlier in this chapter.) This does not mean that compulsory
speech is always wrong; courts and legislatures may rightly compel un-
willing witnesses to give testimony and may rightly punish any failure to
do so that does not invoke a well-established principle of immunity, such
as the bar against coerced self-incrimination. Even here, the point of the
compulsion is to induce individuals to tell the truth as they see it, not to
betray their innermost convictions in the name of a state-administered
orthodoxy.

It is easy for polities, even stable constitutional democracies, to violate
these principles. In that obvious empirical sense, fundamental liberties
are political constructions. But that democratic majorities can deprive
minorities of liberty, often with impunity, does not make it right. Like all
politics, democratic politics is legitimate to the extent that it recognizes
and observes the principled limits to the exercise of democratic power.
The liberties that individuals and the associations they constitute should
enjoy in all but the most desperate circumstances go well beyond the
political rights that democratic politics requires. We cannot rightly assess
the importance of politics without acknowledging the limits of politics.
The claims that political institutions can make in the name of the common good coexist with claims of at least equal importance that individuals
and civil associations make, based on particular visions of the good for
themselves or for humankind. This political pluralism may be messy and
conflictual; it may lead to confrontations not conducive to maximizing
public unity and order. But if political pluralism, thus understood, reflects

the complex truth of the human condition, then the practice of politics must do its best to honor the principles that limit the scope of politics.

## 6.1 The Ambiguities of Conscience

My announced topic in this chapter is freedom of conscience. But what is "conscience," anyway? For James Madison and other eighteenth-century thinkers, the term clearly pointed toward religious conviction. Although Justice Jackson's sphere of intellect and spirit includes religion, it encompasses much else besides. So is conscience to be understood narrowly or expansively?

We may approach this question from two standpoints, the constitutional and the philosophical. Within constitutional law, both the narrow and expansive views have found proponents among able interpreters of the First Amendment. On the narrow side, Laurence Tribe argues that "The Framers...clearly envisioned religion as something special; they enacted that vision into law by guaranteeing the free exercise of *religion* but not, say, of philosophy or science."[73] Christopher Eisgruber and Lawrence Sager object that "to single out one of the ways that persons come to understand what is important in life, and grant those who choose that way a license to disregard legal norms that the rest of us are obliged to obey, is to defeat rather than fulfill our commitment to toleration."[74] In effect, they argue that we must read the religion clauses of the First Amendment in light of the Equal Protection clause of the Fourteenth.

We see this debate playing out in a fascinating way in the evolution of the jurisprudence of conscience-based exemptions from the military draft. Section 6(j) of the World War II-era Universal Military Training and Service Act made exemptions available to those who were conscientiously opposed to military service by reason of "religious training and belief." The required religious conviction was defined as "an individual's belief in a relation to a Supreme being involving duties superior to those arising from any human relation, but [not including] essentially political, sociological, or philosophical views or a merely personal moral code."

In the case of *United States v. Seeger* (1965), however, the Court broadened the definition of religion by interpreting the statue to include a "sincere and meaningful belief which occupies in the life of its possessor a place parallel to that filled by the God of those admittedly qualifying for the exemption."[75] Five years later, in *Welsh v. United States*, a Court plurality further broadened the reach of the statute to include explicitly secular beliefs that "play the role of a religion and function as a religion in life." Thus, draft exemptions could be extended to "those who consciences, spurred by deeply held moral, ethical, or religious beliefs, would give them no rest or peace if they allowed themselves to become a part of an instrument [of war]."[76]

For our purposes, the real action takes place in the penumbra of the plurality's opinion. Justice Harlan, who provided the fifth vote for the expansive reading of conscientious exemption, argued in a concurring opinion that while the plurality's interpretation of the statutory language was indefensible, the Court could and should save the statute by engaging in an explicit act of reconstruction. The reason: It would be a violation of both the Establishment and Equal Protection clauses for Congress to differentiate between religious and nonreligious conscientious objectors.[77] This is the judicial precursor of the Eisgruber/Sager position.

For their part, the three dissenters argued that while Harlan was right as a matter of statutory construction, he was wrong as a matter of constitutional interpretation. They wrote that "neither support nor hostility, but neutrality, is the goal of the religion clauses of the First Amendment. 'Neutrality,' however, is not self-defining. If it is 'favoritism' and not neutrality to exempt religious believers from the draft, is it 'neutrality' and not 'inhibition' of religion to compel religious believers to fight when they have special reasons for not doing so, reasons to which the Constitution gives particular recognition? It cannot be denied [the dissenters concluded] that the First Amendment itself contains a religious classification" – Tribe's point exactly.[78]

To shed light on this dispute, it is useful to move outside the realm of constitutional adjudication and raise more general, even philosophical, considerations. There are, I suggest, two features of religion that figure centrally in the debate about religiously based exemptions from otherwise valid laws. First, believers understand the requirements of religious beliefs and actions as central rather than peripheral to their identity; second, they experience these requirements as authoritative commands. So understood, religion is more than a mode of human flourishing. Regardless of whether an individual experiences religious requirements as promoting or thwarting self-development, their power is compelling. (In this connection, recall the number of Hebrew prophets – starting with Moses – who experienced the divine call to prophetic mission as disruptive of their prior lives and identities.)

My suggestion is that at least in modern times, some individuals and groups who are not religious come to embrace ensembles of belief and action that share these two features of religious experience – identity-formation and compulsory power. It does not seem an abuse of speech to apply the term conscience to this experience, whether religious or nonreligious. My concept of expressive liberty functions, in part, to support the claim that conscience in this extended sense enjoys a rebuttable presumption to prevail in the face of public law. In this respect, though not others, I find myself in agreement with Rogers Smith when he writes:

The only approach that is genuinely compatible with equal treatment, equal protection, and equal respect for all citizens is treating claims of religious and secular moral consciences the same. Fully recognizing the historical, philosophical, and moral force of claims for deference to sincere conscientious beliefs and practices whenever possible, I would place all such claims in a "preferred position" as defined by modern constitutional doctrines: governmental infringements upon such conscientious claims would be sustainable in court only if it were shown that they were necessary for compelling government interests.[79]

What are the kinds of collective interests that suffice to rebut the presumption in favor of individual conscience? I can think of at least two. First, the state cannot avoid attending to the content of conscience. Deep convictions may express personal identity with compulsory power and nonetheless be mistaken in ways that the state may rightly resist through the force of law. Second, even if the content of an individual's conscientious claim is not unacceptable in itself, its social or civic consequences may expose it to justified regulation or even prohibition.

It may well be possible to add other categories of considerations that rebut the presumptions of conscience. In practice, the combined force of these considerations may warrant more restriction than accommodation. My point is only that the assertion of a conscience-based claim imposes a burden on the state to justify its proposed interference. There are many ways in which the state may discharge that burden, but if my position is correct, Justice Frankfurter's argument in *Gobitis* is not one of them. It is not enough to say that whenever a state pursues a general good within its legitimate purview, the resulting abridgement of conscience may represent unfortunate collateral damage that gives affected individuals and groups no legitimate grievance or cause of action. Claims of conscience are not trumps, but they matter far more than Frankfurter and his modern followers are willing to admit.

The ultimate reason is this: In a liberal democracy, the state is not an end in itself but rather a means to certain ends that enjoy an elevated status. The ability of individuals and groups to live in ways consistent with their understanding of what gives meaning and purpose to life is one of those ends. That is what I mean by "expressive liberty." It may rightly be limited to the extent necessary to secure the institutional conditions for its exercise. Beyond that point, the rightful relationship of ends and means is turned on its head. That is the line a liberal democratic state ought not cross.

## Notes

1. *Minersville v. Gobitis*, 310 U.S. 586 (1940).
2. *West Virginia v. Barnette*, 319 U.S. 624 (1943).
3. 319 U.S. 642.
4. *Cantwell v. Connecticut*, 310 U.S. 296 (1940).
5. 310 U.S. 303–4.
6. Some commentators believe that this standard was significantly relaxed by the Court's decision in *Employment Division v. Smith*, 494 U.S. 872 (1990). In this case, five members of the Court held that it was acceptable for the state of Oregon to enforce its drug laws against the use of peyote in Native American religious rites. The five-member majority could not agree, however, on the grounds for this holding, and the case remains bitterly contested in both legislative and judicial forums.
7. *James Madison on Religious Liberty*, Robert S. Alley, ed. (Buffalo, NY: Prometheus Books, 1985), p. 56.
8. Quoted in John Raeburn Green, "Liberty Under the Fourteenth Amendment," *Washington University Law Quarterly* 27 (1942): 497.
9. 310 U.S. 303.
10. *Lochner v. New York*, 198 U.S. 45 (1905).
11. *Gilbert v. Minnesota*, 254 U.S. 325 (1920).
12. 254 U.S. 343.
13. *Meyer v. Nebraska*, 262 U.S. 390 (1923).
14. 262 U.S. 401.
15. *Pierce v. Society of Sisters*, 268 U.S. 510 (1925).
16. 268 U.S. 535.
17. *United States v. Macintosh*, 283 U.S. 605 (1931).
18. 283 U.S. 625.
19. 283 U.S. 633–4.
20. 310 U.S. 591–4; italics mine.
21. 310 U.S. 594; italics mine.
22. Ibid.
23. 301 U.S. 594–5.
24. 301 U.S. 595–6.
25. 301 U.S. 597–8, 599–600.
26. 301 U.S. 598–9.
27. Felix Frankfurter, "Can the Supreme Court Guarantee Toleration?" *The New Republic* 43 (85) (1925).
28. 301 U.S. 599.
29. 301 U.S. 600.

30. Ibid.
31. 301 U.S. 604.
32. 301 U.S. 601.
33. 301 U.S. 606–7.
34. Frankfurter himself received a torrent of abuse. One commentator noted that Frankfurter's supporters, who had long regarded him as the great hope of liberalism, responded to his opinion with amazement, anguish, and outright bitterness. More than one journal compared him to Goebbels mandating the Nazi salute! For an extended discussion of this episode, see Shawn Francis Peters, *Judging Jehovah's Witnesses: Religious Persecution and the Dawn of the Rights Revolution* (Lawrence, KA: University Press of Kansas, 2000), pp. 67–70.
35. William G. Fennell, "The 'Reconstructed Court' and Religious Freedom: the Gobitis Case in Retrospect," *New York University Law Quarterly Review* (19): 31–32.
36. Fennell, "Reconstructed Court," p. 47.
37. 39 *Michigan Law Review* 152 (1940).
38. Robert E. Cushman, *The American Political Science Review* 35(2) (April 1941): 271.
39. Thomas Reed Powell, "Conscience and the Constitution," in *Democracy and National Unity*, William T. Hutchinson, ed. (Chicago: University of Chicago Press, 1941), p. 12.
40. Powell, "Conscience," pp. 28–29.
41. Powell, "Conscience," p. 29.
42. Powell, "Conscience," p. 26.
43. Powell, "Conscience," pp. 23–6.
44. Powell, "Conscience," p. 30.
45. Powell, "Conscience," p. 29.
46. *Jones v. Opelika*, 316 U.S. 584 (1942).
47. 316 U.S. 597.
48. 316 U.S. 598.
49. 316 U.S. 600–8.
50. 316 U.S. 618.
51. 316 U.S. 620.
52. 316 U.S. 621.
53. 316 U.S. 623–4.
54. Green, "Liberty Under," p. 525.
55. *Murdock v. Pennsylvania*, 319 U.S. 105.
56. 319 U.S. 630.
57. 319 U.S. 633–4.
58. 319 U.S. 635–6.
59. 319 U.S. 637.
60. 319 U.S. 641.
61. 319 U.S. 639.
62. 319 U.S. 641.
63. 319 U.S. 643–4.
64. 319 U.S. 644–6.

65. 319 U.S. 646.
66. 319 U.S. 646–7.
67. 319 U.S. 651.
68. 319 U.S. 653–4.
69. 319 U.S. 655.
70. 319 U.S. 656.
71. 319 U.S. 659, 661.
72. 319 U.S. 670–671.
73. Laurence Tribe, *American Constitutional Law; Second Edition* (Mineola, NY: Foundation Press, 1988), p. 1189.
74. Christopher L. Eisgruber and Lawrence G. Sager, "The Vulnerability of Conscience: The Constitutional Basis for Protecting Religious Conduct," *University of Chicago Law Review* 61 (1994): 1315.
75. *United States v. Seeger*, 380 U.S. 163 (1965), at 176.
76. *Welsh v. United States*, 398 U.S. 333 (1970), at 339, 344.
77. 398 U.S. 345, 356–7.
78. 398 U.S. 372.
79. Rogers M. Smith, "'Equal' Treatment? A Liberal Separationist View," in *Equal Treatment of Religion in a Pluralistic Society*, Stephen V. Monsma and J. Christopher Soper, eds. (Grand Rapids, MI: Eerdman's, 1998), p. 193.

PART II

LIBERAL PLURALISM AND PUBLIC ACTION

# 5

## Value Pluralism and Political Means

### *Toughness as a Political Virtue*

### 1 INTRODUCTION: VIRTUE AND POLITICAL LIFE

My topic in this chapter is political virtue: more precisely, a political virtue – a disposition of mind and character I will call "toughness."[1] My contention is that in spite of its well-advertised disquieting aspects, this disposition fully deserves the honorific term "virtue," and that individuals lacking this virtue who seek to attain and exercise political leadership will bring themselves and others to grief. If true, this contention reveals a dimension of value pluralism with deep and often troubling implications for the practice of politics.

The need for toughness arises from an unpleasant but pervasive fact about politics: The attainment of even the worthiest ends will sometimes require the employment of distasteful means. While Machiavelli was by no means the first student of politics to make this observation, his relentless concentration on it has led many to regard it as his distinctive contribution to political wisdom. In deference to this common view, I will call the perplexed relation between public ends and public means "Machiavelli's problem." This problem preoccupied – one might almost say transfixed – Max Weber. More recently, it has gained the attention of some of our most talented moral philosophers – Michael Walzer, Bernard Williams, and Thomas Nagel, along others – and I shall have occasion to discuss their views.

As Stuart Hampshire observed, we cannot dissolve Machiavelli's problem simply by rejecting the broader valuational frame of Machiavelli's politics. Even if we reject the understanding of the human good as the quest for "glorious worldly achievements which will be recognized in history," however noble and public-spirited the goals or goods we put in place of memorable glory, the problem of political effectiveness will remain, undiminished.[2]

In the face of this problem, how is the actual or would-be leader to keep his moral balance? My answer takes the form of an Aristotelian schema: by embracing toughness as the mean between extremes. Three continua seem especially relevant. One ranges from squeamishness (excessive sensitivity to inflicting harms and deprivations on others) to callousness (indifference to such occurrences). A second continuum ranges from wishfulness (deliberate avoidance of the harsher aspects of political life) to cynicism (obliviousness to the aspirational possibilities of politics). The third ranges from what Hampshire calls "innocence" (the focus on maintaining the unsullied purity of one's soul) to calculation (the focus on attaining external objectives, whatever the consequences for one's soul). So the toughness required for political leadership stands between squeamishness, wishfulness, and innocence, on the one hand, and callousness, cynicism, and calculation, on the other. It is this disposition that enables leaders to recognize harsh necessities without blinding themselves to moral costs.

My account of toughness takes place within the context of broader theses about the virtues in general. To begin with, I cannot accept Kant's demand for a moral understanding that is freed from propositions about "the nature of man or . . . the circumstances in which he is placed."[3] While I am sympathetic to the considerations that moved Kant, his conclusion seems unsustainable. If the human species had basic characteristics very different from the ones it now possesses, or had to deal with challenges very different from the ones it now confronts, the character of our virtues and duties would surely shift as well. As Aristotle suggests, our morality reflects our emotions, our bodily constitution, and our sociality, not just our rational capacities; the human virtues are the virtues of our "composite nature," which stands between the beasts and the gods.[4]

The Kantian proposition is valuable, however, in pointing to an important duality in our understanding of the virtues, a duality that decisively affects Aristotle's discussion. If we look to human nature, we are led to focus on the virtues as intrinsic goods – that is, as the active dispositions that constitute our good, excellence, or perfection *qua* human beings. If we look to human circumstances, we emphasize the virtues as instrumental goods – that is, as dispositions that enable us to perform well the specific tasks presented by our situation.

As avenues for philosophical exploration, each possibility seems promising. In an article entitled "Non-Relative Virtues," Martha

Nussbaum offers a compelling, if not uncontroversial, reconstruction of the Aristotelian thesis that many virtues can (must) be understood as intrinsic, hence universal, even as they come under the gravitational influence of local particularity.[5]

Nussbaum offers her thesis in explicit opposition to contemporary virtue theorists (MacIntyre, Williams, Foot) who oppose the "localism" of virtues embedded in the traditions and practices of specific communities to what they take to be the false universality (or dangerous abstraction) of deontological or utilitarian theories. Nussbaum implies, though she does not quite say, that if we want nonrelative virtues, we must look for intrinsic virtues, the constitutive dimensions of human flourishing; and conversely, that if we look at instrumental virtues, we are necessarily led toward relative virtues.

In one sense, of course, this is true by definition: Instrumental virtues are inherently relational – relative to tasks or roles that are themselves situated within social contexts. But in another sense, the suggestion I am imputing to Nussbaum is not necessarily true. If some activities and contexts enjoy a normative superiority to others, then the virtues that sustain the preferred activities and contexts themselves have a plausible claim to be superior. If all activities and contexts are not created equal, then not all instrumental virtues are relative in the second, nontrivial sense of the term.

Now it may be contended that my argument merely displaces, without resolving, the problem of virtue-relativism. Suppose that the normative worth of a political context rests ultimately (as many have taken Aristotle to argue) on its propensity to foster individuals who develop and exercise the intrinsic virtues. If this were the case, then the existence and content of nonrelative instrumental virtues would depend on the specification of a rationally preferred account of the intrinsic virtues.

But what if this is not the case? What if it is possible to offer arguments for the normative superiority of a political context that rest on other than the cultivation of intrinsic virtue? Many defenses of constitutional government and of liberal democracy have this character; indeed, Aristotle himself partially lays the basis for it when he notes that the political community comes into being for the sake of life, as distinguished from the *good* life, and never wholly sheds the primordial concern for preservation, stability, and at least a minimum level of material decency. Judith Shklar's defense of rights as bulwarks against tyrannical oppression; Stuart Hampshire's embrace of procedural justice as the antidote to coercion; James Fishkin's linkage of liberal legitimacy with the generalized receipt of essential benefits – these and related approaches suggest the possibility of a vindication of liberal constitutional democracy that does not rest on any preferred or unique conception of intrinsic virtues.[6] I have some quarrels with each of these accounts, but I shall assume what I argue elsewhere – that some such account is possible.

To avoid any misunderstanding, let me make it clear that I am not suggesting that the defense of liberalism, or of any form of political organization, can be purely formal or procedural. Any viable defense must rely on some substantive conception of what is good for human beings. My suggestion is rather that the intrinsic virtues form only a part of such a conception and that political justification may find it more promising to begin with the other part, which I shall call "nonvirtue goods."[7]

I would suggest further that our understanding of nonvirtue goods might well begin with an inventory of the greatest evils that can afflict us: death, suffering, oppression, isolation, and a handful of others. Even if we cannot identify a *summum bonum*, we can still specify the *summum malum*, the great evils of the human condition the avoidance or minimization of which constitutes the central purpose of politics, and therefore the prime criterion in light of which the performance and value of political institutions are to be judged.[8]

At any rate, I shall suppose that certain forms of political organization – liberal constitutional democracies prominent among them – have a substantial propensity to meet this criterion. The next step in the argument is to note that every society contains a variety of "essential roles" – a variety of structured human activities without which the political community could not hope to conduct its affairs and accomplish its objectives. As Aristotle argued, political society is not a multiplicity of individuals performing the same or similar functions, but rather a collectivity of individuals performing different functions, each with its own characteristic excellences.[9]

Among the essential roles is political leadership. Not even in a pure democracy can everyone wield equal power at all times; pure democracy is, in Aristotle's phrase, ruling and being ruled in turns (with the proviso, of course, that no one spends a disproportionate time in the former as opposed to the latter status). *A fortiori*, political leadership is an essential role in forms of government other than pure democracies. And therefore – to assemble the parts of the argument thus far – in forms of government that broadly promote the attainment of nonvirtue goods for their citizens, the functional excellences of political leadership should be regarded as among the important virtues.

We may now rejoin our point of departure – the proposition that toughness (as defined earlier) is one of these functional excellences of leadership. To recapitulate: It is a necessary excellence because of the steady and unavoidable tension between even the most worthy ends and the significantly less worthy means often required for their pursuit. Let me offer an account of circumstances calling for toughness that are therefore regularly encountered in the ordinary course of politics.

However open and consensual the processes may be by which collective decisions are made, their implementation requires a substantial degree of coordinated action, both within the government and in the larger society. The possible bases of coordination are various. Some individuals will fall in line because of personal loyalty to the leader; others because they seek the leader's personal recognition and approval; others because they are rationally persuaded of the wisdom of the contemplated course of action; still others because the leader correctly divines their material interests and provides what Mancur Olson calls "selective incentives."[10] My own political experience confirms, however, what the reading of history so strongly suggests – that in each instance, for some individuals whose cooperation is essential, none of these relatively benign forms of coordination will succeed. The leader will then be faced with the choice between failure and the use of a means of coordination not yet mentioned – namely, fear. No one who is incapable of employing targeted fear as an instrument of policy can hope to succeed as the leader of any political group numbering more than a handful.

The ability to use fear selectively is a crucial aspect of what I am calling toughness. At one extreme is the temptation to use it habitually, even when unnecessary, as a way of husbanding material resources and maximizing personal control. Far more usual, at least in democratic societies, is the other extreme – the reluctance to use fear, even when necessary, stemming from the desire to avoid giving offense and breeding resentment. Many politicians are driven by a craving to be liked, or even loved, universally. While humanly understandable, this craving amounts to a political vice to the extent that it prevents the political leader from carrying out the functions appropriate to his role.

A few comments on what I have just said. To begin with, I am not embracing Machiavelli's dictum that it is better to be feared than to be loved. I am offering a much more modest proposition – that the psychological aversion to ever being feared, and to acting so as to engender fear, is a deep political disability. Nor, I think, am I offering a gender-bound thesis. Golda Meir and Indira Gandhi had the capacity to inspire fear; Margaret Thatcher had it and used it, many thought to excess. Given what I take to be certain basic and enduring features of political life, pervasive in constitutional democracies as well as in tyrannies, anyone, female or male, who seeks to lead successfully for any length of time will need this capacity in full measure.

At this point, some readers will be inclined to raise an Aristotelian objection: Am I not overlooking the distinction between the good human being and the good citizen? We are interested in the virtues, after all, as guides to (or aspects of) living well. Perhaps the capacity to inspire fear as well as many other elements of toughness are part of leading well. But are they part of living well? Are we, that is, simply prepared to endorse as desirable human qualities the kinds of traits political leaders cannot do without?

I must acknowledge the force of this objection. Many politicians I have admired as human beings have proved unable, in part because of their human qualities, to deal effectively with the harsher realities of power. But I hasten to add that I mistrust my own sentiments in this matter. It is natural to judge others on the basis of how one is treated by them, to value highly those who deal with you on the basis of friendship and respect. But politics is not a realm in which human relationships can be invariably, or even usually, conducted on the basis of friendship and respect. Max Weber has argued, I think correctly, for a "sense of proportion" as one of the essential qualities of the political leader. This he defines as the "ability to let realities work upon him with inner concentration and calmness." He goes on to note that this quality requires "*distance* [Weber's emphasis] to things and men."[11] The desire for intimacy, in short, is out of place in a realm that requires a very substantial amount of detachment. Perhaps that is why our most successful presidents have had many acquaintances but almost no friends in the political sphere, and why those presidential associates who interpret the political relationship as one of friendship are so regularly and profoundly disappointed.

But let me be a bit more systematic, and reply to this Aristotelian objection in an Aristotelian spirit. It was Aristotle, after all, who famously argued (against Plato) that the good is not one but many: A good knife and a good song have something in common, of course, but it is nothing like participation in a single "Idea of the Good." Perhaps this is true as well of the good leader and the good friend. We want and need both, but it would be foolish indeed to expect the same excellences of both.

Yet (it will be objected) friends and leaders have something very important in common: They are both human beings. Are there no virtues of human beings *qua* human beings? Yes, of course there are. But my point has been that our understanding of the virtues is by no means exhausted by such virtues for the simple reason that the variety of roles and functions coexists with the bare fact of our common humanity. I would add that there is nothing to prevent political leaders from having and exercising the capacity for friendship. The point is rather that this capacity is most likely to be manifested alongside, not within, the political sphere.

What I have said relaxes, but by no means dissolves, the tension between the good human being and the good leader. The remaining difficulty rests on the fact that at least some acts, considered in themselves, abstracted from functional relationships and consequences, have intrinsic properties that render them distasteful and objectionable, the sort of thing that any decent person would regard with aversion and hesitate to do. (Standard examples include lying, coercion, and acquiescing in or failing to prevent evil acts by allies and confederates.) There is a plausible suspicion that the practice of political leadership continually tests our sense of where to draw the line, and tends over time to corrode our conviction that the line exists.

That is precisely why toughness is such an essential virtue: It allows the agent to contemplate the performance of intrinsically distasteful and objectionable acts, but only at the right time and in the right manner. As Bernard Williams puts it, "Only those who are reluctant or disinclined to do the morally disagreeable when it is really necessary have much chance of not doing it when it is not necessary."[12] This moral balance is what enables political leaders to avoid Machiavelli's choice between their fatherland and their soul, to remain decent while doing intrinsically distasteful things when required by circumstances.

There is a family resemblance between my argument and Weber's notion of an ethic of responsibility as opposed to an ethic of intention or purity of soul. But two distinctions are worth noting. Weber focuses on violence as the defining characteristic of politics and as the locus of the most troubling means, while I think an important part of the problem lies elsewhere – in deception, betrayal, and appeals to unreason and prejudice. Second, while Weber emphasizes the responsibility for foreseeable consequences of actions (as opposed to a focus on inner intention), I believe (as I shall argue more fully in Section 2) that we must also focus on the politician's self-assumed responsibility to particular individuals, groups, or causes. If we want the analysis to be applicable to contemporary circumstances, that is, we must undertake a revision of Weber's quasi-Nietzschean image of the politician as solitary hero.

The need for this revision raises three points of general importance. First: The nature, and therefore the virtues, of leadership vary

considerably across forms of organization. A good Pope differs significantly from a good president. And even within democracies, constitutional differences fundamentally affect the substance of leadership. In
most Western countries, for example, the head of state and head of government are different persons (in England, the Queen and the Prime
Minister; in West Germany, the President and the Chancellor; and so
forth). In the United States, by contrast, the functions of head of state
and head of government are combined in the same presidential office.
An excellent president (Franklin D. Roosevelt comes to mind) will therefore need the virtues corresponding to both these public functions, while
other talented but less excellent presidents have been much stronger
along one dimension (Lyndon Johnson as prime minister, Ronald Reagan
as king) than along the other.

Second: The language of virtue and the language of obligation are
not, as some have supposed, disjoint or antithetical. A virtue, after all, is a
disposition to act rightly within a particular sphere of human experience.
But in many (though perhaps not all) cases, the content or specification of
right action will be furnished by natural duties, self-incurred obligations,
or particular responsibilities. This is seen most clearly in the case of justice:
The individual disposition to behave justly has as its necessary supplement
the rules or considerations on the basis of which the requirements of
justice may be understood in particular instances.

The third point bears on the classic distinction between the Aristotelian image of the virtuous human being as internally harmonious
and the Christian–Kantian image of the moral impulse wrestling with
inexpungible opposing impulses. Some virtues may well be "easy" in the
Aristotelian sense – that is, they may so constitute the individual soul as
to efface all contrary dispositions and desires. But many of the political
virtues – toughness among them – are "hard" in the sense that it is difficult
to imagine how the opposing dispositions and desires could wholly lose
their force. To all such cases we may apply Kant's description of virtue as
"fortitude": the strength needed to successfully oppose the inner forces
that (tend to) prevent us from doing what is good or right. To which
we must add, in a somewhat un-Kantian spirit, that virtue is not one but
many, and that the plurality of the virtues corresponds, in part, to the
plurality of inner forces of resistance to right conduct.

Beyond these points of tangency and difference with Max Weber, my
argument also overlaps the notion of "dirty hands" discussed by Michael
Walzer. But I diverge from his account in a crucial respect. Walzer believes
that the decent leader who is compelled to perform objectionable acts
becomes a "guilty" person, both in the subjective sense of feeling that

he has done something wrong and in the objective sense of owing some reparation to those he has wronged.[13] I don't agree: The anti-utilitarian premise, which I share with Walzer, that some acts are intrinsically distasteful does not warrant the conclusion that I have acted wrongly, in a manner rightly productive of guilt (as opposed to regret), when circumstances compel me (and would compel any other decent person in my shoes) to perform them.

I am closest, I suppose, to the position marked out by Bernard Williams. It is, he states, "a predictable and probable hazard of public life that there will be these situations in which something morally disagreeable is clearly required. To refuse on moral grounds to do anything of that sort is more than likely to mean that one cannot seriously pursue even the moral ends of politics." To be sure, only those politicians who preserve a lively sense of the disagreeableness of what they are required to do will be able to refrain from doing is when it is not required. Still, the ability, in full awareness, to hold ends and means in balance, is a core element of what Williams and I seek to define and encourage: a workable space "between cynicism and political idiocy."[14]

## 2 POLITICAL LEADERSHIP IN CONSTITUTIONAL DEMOCRACIES

Let me bring some of these general considerations down to earth by reflecting on the conduct of political candidates in constitutional democracies. The reader will quickly see the nexus between my practical involvements and my theoretical concerns. Also, and immediately obvious, is the movement back and forth between dispositional and deontological language. For the reasons sketched in Section 1, this movement is both possible and necessary. It is especially necessary, I would say, in constitutional democracies with their special procedures for the acquisition and exercise of power, procedures in and through which leaders incur special responsibilities toward those whom they would lead.

The basic argument is this: In most, if not all, circumstances, a democratic politician does not stand alone, but rather acts on behalf of others, or acts in ways that affect others, in pursuit of certain ends that others have good reason to expect him to pursue. To become a politician is in most circumstances to say to others that you take seriously the acquisition and maintenance of power and its employment to further the goals you share with them. You take upon yourself the responsibility to act effectively, which not infrequently entails the obligation to use the kinds of tactics a decent person will regard as intrinsically disagreeable.

To ward off possible misunderstanding, let me emphasize at the outset that I do not mean to be offering a thesis applicable to democratic politics as a whole. There are, after all, candidacies and campaigns with aims other than the immediate acquisition of power – Norman Thomas's socialist insurgencies, for example, or John Anderson's 1980 presidential effort. If the point is to offer new ideas, to ensure that hitherto silent voices are heard, to expound important but unpopular principles and to expand future possibilities, then certain kinds of disagreeable tactics may well be pointless, even counterproductive. My thesis is restricted to the portion of political life for which winning and holding power, here and now, is essential.

Nor do I mean to suggest that the politician's only responsibility is to his constituents or party. Everyone, for example, is expected to place citizenship before partisanship – that is, to refrain from pursuing and exercising power in ways that betray core democratic norms, undermine basic institutions, or violate the fundamental rights of individuals. The balance between factional and broader responsibilities varies with circumstances, however. An incoming president will typically, and appropriately, pledge in some fashion to be president of "all the people." By contrast, a victorious candidate for his party's presidential nomination begins his convention speech by saying "I accept your nomination." By doing so, he acknowledges the special weight of the responsibility he bears to his supporters, at least for the duration of the general election campaign.

To illustrate and extend this thesis, let me reflect for a few moments on the 1988 presidential campaign. There is, I think, a general agreement that Michael Dukakis failed to campaign effectively. I want to argue that this and other such failures are more than tactical blunders. To the extent that they are rooted in certain erroneous conceptions of political practice, they represent a moral failing and a failure of responsibility.

I don't want to suggest that Dukakis's failure was rooted in a single belief or trait of character. In fact, many motives were at work. For quite a while, anyway, he didn't believe that anyone would take George H. W. Bush's attacks seriously – a belief that reflected both an error of judgment (rooted in ignorance of public opinion outside Massachusetts) and a degree of arrogance. To some extent, he and his advisors feared that the attacks would be taken seriously only if he dignified them with a reply.

But something else was going on as well. Dukakis didn't want to conduct the campaign on the terrain defined by Bush, either by defending himself against charges or by responding with charges of his own. He wanted to be affirmative, not negative; he wanted to talk about what he regarded as real issues, not phony ones; and he wanted discourse to be rational, not emotional or demagogic.

These are understandable desires. But my contention is that they reflected a kind of recoiling from the rigors of the combat he had willingly entered. The party that nominated him had every right to expect that he would do what was necessary to maximize his chances of winning. He undertook a responsibility to be as effective as possible in the pursuit of power. In carrying out that responsibility, he had an obligation to shape his tactics in relation to the world as it was, not as he wanted it to be.

In politics as in other forms of competition, the immediately relevant world – the arena of combat – is defined by the decisions of your adversary, not just by your own desires. To believe otherwise is to assume that your most preferred tactics, the ones with which you are morally most comfortable, will be effective in all circumstances and that it will never be necessary to consider using tactics with which you are less comfortable. This is to give moral comfort priority over political effectiveness. It is to pursue an illusory ideal of individual moral purity, retained at the expense of one's responsibility to others. It is, in short, a form of moral self-indulgence.

If I am even partly right about all of this, Michael Dukakis had an obligation to respond far more forcefully to the Republican attacks than he actually did. Let me offer an example. As readers may recall, Bush attacked Dukakis for his stance on the mandatory recitation of the Pledge of Allegiance, and Dukakis responded with a statement that sounded like a page from Laurence Tribe's constitutional law textbook. Suppose Dukakis had taken another tack. Suppose he had said, "Let me tell you what's really going on here. The real issue isn't the Pledge – it's my character. Vice President Bush is impugning my patriotism, and I resent it. And I think I know why he's doing it. He's trying to suggest that because his ancestors have been in this country for 200 years while my parents were Greek immigrants, because my nose is a bit bigger than his and my skin is a bit darker, he's somehow more American than I am. Well, I really resent that, and so should every American whose parents and grandparents arrived here in search of freedom and opportunity. I'm proud of my heritage, I'm proud of America's diversity, I'm disgusted by these tactics, I think the Vice President owes the American people an apology, and I hope he won't stoop to this again." Emotional? Yes. Unfair? Arguably. A stretch beyond the verifiable facts of the case? Certainly. Warranted – indeed, required – by the circumstances and by the tactics of the opposition? Without a doubt.

Whether or not you find what I just said compelling, it may strike you as the easy part of the question. What about George Bush? Did he have an obligation to campaign as he did? I am a partisan, activist Democrat, but I am compelled to answer that question in the affirmative. In accepting his party's presidential nomination, Bush took on the same responsibility for effectiveness that Dukakis had earlier assumed. In discharging this responsibility, moreover, he had to work within a context largely created by others. The media, led by *Newsweek* magazine and CBS News, had described him as vacuous and weak – a "wimp." Beginning with Ann Richards's no-holds-barred keynote address, the Democratic convention had portrayed him as feckless and contemptible. And Governor Dukakis sought to define the general election as a contest over competence, not ideology – a theme designed both to play on perceptions of Bush as incompetent and to shift attention away from ideological disputes where Democrats had been at a disadvantage since the 1960s.

Bush's challenge, then, was twofold: He had to overcome the wimp factor by projecting guts and strength, and he had to reestablish the political centrality of disputes over basic values. The issues he chose to emphasize, and the manner in which he chose to discuss them, were calculated to achieve these two objectives. And he succeeded.

I would be the first to concede that the spectacle wasn't exactly edifying. And I freely grant that the use of such tactics in pursuit of efficacy would have been wrong if other, loftier, less distasteful means had held out a reasonable prospect of working. But a reasonable person surveying the terrain in July of 1988 could well have come to the conclusion that nothing else was likely to work. The electorate was in no mood to hear a serious discussion of the long-term problems facing the country; emotional issues such as drugs and crime dominated the agenda, and the media, bored as always by substance and driven as always by the exigencies of Nielsen ratings, was determined to focus on tactics and personalities.

Given our founding tradition of populist suspicion, it is natural for us to blame our leaders for these ills. I think the truth lies elsewhere. George Bernard Shaw once defined democracy as the only form of government in which the people get exactly what they deserve. Walt Kelly's Pogo put it even more pungently: "We have met the enemy, and they is us." Our politicians will lose all incentive to employ negative advertising when it stops being effective. They will talk to us seriously about serious things only if we give them good reason to believe that they will be rewarded – or at least not punished – for it. The occasions for this kind of public discourse are more rare than one might suppose.

### 3 TOUGHNESS AS A MEAN BETWEEN EXTREMES

But are there no limits? Can we better define the dimensions of Bernard Williams's space between cynicism and political idiocy? Let me begin my answer by reviewing, in summary form, some of the features of democratic political life that have guided my comments thus far.

In my view, democratic politics as an honorable calling is first and foremost a struggle to acquire and maintain power in order to do good. Although rational inquiry and persuasion have a role in politics, it is not properly modeled as a truth-oriented university seminar. Deception, appeals to irrationality, pressure, and even force may at certain junctures properly play key roles.

Democratic political life, next, entails a dense network of responsibilities to supporters, other politicians, and ordinary citizens. It is misconceived if seen as a realm of individualistic entrepreneurship. Nor (*pace* Hannah Arendt) is it primarily an arena for displaying the beauty or excellence of one's soul.

Finally, democratic politics carries with it a complex weave of responsibilities for certain goals: to victory and the power attendant on victory; to the cause for which one seeks power; and to the basically decent (though surely improvable) institutions within which power and the public good are pursued. These responsibilities entail an obligation, felt keenly by the most morally serious leaders, to be effective in an arena where many agents are not good, in circumstances in which the effective pursuit of power and the good necessarily entails acts that a decent person will regard as morally distasteful.

Within this context, how are we to understand the nature and limits of morally acceptable political tactics? A sports analogy may prove illuminating.

In baseball, there is a threefold distinction: Hardball is understood in distinction from softball, but also from dirtyball. Consider two examples. Case 1: hardball means sliding into the second baseman to break up a double play; softball means sliding around the second baseman to avoid potentially injuring him; dirtyball means sliding into him spikes up with the intention of knocking him out of the game. Case 2: the hardballer throws a high inside pitch to brush the batter back from the plate; the softballer refrains from brush-back pitches to minimize chances of hitting the batter; the dirtyballer throws right at the batter.

As I stated at the outset, the political import of these sports examples may be expressed in a quasi-Aristotelian formula: Playing hardball requires the virtue of toughness, which is flanked (along one dimension) by the opposing vices of squeamishness and callousness. It is possible also to give an account of the vices in Machiavellian terms. Squeamishness invites the victory of evil – that is, more of the evil from which it averts its gaze. For example: The failure to apply force vigorously when necessary may open the door for greater disorder, doing greater damage or necessitating more force than would earlier have been the case. Callousness involves inflicting pain and injury beyond the minimum needed to attain an appropriate objective. At best, it implies a kind of indifference to others' suffering. At its most perverse, it can even become a kind of pleasure or end in itself. A decent political act, by contrast, is one that a morally serious and responsible person with adequate knowledge of the facts could perform in the specific circumstances in which the decision must be made.

### 4 TOUGHNESS IN HARD CASES

This rough and ready characterization of political hardball suggests two very different kinds of cases in which it must be employed.

First: Within a static set of rules to which all adhere, you have a responsibility to play hardball as necessary. Yes, the decision to use a brush-back pitch on the other team's leading hitter appreciably raises the odds that you will hit him, a prospect you understandably view with distaste. But if you don't use the pitch, you will raise the odds that the slugger will make solid contact, and you have a responsibility to your teammates to minimize those odds, within the framework of the tactics generally specified as acceptable.

Let me offer another example from the 1988 presidential campaign. Well before the Iowa caucuses, there surfaced a now-famous "attack video," which graphically drew the attention of the press to the remarkable similarity between some of the speeches of Sen. Joseph Biden, a candidate for the Democratic nomination, and orations previously delivered by Neil Kinnock, the head of the British Labour Party. These revelations drove Sen. Biden from the race. They also led to the resignation of John Sasso, the manager of the Dukakis campaign, who had masterminded the release of the fatal videotape.

A strong case can be made that Sasso in fact did nothing wrong. After all, the video did not lie; if it had, it would not have induced Sen. Biden to withdraw. Nor did it raise an irrelevant issue: The question of whether Sen. Biden was morally and intellectually serious was already in the air.

Nor, finally, did the tape breach accepted limits of political tactics: It represented hardball but not dirtyball.

Why, then, was Sasso compelled to resign? A clue may be found in the fact that he had caused the tape to be delivered anonymously to the press and had subsequently concealed this both from the press and from Gov. Dukakis. He proceeded in this fashion, not because he felt that he was doing anything shameful, but because he was violating his boss's instructions. Early on, Dukakis had forsworn negative campaigning and had pledged to crack down hard on any member of his campaign caught indulging in it. Sasso evidently felt that this self-denying ordinance was incompatible with the responsibility incumbent on a serious candidate to maximize his effectiveness within the limits of accepted practices. He therefore took it on himself to play hardball in the interests, though against the instructions, of his master. When the entire matter became public, Dukakis was forced to expel Sasso from his campaign to honor his own misguided pledge.

I want to suggest that the Dukakis pledge, the refusal to play hardball, represents an instance of the political vice I have called squeamishness. The denouement also calls our attention to a difficulty suggested by Machiavelli: A politician who wishes to remain undisturbed by moral discomfort must either reconcile himself to the failure of his enterprises or engage the services of a lieutenant who is not similarly disturbed. If the politician then says (as many do), just get the job done, and if the lieutenant keeps the details secret, his boss may bask in the sunlight of rectitude. But he is not thereby rendered more righteous than the politician who takes responsibility for the hardball tactics of his organization, In fact, I believe, he is less admirable, both because of his hypocrisy and because he has selfishly shifted the moral burden onto others' shoulders.

The second kind of hardball case involves circumstances in which the political rules are fluid rather than static. If your adversary systematically and intentionally crosses the line separating hardball from dirtyball, the location of the line may be said to shift, and you may now have a responsibility to consider the use of previously forbidden tactics, either to give your adversary an incentive to return to the status quo ante or to maintain competitive effectiveness in the circumstances your adversary has unilaterally altered to his advantage.

This is less likely to be the case if there is an umpire who enforces the rules by imposing a meaningful penalty on the violator. In some circumstances, therefore, politicians may have a responsibility to create such an umpire. For example, early in 1989, the nine candidates for mayor of

New York city signed a pledge, drafted by a nonpartisan Committee on Decent Unbiased Campaign Tactics, to avoid appeals based on race, ethnicity, and other emotional divisions among the electorate. It is at least possible that each candidate's fear of being publicly cited by the Committee for breaches of the pledge served as sufficient incentive to honor it. Whatever the cause, the campaign was noticeably freer from inflammatory appeals than many had feared, and those lieutenants (such as Jackie Mason and Sonny Carson) who crossed the line were quickly fired by the candidates they served.

But matters are different when rules are breached in the absence of an effective, timely, reliable enforcer. Toughness then requires the nonviolator to consider some action, outside the rules if necessary, to restore fairness and balance to the competition. I say "consider" because there may be other compelling reasons not to engage in such behavior. The point is only that it cannot be ruled out in principle.

A good example of this would be the rise of negative political advertising. Much of it violates norms of integrity and civility that had previously had some currency in political campaigns, particularly at the national level. It is easy to understand why decent persons with a healthy respect for democratic ideals would want to refrain from such practices. The problem is that negative advertising works and (in a political version of Gresham's law) tends to drive out more elevated forms of discourse. In current circumstances, to forswear negative advertising, especially if one's opponent is determined to use it, is to heighten unacceptably the risk of defeat.

At this juncture, I anticipate an anguished and perhaps angry outcry. How far can the requirements of efficacy drive us? Are there no limits? Doesn't a healthy and proper regard for our own decency at some point lead us to say that enough is enough?

To illustrate this tension between moral self-regard and responsibility to others, let me offer a somewhat less-charged example from my own life. My wife and I bicker, more or less amiably, whenever we encounter two lanes of traffic merging into one. Some people zip along the disappearing lane until the last possible moment, then wedge themselves into the surviving lane, obtaining a significant advantage over drivers who wait their turn. My wife frequently wants me to do the same thing, but I refuse. I would like to be able to say that I'm employing the categorical imperative and recoiling in horror from the world of vehicular anarchy my own lane-jumping would implicitly endorse. But in fact that's not what's going on. What really holds me back is my desire to be able to say to myself that I'm not the kind of person who engages in that kind of un-fair, self-aggrandizing behavior. Because I regard the rules as fair and sensible, I want to be able to see myself as a person whose character is defined/expressed by adherence to them, even at some cost.

Some may regard this behavior as a sign of terminal idiocy on my part, but note that at least in the limit case – if I am in the car by myself, driving for personal pleasure or on some personal errand – it seems morally unobjectionable. The focus on my desire to view myself in a certain way becomes steadily less defensible, however, as my responsibility to others escalates. Consider a case at the other extreme: If I were rushing my son to the hospital, it would be almost unimaginable to impede my progress by refusing to breach some rules of the road.

Note also that our judgment is shaped by assumptions about the nature and status of the rules. Some are purely conventional, in two senses: There is no compelling moral reason why they couldn't have been different (driving on the right versus driving on the left); and the fact that there is a general propensity to obey them is a necessary condition of their being binding on me. Other rules are quite different in both respects: We assent to them because we regard them as rationally or morally correct, and the behavior of others may not be a necessary condition of bindingness for me, even though others' violations may impose costs on me.

Now, clearly, the rules demarcating hardball from dirtyball are of the second sort. We quite properly regard an appeal to public ignorance, prejudice, or passion as wrong in itself and not merely by agreement: witness the outraged bipartisan response to a 1989 Republican National Committee memo smearing the incoming Speaker of the House, Tom Foley. We would try to resist as long as possible the conclusion that such appeals by others have left us with the unpalatable alternatives of retiring from the fray or responding in kind. Nevertheless, we may ultimately be driven to confront just such a choice.

For example, in the midst of the 1984 North Carolina Senate race between Jim Hunt and Jesse Helms, the Senate took up legislation to create a national holiday honoring Martin Luther King. Helms went all out against the bill; Hunt knew that supporting it would cost him severely, but he felt he had no other morally acceptable course. One of Hunt's advisors is reported to have said to him at the time, "If the election is about race, if that's what you've got to do to win, we just won't win, and just be prepared to accept that."[15]

Hunt's decision strikes me as defensible, for two reasons. First, it might be argued that his responsibility to his supporters was not only to win, but also to represent certain values about which they deeply cared. If the price of victory were the public abandonment of one of those values, then his victory could well be thought to lose much of its point. Second, race was not just any issue. It involved historic injustices, dangerous passions, and a legacy of dishonor. A decent politician – and particularly a Southerner – had ample reason to believe that compromise on race would be unconscionable.

Still, the result of Hunt's decision was the defeat of an intelligent and honorable man at the hands of someone who used race systematically and indefensibly as a tool of political combat. If trimming on the King holiday bill could have secured Helms's defeat, I believe that a decision (however painful) on Hunt's part to do so would have been morally permissible.

What are we to make of all this? Where, if anywhere, is the line between forbidden means and acceptable politics? I offer the following list of general principles as a summary guide.

1.  Every political context will contain some version of the triadic softball/hardball/dirtyball distinction.
2.  Whatever your adversary does, it is permissible to play hardball, and it is sometimes obligatory to do so, especially when one's opponent has initiated the use of hardball tactics and is wielding them effectively.
3.  It is hardly ever right to initiate the use of dirtyball tactics. If your opponent goes first, it may be permissible to reply in kind. Rarely, if ever, however, may a politician be said to have an obligation to play dirtyball, because countervailing responsibilities – to the basic values of his supporters and to the long-term health of the political system as well as to his personal integrity – will always weigh heavily on the other side of the scale.[16]

## 5 CONCLUSION

I close by recalling to the witness stand Max Weber, perhaps this century's prime exponent of the distinction between political ethics and the concern for purity of soul (Hampshire's "innocence"):

It is immensely moving when a mature man – no matter whether old or young in years – is aware of a responsibility for the consequences of his conduct and really feels such responsibility with heart and soul. He then acts by following an ethic of responsibility and somewhere he reaches the point where he says: "Here I stand; I can do no other." That is something genuinely human and moving. And every one of us who is not spiritually dead must realize the possibility of finding himself at some time in that position. In so far as this is true, an ethic of ultimate ends [the ethics of the Gospel or of Kant] and an ethic of responsibility are not absolute contrasts but rather supplements, which only in unison constitute a genuine man – a man who can have the "calling for politics."[17]

## Notes

1. I choose this in preference to Thomas Nagel's "ruthlessness," which seems to me (somewhat against his philosophic intention) to stack the moral deck. See Thomas Nagel, "Ruthlessness in Public Life," in *Public and Private Morality*, Stuart Hampshire, ed. (Cambridge, MA: Cambridge University Press, 1978), chapter 4.

2. Stuart Hampshire, *Innocence and Experience* (Cambridge, MA: Harvard University Press, 1989), pp. 165–7.

3. Immanuel Kant, *Foundations of the Metaphysics of Morals*, Robert Paul Wolff, ed. (Indianapolis: Bobbs-Merrill, 1969), pp. 5–6.

4. *Nicomachean Ethics* 1178a 8–21. For a more extensive discussion, see my "What Is Living and What Is Dead in Kant's Practical Philosophy?" in *Kantian Politics*, Ron Beiner and James Booth, eds. (New Haven: Yale University Press, 1995).

5. Martha Nussbaum, "Non-Relative Virtues: An Aristotelian Approach," in *Midwest Studies in Philosophy, Volume XIII; Ethical Theory: Character and Virtue*, Peter French, Theodore Uehling, Jr., and Howard Wettstein eds. (Notre Dame: University of Notre Dame Press, 1988), pp. 32–53.

6. Judith Shklar, *Ordinary Vices* (Cambridge, MA: Harvard University Press, 1984); Hampshire, *Innocence and Experience*; James Fishkin, *The Dialogue of Justice: Toward a Self-Reflective Society* (New Haven: Yale University Press, 1992).

7. For my thoughts, see *Liberal Purposes* (New York: Cambridge University Press, 1991). For related arguments linking the moral valuation of political acts and roles to the overall moral character of the political institutions within which they occur, see Nagel, "Ruthlessness," pp. 82–5, and David Luban, *Lawyers and Justice* (Princeton: Princeton University Press, 1988), chapters 6–7.

8. Hampshire, *Innocence and Experience*, pp. 90–1; Judith Shklar, "Giving Injustice Its Due," *Yale Law Journal* 98(1989): 1135–51.

9. Aristotle, *Politics* (London: Penguin, 1992), Book III, chapter 4.

10. See Mancur Olson, *The Logic of Collective Action: Public Goods and the Theory of Groups* (Cambridge, MA: Harvard University Press, 1965).

11. Max Weber, "Politics as a Vocation," in *From Max Weber: Essays in Sociology*, H. H. Gerth and C. Wright Mills, eds. (New York: Oxford University Press, 1946), p. 115.

12. Bernard Williams, "Politics and Moral Character," in *Moral Luck* (Cambridge: Cambridge University Press, 1981), p. 62.

13. Michael Walzer, "Political Action: The Problem of Dirty Hands," in *War and Moral Responsibility*, Marshall Cohen, Thomas Nagel, and Thomas Scanlon, eds. (Princeton: Princeton University Press, 1974), pp. 69–70.
14. Williams, "Politics and Moral Character," pp. 60, 66.
15. I am indebted to my colleague Robert Fullinwider for bringing this case to my attention.
16. This is the way in which I would begin to strike the politically relevant balance between acts and outcomes that is the focus of Nagel's argument. See "Ruthlessness," pp. 82–86.
17. Weber, "Politics as a Vocation," p. 127.

# 6

## Value Pluralism and Motivational Complexity

### *The Case of Cosmopolitan Altruism*

## 1 INTRODUCTION

This chapter focuses on what I shall call "cosmopolitan altruism" – the motivationally effective desire to assist needy or endangered strangers. Section 1 describes recent research that confirms the existence of this phenomenon. Section 2 places it within interlocking sets of moral typologies that distinguish among forms of altruism along dimensions of scope, interests risked, motivational source, and baseline of moral judgment. Section 3 explores some of the relationships between altruism – a concept rooted in modern moral philosophy and Christianity – and the understanding of virtue and friendship characteristic of Aristotelian ethical analysis. Finally, Section 4 argues that cosmopolitan altruism does not represent moral progress *simpliciter* over other, less inclusive views, and that the widening of moral sympathy to encompass endangered strangers entails significant moral costs.

The underlying purpose of this chapter is to explore the implications of value pluralism for our understanding of motivation. Descriptively, value pluralism is linked to a diversity of motivations for action and of dimensions along which these motivations vary. Normatively, value pluralism suggests the hypothesis that there is unlikely to be just one account of motivation that is best for, or required of, all individuals at all times. Rather, there is likely to be a range of legitimate variation, representing different combinations and weightings of dimensions of motivation, and a heavy emphasis on any single dimension will entail sacrifices along others.

## 2 THE ACTUALITY OF ALTRUISM

The debates over altruism during the past generation revolved around two issues: the *possibility* of altruistic behavior, and the *desirability* of such behavior. The relationship between these issues was clear enough. If altruism were impossible (as the proponents of "psychological egoism" insisted),[1] it was not much use arguing about its merits. Indeed, all talk of altruism would be diversionary if not obfuscatory. (Nietzsche's understanding of the Sermon on the Mount as expressing the concealed vengeful self-love of the powerless is an extreme but by no means illogical working-out of this possibility.)

In part because the debate over the possibility of altruism was so strongly empirical as well as conceptual, it proved possible to make progress. In fact, it has now been resolved: In a series of articles artfully blending open-ended interviews and rigorous hypothesis-testing, Kristen Monroe has demonstrated the existence of a class of individuals (gentile protectors of Jews during World War II) whose acts simply cannot be explained through any nonvacuous account of self-interest.[2]

Monroe's procedure is ingenious but straightforward. She begins by defining a class of "rescuers" whose acts on behalf of endangered Jews continued over an extended period, required enormous sacrifice of resources, entailed huge risks to liberty and life itself, and yielded condemnation and even ostracism from family and former friends and associates. She then inventories the numerous theories from various disciplines (economics, sociology, developmental psychology, evolutionary biology, and anthropology, among others) that seek to explain apparently altruistic behavior as the product of deeper self-interest, variously understood. She tests these theories against evidence developed from interviews and surveys administered to individual rescuers (identified through Yad Vashem, the Israeli agency established to honor Holocaust victims and those who sought to save them) as well as to individuals identified as entrepreneurs, philanthropists, and heroes. The evidence clearly indicated differences of psychology and outlook among these four groups, and it failed to support, let alone confirm, any of the self-interest theories of altruism. Monroe concludes, plausibly, that the rescuers did indeed act altruistically, and she traces their acts to a distinctive sense of personal identity that erodes typical divisions between self and others. While various methodological questions can be raised about this line of research, I shall proceed on the assumption that its principal conclusions are (at least roughly) valid.

The fact that altruism is possible for some individuals does not prove that it would be possible for all, even under the most favorable formative circumstances. On the contrary: I do not have a knock-down argument, but I defy anyone to read Monroe's depiction of the rescuers without seeing just how exceptional they are, and how misguided it would be to expect such behavior of everyone. The diversity of human character-types constitutes an obstacle to any understanding of altruism as a universal moral obligation. The dictum that "ought implies can" must be applied in a manner that is sensitive to deep differences of individual moral capacity. For example, the solitary, self-willed courage most rescuers displayed would simply be beyond the powers of most individuals. I would hazard the conjecture that this crucial difference is not (entirely) the product of upbringing or social context but represents the expression of deepseated differences of temperamental endowment. If true, this conjecture would not reduce our admiration for the rescuers, but it would relax the rigorous judgment we might otherwise want to pass on those who had the opportunity to rescue, but out of fear failed to seize it.

Moral diversity also complicates relations between ethics and politics. If political theorists (or political actors) expect too much of the citizenry taken as a whole, the result is bound to be unappealing. From the French Revolution to the "New Soviet Man" to Mao's Cultural Revolution, the history of utopian efforts to require constant selfless dedication to the common good on the part of everyone suggests that failure is inevitable, and that efforts to avert it are bound to turn tyrannical.

But there is an opposing error – expecting too little of human beings and citizens – to which anti-utopians (and economists) often fall prey. From the fact that altruism will be the exception rather than the rule, it does not follow that the rest of us will be guided by naked self-interest. "Selfishness/altruism" describes, not a dichotomous set of possibilities, but rather a behavioral continuum ranging from complete indifference to the interests of others (at one extreme) to complete responsiveness (at the other), with innumerable gradations in between. For all but the most insensate, the suffering of others constitutes, not just a reason, but also a felt motive, for other-directed acts. The question then becomes how strong or effective that motive is – *how much* cost, or risk, the agent is willing to accept while acting on behalf of others.

By thus characterizing a behavioral continuum, I do not want to be taken as endorsing a conceptual opposition between self-interest and altruism. In some cases, at least, a high degree of responsiveness to others is so integrated into individuals' character that altruism coincides with self-affirmation. As Neera Kapur Badhwar rightly suggests, there are forms of moral integrity or self-expression that are not self-focused.[3] The fact remains (as Badhwar recognizes) that most forms of self-interest – financial, psychic, even self-perfective – are self-focused in a way that hinders their integration into altruistic behavior.[4] It is this fact that gives rise to the commonplace, if overly sweeping, assertions of opposition between altruism and self-interest.

There is a second potential misunderstanding I wish to avoid. In offering a selfishness/altruism continuum, I do not mean to suggest that acts of agents necessarily improve morally as they move away from the former pole toward the latter. Indeed, I shall later argue that certain kinds of concern for others are rooted in a lack of concern for, or undervaluing of, oneself that is more nearly a vice than a virtue. I quite agree with Jean Hampton that not all self-sacrifice is worthy of moral commendation, and in particular, not the self-sacrifice that stems from self-abnegation.[5] Our judgment must not be blanket, but rather case-by-case: It will depend, not only on the specific sacrifice, but also on the constitution and circumstances of the self performing that sacrifice.

Distinguishing between selfishness and altruism in behavioral terms brings us to the classic distinction between act and motive. We may wish to reserve the term "altruism" for acts in which the inner impulse to assist others comes to dominate self-regarding desires that counsel inaction. If so, we shall have to employ some other term (perhaps "empathy" would do) to characterize the very real effects the interests of others may produce even when we are not sufficiently moved to act. One sign of this is the discomfort many of us feel when we fail to go to the aid of someone who appears to be in need. The fear (of injury, financial loss, emotional entanglement, or whatever) that holds us back may seem reasonable enough, but it does not erase the empathy that initially posed the choice for us.

This conception of the behavioral continuum, in which empathy may (but need not) prove strong enough to issue in altruistic acts, relies on two propositions defended most persuasively by Thomas Nagel. The first is that human beings simultaneously experience the force of subjectivity and objectivity – that is, they put themselves at the center of the universe *and* see themselves as but one entity, or point of view, or claimant, among myriad others. The question then becomes how these two standpoints are to be integrated into a single way of seeing or acting. The mode of integration, the balance struck, will vary from individual to individual. Some (the full-blown altruists) will give pride of place to the "view from nowhere"; others (the full-blown egoists) will focus exclusively on their personal standpoint; the rest of us will give weight to both, with the balance shifting in response to particular circumstances and to the vagaries of what might be termed our moral mood.

It is not the case, however, that the balance can be purely subjective or personal. This brings me to Nagel's second proposition: Some interests have objective value (or disvalue) regardless of the identity of individuals to whom they are linked at any given moment, and these interests therefore make a rational claim on us regardless of our personal relationship to them. Because pain is objectively bad from an impersonal standpoint, my desire for the cessation of my pain at least overlaps my desire for the cessation of your pain. I may well give more attention to my plight than to yours, but that does not mean that I am, or can reasonably be, wholly indifferent to yours. Indeed, I can ignore yours only at the cost of undermining the rational basis on which I care about my own.[6]

This is not to say that all interests have impersonal or objective value. Some are valuable only because they have been adopted as ends by individual agents. As T. M. Scanlon has argued, such agent-relative values make far weaker claims, if any, on others who may be in a position to aid or to frustrate their achievement. For me to take your agent-relative interests as grounds for action is, as Nagel puts it, "a matter of personal sympathy rather than objective acknowledgement."[7] This distinction may help draw the line between the kinds of regard for others that are to some degree required and those that are purely optional or supererogatory.

The distinction between impersonal and agent-relative interests is far from exhaustive. A third possibility is that needy agents can simply be mistaken about their interests, or about the specific steps that might promote them. Similar mistakes are possible on the part of those who are motivated to assist those who appear needy. It seems odd to say that well-intentioned acts built on such mistakes cease to be altruistic. The point is rather that there is a gap between acting with the intention of benefiting others and actually doing so; successful altruism includes a cognitive dimension (of practical and moral understanding) that may be less common than is the raw impulse to do good.

One may object, more radically, to Nagel's entire framework. Christine M. Korsgaard argues that an ambiguity lurks in the concept of impersonal or agent-neutral values. On one interpretation (Objective Realist), an agent-neutral value would be independent of agents in general; on the other (Intersubjectivist), such values would exist equally for all rational agents but would be neutral with respect to the individual identities of agents. On Korsgaard's preferred Intersubjectivist view, the projects

Nagel characterizes as agent-relative are not rightly understood as brute or unmotivated; "There are reasons for caring about these things, reasons which are communicable and therefore at least potentially shareable." And if the desires that provide A with reasons to act are shareable, then they provide B with reasons to help A – at least if B happens to be in A's neighborhood.[8]

This is a persuasive argument as far as it goes, but it generates a new ambiguity of its own. Reasons can be "shareable" in the sense that I can (come to) understand why you care about your project, or in the sense that I (come to) care about what you care about. The former sense is necessary for the latter, but not obviously sufficient. The gap between them mirrors the practical force of Nagel's agent-relative/agent-neutral distinction. In the first sense of shareability, I am enabled to take an interest in your interests; in the second sense, I am all but compelled to do so, on pain of losing touch with my own. This does not mean that I am always required to act in support of your agent-neutral interests. It does mean that when confronted with such interests, I must have reasons for not coming to your assistance that are far weightier than the reasons that would justify not helping with your more optional projects. (This is not to deny that it would be wrong for me *never* to help neighbors or associates with personal projects.)

It would be absurd to suggest that the primary threat facing European Jews during World War II was interference with optional life-plans. The threat was to family ties, security, and life itself – hardcore agent-neutral interests. What distinguished the rescuers from others who stood by was their ability to give their own agent-neutral interests no greater weight (in many cases *less* weight) than the comparable interests of endangered strangers. In Nagel's terms, they were unusually capable of adopting the impersonal standpoint as the basis of moral action, and of setting aside the kinds of personal considerations that proved decisive for most people. The question is no longer whether they behaved in that fashion – Monroe's work has settled that – but rather how it was possible and what we can learn from it.

## 3  DIMENSIONS OF ALTRUISM

To bring these issues into sharper relief, I want to turn more systematically to problems of description and conceptualization. "Altruism," I will argue, is not the name of a specific moral requirement or pattern of behavior. Rather, it points toward a family of possibilities.

### 3.1  The Objects of Altruism

To begin with, altruism can vary in its objects. Three main variants may be discerned. *Personal* altruism is directed toward individuals near at hand, such as family members and friends. *Communal* altruism is directed toward groups of individuals possessing some shared characteristics: members of an ethnic group, coreligionists, and fellow citizens, among others. *Cosmopolitan* altruism, by contrast, is directed toward the human race as a whole, and hence toward individuals to whom one has no special ties. (One could imagine a fourth variety – a *comprehensive* altruism directed toward all entities with interests. This possibility raises important issues that I cannot explore in this chapter.)

The steady expansion of scope from the personal to the communal to the cosmopolitan does not (necessarily) represent moral progress. While the form of altruism directed toward family and friends may be more common than is altruism embracing all humanity, it does not follow that the former is in any simple sense less worthy than the latter. This point is of particular importance because, as we shall see, forms of altruism can come into conflict with one another. While philosophical discussion typically induces us to focus on the clash between self-interest and altruism, conflicts between competing objects of altruism are equally pervasive, and perhaps even more wrenching. (As a parent, one wishes the best for one's child; as a citizen, one may believe in forms of military conscription that place that child at risk; and so forth.) If enlarged scope does not translate into moral priority, there may be no way to resolve such clashes without moral loss; each course of action, including the all-things-considered best, may require the agent to forego some significant impersonal good.

### 3.2  Varieties of Sacrifice

Second, forms of altruism can vary, with regard to the kinds of personal goods agents are willing to sacrifice on behalf of others. In differing circumstances, altruism may entail the sacrifice of life, wealth, liberty, convenience, or many other goods. This variation is significant because individuals may find it less difficult to act altruistically along some dimensions than others. I know people, for example, who freely donate their time and energy to others but who cannot bear to part with their money. This phenomenon of good-specific altruism suggests intriguing links with the traditional vocabulary of the virtues. Risking one's life for others might be thought akin to (or at least to depend on) a species of courage; the sacrifice of wealth, liberality; of pleasure or personal convenience, moderation; and so forth.

### 3.3 Motives for Altruism

Forms of altruism also vary in their personal source or motivation. One form seems rooted in some individuals' highly developed capacity for *sympathy*. Because they cannot maintain emotional distance, because they keenly feel the pain and suffering of others, they are more inclined than are most of us to come to the aid of those in need.[9] Another form reflects *rationality* – the capacity to understand the ways in which claims made on one's own behalf can entail equally valid claims by others, and to act on the basis of that understanding.[10] A third, perhaps less familiar, form rests on *identity*. Monroe's study of rescuers, for example, found that these individuals without exception acted instinctively rather than reflectively, expressing a perception of self as at one with all mankind: "Their perception of themselves as part of a common humanity formed such a central core of their identity that it left them no choice in their behavior toward others."[11]

This conception of identity-based altruism combines two dimensions, which I shall call "expression" and "identification." The former is the idea of a kind of action that directly and spontaneously reflects the character of the agent, such that to act otherwise would be to deny what one is. The latter is the idea of a special sense of self in which the customary boundary between self and others becomes indistinct.

### 3.4 The Baseline for Altruism

The foregoing varieties of altruism are dimensions of observed empirical variation. I want to turn now to a conceptual issue: the baseline relative to which altruistic behavior is defined. I have already observed that the mix of self- and other-regarding motives generates a continuum of possibilities rather than a two-valued choice. Still, there are a number of competing conceptions of full or complete altruism.

The first, and probably the most stringent, is self-abnegation: Your actions are wholly defined by (your perception of) the interests of others, and your own interests are given less weight than those of others, perhaps no weight at all. Examples of this include some of the sacrifices parents make for their children.

A less stringent but nonetheless quite demanding baseline is the requirement, characteristic of utilitarian theories among others, that we regard ourselves as but one among equals and give our own interests the same weight as those of others. Altruism then means making the point of view of the impartial spectator effective as a motive of personal conduct. On this understanding, self-abnegation is not only not required, but is not even regarded as supererogatory; it is actually ruled out as arbitrary and irrational.

Less stringent still is a baseline defined relative to justified self-regard. On this account, morality itself incorporates a measure of self-preference: You are permitted to give your own interests greater weight than those of others, up to a point. If you and someone else are contending for a good that only one of you can get, and if there is no special factor that gives your foe a superior moral claim, then you are not required to be impartial. You are not, for example, required to resolve the matter through some randomizing device such as a coin-toss. The fact that you are one of the contending parties makes a moral difference that you are allowed to take into account. But while self-preference is permitted, it is hardly required. You may recede from permissible self-preference in the direction of (say) giving equal weight to self and others, and this moral shift would count as a species of altruism.

Still another variant of altruism might be termed "justice-based." Assume that some theory of justice plausibly defines your just share S of some good. You could be said to act altruistically whenever, and to the extent that, you claim less than S for yourself and are willing to surrender the remainder to others. (I assume here that you are acting on principle; surrendering a portion of your share out of fear, or confusion about what you are entitled to, or desire to curry favor with someone else can hardly be considered altruistic on any interpretation. I also assume what can in principle be denied – that those who receive the portion of your share that you have relinquished are better off as a result.)

Justice-based altruism connects up in interesting ways with classical accounts of the virtues. The primary Greek antonym of justice is *pleonexia* – grasping, overreaching, claiming more than one's share. Aristotle does discuss the other possible antonym – claiming less than one's due – in his account of "equity," but he does not there explain the basis of such conduct *(Nicomachean Ethics* [hereafter *NE*], 1137a32–1138a4). The explanation is suggested, rather, in the discussion of *megalopsychia* (greatness of soul). Some human beings are justifiably proud: They think well of themselves, for good reason. Others are foolishly arrogant, thinking better of themselves than the facts would warrant. Still others err in the reverse direction by undervaluing themselves (*NE*, 1123b). While Aristotle does not make the connection explicit, on the level of moral psychology a link is at least implied between undervaluing and underclaiming. From this standpoint, what I have called justice-based altruism would have to be regarded, not as a virtue, but rather as the outgrowth of a vice.

But this is not the end of the matter. To think well of oneself, Aristotle believes, is also to care less about the external goods that less-confident individuals crave as sources of identity, worth, and power. So self-undervaluing can also lead to overclaiming. By contrast, great-souled individuals may be more willing to yield their share of resources, opportunities, and even life itself. Something that looks like altruism can be the byproduct of diminished concern for the usual objects of desire. This is not to say, however, that great-souled individuals are selfless. Rather, their concerns are so focused on a single external good – honor – that the importance of other goods is diminished (*NE*, 1124a, 1136b). More generally, it is not clear that Aristotle's moral psychology has room for the uncompensated surrender of individual advantage on behalf of another.

#### 4 ALTRUISM, VIRTUE, AND FRIENDSHIP

This gesture toward the classical virtues may well seem inconclusive, but it suggests something important about the moral geography of altruism. As we have seen, "selfishness/altruism" names a moral continuum along which the relative weight of self- and other-regarding motives shifts. Omitted from this calculus are substantive differences among the selves to which the interests of others are counterposed. On one interpretation, for example, the Aristotelian virtues constitute an account of self-perfection – that is, of self-interest rightly understood. And yet this higher-order self-interest can yield patterns of conduct not easily distinguished from regard for others. The interests of the purified self are likely to be more compatible with the interests of others than are those of the brute, unrefined self, especially if, as Aristotle argues, justice is a part of rational self-perfection.

Still, a gap remains. Of all the classical virtues, friendship most closely approaches the contemporary understanding of altruism. Yet here too, self-regard, even rightly understood, places limits on what we are willing to wish, or do, for our friends. True friendship requires equality, and thus, Aristotle suggests, we would not hope that our friends would achieve a degree of excellence or perfection that would move them outside the circle of possible friendship with us: "One will wish the greatest good for his friend as a human being. But perhaps not all the greatest goods, for each man wishes for his own good most of all" (*NE*, 1159a11–13).

This might seem to mark the limits of possible reconciliation between altruism and the classical virtues. But it turns out that the boundaries of the self whose good is primarily sought can shift in morally significant ways. In a remarkable passage, Aristotle reflects on the relationship between friendship and self-love. The good man (indeed, *only* the good man) truly loves himself; but "he has the same attitude toward his friend as he does toward himself, *for his friend is really another self.* . . . [T]he extreme degree of friendship can [thus] be likened to self-love" (*NE*, 1166a30–b2). Because the self whose interests we seek to promote can come, in the best case, to include the interests of others, the boundary between self-regarding activities and what I earlier called particular altruism begins to blur.

The question is how this merger of self and other can occur. Aristotle suggests a triadic model: Two individuals are brought together through their common possession, or pursuit, of something each regards as objectively good. This triadic (or classical) model contrasts with a dyadic (Romantic) account in which individuals become directly merged with, lost in, one another without the mediation of an independent good. In the two-person case, romantic love, this takes the form of mutual intoxication.

This experience, while real, is notoriously hard to sustain in the absence of truly shared tastes, activities, or objectives. Children can provide the third pole of the triad; so can commonalities of religion, creed, and ethnicity. From this point of view, while the practice of arranged marriages constitutes an extreme example of anti-Romanticism, it is not entirely crazy. It reflects the belief that if due attention is given to objective commonalities, the individuals chosen for one another will come over time to experience sharing subjectively.

As Aristotle emphasizes, the triadic account rests on a distinction between competitive and noncompetitive goods – that is, between (on the one hand) finite or inherently scarce goods and (on the other) inexhaustible goods whose possession by one individual does not impede their acquisition by others. This is why Aristotle lays such stress on knowledge and virtue as those shared goods most conducive to enduring friendship: My attainment of (some part of) virtue or wisdom does not diminish (may even enhance) your opportunity to attain the same objective good.

Of course, this cannot be said of the external rewards (such as public honor) that may be attached to these goods. For example, in a particular military situation that calls forth extraordinary heroism, it is unlikely that more than one individual will be considered for the Congressional Medal of Honor, even if several have behaved in an exemplary manner. Even more dramatic examples occur in the arena of knowledge, when the identity of the first discoverer of some phenomenon or theory (differential calculus in the seventeenth century, the AIDS virus today) becomes a matter of intense controversy. (The competition to make the discovery is correspondingly intense; recall James D. Watson's narrative of the race for DNA in *The Double Helix*.[12]) When an inexhaustible good is valued, not just for itself, but also as a means to a finite good, such conflicts are all but inevitable.

This triadic account of the extended self gives rise to perplexities. For example, why isn't the common pursuit of an inexhaustible good merely the adult version of the side-by-side but unengaged ("parallel") play characteristic of very young children? How does it lead to a partial merging of separate selves? The answer lies, I suggest, in the shared awareness that the other person is having an experience akin to one's own, and in the sense of identification that this awareness can produce. As an analogy, consider two people on a beach watching a gorgeous sunset. Each experiences, not only the sunset, but also the fact of its being shared by and with another. The result is a kind of merged consciousness – partial and fleeting, to be sure, but nonetheless real and significant.

A deeper perplexity is whether, and how, the kind of self-extension based on shared participation in an objective good can become particularized. If the commitment is to the good, then why does it not extend to all persons similarly situated with respect to that good? The answer is that it does, to *some extent*. Aristotle describes the kind of sentiment ("good will") that is apt to arise whenever we become aware of individuals or groups who possess what we take to be desirable attributes, whether or not we know them. This good will represents the universalizing tendency inherent in the classical account.

The difficulty, according to Aristotle, is that this wide-ranging feeling lacks "intensity and desire." The bearers of good will "only wish for the good of those toward whom they have good will, without giving them active assistance in attaining the good and without letting themselves be troubled in their behalf." While good will activates altruistic sentiments, it is insufficient to motivate altruistic deeds (*NE*, 1166b33–1167a5).

The reason, Aristotle argues, is rooted in the finitude of our consciousness. Acting on behalf of others requires effective identification with them, which requires in turn that we be able to experience their feelings as our own. But it is "difficult to share the joys and sorrows of many people [not just a few friends] as intensely as if they were one's own . . . [for example] it might well happen that one would have to share the joy of one friend and the grief of another all at the same time" (*NE*, 1171a5–8). That we effectively identify with one virtuous individual rather than another may be an accident of personal history, but once the available psychological space has been filled, it is impossible to further broaden the sphere of deep connection.

Let me translate this thesis into the typologies developed earlier in this chapter. Aristotle is arguing, in effect, that rational altruism provides at most a motive for desiring the good of others, but not for acting on that desire. The movement from desire to action is mediated by sympathy, but sympathy is inherently limited in scope. Even at its best, altruism is necessarily particular altruism; full-blown cosmopolitan altruism is virtually inconceivable.

This is not to say that there is nothing corresponding to cosmopolitanism in the classical understanding. Not only can good will link us to strangers; there is a kind of fellow-feeling based on common membership in the human species: "That is why we praise men for being humanitarians or 'lovers of their fellow men'." This sentiment goes well beyond the specific feeling ("concord") that can arise through common membership in a political community: "Even when traveling abroad one can see how near and dear and friendly every man may be to another human being" (*NE*, 1155a21).

Still, this is a far cry from Monroe's rescuers – cosmopolitan altruists who not only care about strangers *qua* fellow human beings but who are ready to risk everything to save them. How are we to explain this apparent gap in Aristotle's account? One possibility is that the principle of rational altruism extends farther than he thought. Human beings can share an orientation, not just toward lives lived in particular ways, but also toward human existence itself. The fact – and Aristotle takes it to be a fact – that most of us prize our own existence may lay the foundation for considering the existence of other human beings, and threats to that existence, with utmost seriousness, and for assisting threatened individuals. Not everyone will go to the aid of an endangered stranger (as the Kitty Genovese case so graphically demonstrated),[13] but some will, at least some of the time.

Another possible explanation would expand the sphere of potential sympathy. On this account, Aristotle erred in believing that our psychic space could accommodate only a small number of intense relationships. In fact, at least some people are capable of extended sympathy and of acting in response to the suffering of distant strangers. Those individuals have the capacity that Aristotle questioned – to feel a wide range of joys and sorrows more or less simultaneously.

One may at least speculate about the link between this enlarged capacity and the spread of Christianity. The picture of Jesus, who could feel the sufferings of all humanity and who made the ultimate sacrifice so that others might be redeemed, powerfully influenced the European moral imagination. Conversely, Christianity appealed to aspects of human moral capacity that classical philosophy had largely overlooked. And, of course, the idea of the impartial and benevolent spectator, though turned to secular use, drew much of its force from the understanding of divinity as aware of and concerned about individual human beings, which Aristotle's Unmoved Mover assuredly was not.

A third possible explanation for acts of altruism is that Aristotle may have overstated the extent to which the understanding of the self and its interests is congruent with the physical boundaries of individuals. His assumption was that individuated self-love was the universal norm and that only intense particular relationships could come close to overcoming it. But if Monroe's findings are to be believed, this is simply not the case for at least some individuals: The ordinary boundaries between self and other are relocated, and numerous physical individuals are seen as within the perimeter of the psychological self.

These three explanations track the trichotomy of reason-based, sympathy-based, and identity-based altruism sketched earlier. They need not be viewed as mutually incompatible or, for that matter, as jointly exhaustive. My point is only that because the actuality of cosmopolitan altruism implies its possibility, some relaxation of Aristotle's rigorously skeptical view is necessary, and that these three hypotheses are among the most plausible ways of proceeding in that direction.

## 5 THE VICISSITUDES OF COSMOPOLITAN ALTRUISM

The discussion thus far has revolved, albeit at varying distance, around the question of possibility. The second major issue I mentioned at the outset – the desirability of cosmopolitan altruism – raises different questions. Even if (or when) not obligatory, such altruism might still be (and frequently is) considered exemplary. For example, while Richard Rorty is at pains to debunk traditional philosophical accounts of moral cosmopolitanism, he has no doubt that "there is such a thing as moral progress, and that this progress is indeed in the direction of greater human solidarity," where solidarity means the ability to identify with, and respond to, the pain and humiliation of others.[14] At the end of Rorty's road is a world in which our capacity for solidarity overrides boundaries of family, class, ethnicity, politics, and religion – everything that can distance us from the sufferings of the most distant strangers.

Rorty seems to believe that cosmopolitan solidarity represents an unqualified gain over other, less inclusive principles. In his optimistic view, we can indefinitely widen the circle of our concern without giving up any previously held value. I doubt it, for all the reasons Isaiah Berlin has so memorably expressed: Not only is moral value pluralistic and multidimensional, strong gains along one dimension almost always involve costs along others. As Berlin puts it: "If, as I believe, the ends of men are many, and not all of them are in principle compatible with each other, then the possibility of conflict – and of tragedy – can never wholly be eliminated from human life, either personal or social."[15] There are general considerations, rooted in what Nagel calls the fragmentation of value, for believing this to be so. And there are particular reasons, based on empirical research, for believing it to be true in the case of cosmopolitan altruism.

I want to distinguish this argument from another with which it can easily be conflated. In her well-known essay "Moral Saints," Susan Wolf argues that moral perfection (of which altruism is a species) does not constitute a model of personal well-being toward which it would be rational or good to strive. There is human value other than moral value – wit, charm, or general agreeableness, some excellences of skill, some aspects of self-perfection, *inter alia* – that the moral saint cannot achieve.[16] While I believe there is much to be said in favor of this proposition, my claim is different: Without invoking nonmoral goods, even within what we would all regard as the sphere of morality, there are grounds for doubting that cosmopolitan altruism represents a comprehensively worthy ideal.

I build my case on three features of this moral stance that emerge from Monroe's research. First, the rescuers were willing to place at risk not only their own lives and well-being but those of their families as well, frequently over the family's passionate objections.[17] This would not be troubling if cosmopolitan altruism could be understood as a universal moral obligation, but (as we saw earlier) there are many reasons to believe that it cannot be – that it is not a general moral possibility and must instead be regarded as extraordinary, hence as supererogatory. It is, to say the least, morally questionable to compel others to risk profound sacrifices that they are not required to make and to which they have not consented.

These doubts only deepen when we reflect on the identity of those forced to run risks against their will. It is one thing for me to be indifferent between my own life and that of a stranger, and quite another to be indifferent between that stranger and my own brother. Cosmopolitan altruism seems to require the negation of particularistic obligations and the attenuation of special emotional ties, but these forms of human connection can hardly be set aside without moral loss.

Another feature of cosmopolitan altruism points in the same direction. Monroe reports, astonishingly enough, that the rescuers felt they had done nothing extraordinary. From an internal perspective, this is easy to understand. The rescuers' personal identity was so intimately bound up with others that their altruistic behavior was direct, immediate, and unreflective. They felt that they had no choice but to help the endangered Jews, whatever the risk. Their acts expressed their identity in a manner that they experienced as natural and unforced – the reverse of the kind of exertion experienced as demanding and extraordinary.[18]

From an external point of view, however, the rescuers' view constitutes an astounding absence of moral perspective. They seem not to understand that their personal no-man-is-an-island definition of selfhood is extraordinary. Precisely because they identify so closely with others, they lose sight of the profound differences between themselves and others. We may speculate that this lack of perspective contributed to their willingness to place the lives of family members at risk: The rescuers may have assumed that, at bottom, their kin were just like themselves.

In part because they denied the extraordinariness of their deeds, the rescuers tended to be indifferent to – and in several cases rebuffed – postwar efforts to honor them.[19] This is the third feature of cosmopolitan altruism I find troubling. After all, what could be more natural than the desire of those rescued, and of their communities, to recognize and thank those who had saved them? The victims' sense of gratitude and desire to do what they could to express it – to equalize the moral balance-scales as best they could – was overwhelming. But the rescuers found it difficult, if not impossible, to respond to these desires in the ordinary human way.

Once again, it is not difficult to understand why. To do what they did during the war, the rescuers had to disregard the opinions of others – not only of family and friends, as we have seen, but also of the broader community in which they had grown up.[20] It was their strong, inwardly sustained sense of self that enabled them to do this, and it was this inner self that continued to guide their postwar behavior. The very source of their extraordinary wartime conduct generated a kind of imperviousness to ordinary human connections afterward.

I want to stress that these observations are not intended as a case against cosmopolitan altruism. Speaking as a Jew, I am thankful for the rescuers' existence; I only wish there had been more of them. My point is rather that their moral excellence was not comprehensive, that the inner constitution that enabled them to risk their lives on behalf of endangered strangers was intimately connected to what might well be regarded as moral deficiencies. Precisely because moral worth is multidimensional, extraordinary excellence along one dimension is apt to produce loss along others.

To avoid misunderstanding, let me restate what I hope is already clear: Moral loss is hardly a phenomenon confined to cosmopolitan altruism, but rather is characteristic of a very wide range of moral choices. The identification of forms of moral loss characteristic of cosmopolitan altruism does not in itself constitute, and is not intended as, a criticism of that choice or an argument for some other choice. The point, rather, is this: Because cosmopolitan altruism is not infrequently regarded as a peak of moral excellence, it is especially important (and perhaps even surprising) to discover that it too encompasses acts and attitudes that may well be judged less than fully admirable.

The proposition that moral loss is ubiquitous, moreover, does not entail the casually relativistic conclusion that no choices can be rationally preferred to others. Some alternatives may straightforwardly dominate others: B may simply outrank A along every relevant moral dimension. And even if there is no single dominant option, even if qualitatively diverse dimensions point in different directions, there may still be an identifiable right thing to do, all things considered. If, as seems plausible in most cases, the morally relevant dimensions cannot be reduced to a common measure, then all-things-considered judgment rests on trained moral deliberation, a fully adequate account of which remains elusive.

The multidimensionality of value and agency characteristic of value pluralism allows us to raise some hard questions about cosmopolitan altruism. If rescuing cannot be understood as obligatory, it would appear questionable at best for rescuers knowingly to endanger others without their consent. I do not believe that it is right to place one's children at risk in this manner. It is certainly not right to conceal one's activities from (say) one's fiancé, depriving him even of the opportunity to offer considered approval to deeds in which he is likely to be implicated. Identification with all of humanity can be an admirable ground for personal action, but by itself it does not entitle the agent to act for, or involve, others.

The principal conclusion I draw from the ubiquity of moral loss concerns, not the substance of moral choices, but the manner in which they should be made. Within a given situation, the fact that some considerations override others does not mean that the losers simply vanish without a trace, morally speaking. The considerations that could not be reflected in our action retain a claim on our attention. Moral choices, I suggest, should be made and carried out with continuing awareness of, and sensitivity to, their costs. If we find ourselves compelled to disregard certain personal or communal ties in the name of cosmopolitan considerations, we should nonetheless experience the continuing force of those ties. When the considerations that determine our choices also dominate our consciousness, the result can often be a dangerous moral tunnel vision.

This is not to say that we ought to feel guilt when we do what is right, all things considered. When we do what is right, we have done the best we can, given (so to speak) the structure of the universe. We have done nothing for which to reproach ourselves. While we may yearn for a less pluralistic world in which moral loss is less pervasive, that loss is neither our product nor our responsibility. The point is rather that we should not seek to gratify our understandable desire for moral harmony by obliterating our awareness of unavoidable moral costs.

I close with two suggestions concerning the sources of moral loss within cosmopolitan altruism. First, moral universality is (can only be?) purchased at the cost of moral particularity; the ability to act on behalf of strangers conflicts with, and may often crowd out, other forms of human connection. Second, there is, if not classic egoism, at least a form of self-centeredness, in self-expressive action, for through such action individual inwardness is in a sense imposed on the world. Thus, while the rescuers' personal identity encompassed humanity as a whole and their acts expressed that inclusiveness, their moral stance was nonetheless unresponsive to the moral sentiments of human beings unlike themselves.

This unresponsiveness was necessary. As we have seen, if the rescuers had been effectively responsive to family and community, they could not have done what they did. Still, an important variant of moral inclusiveness is being able to take seriously other human beings, not as abstract homogenized entities identical to oneself, but rather as particularized individuals who may be very different. Responsiveness to particularity may undermine cosmopolitan altruism, but it may also pave the way for other worthy forms of moral action.

## Notes

1. For a general discussion, see Ronald D. Milo, "Introduction," in *Egoism and Altruism* (Belmont, CA: Wadsworth, 1973).
2. See Kristen Monroe, "John Donne's People: Explaining Differences between Rational Actors and Altruists through Cognitive Frameworks," *Journal of Politics*, 53 (2) (May 1991): 394–433; and Kristen Monroe, Michael C. Barton, and Ute Klingemann, "Altruism and the Theory of Rational Action: Rescuers of Jews in Nazi Europe," *Ethics* 101 (1) (October 1990): 103–22.
3. Neera Kapur Badhwar, "Altruism Versus Self-Interest: Sometimes a False Dichotomy," *Social Philosophy and Policy* 10 (1) (1993): 90–117.
4. Ibid.
5. Jean Hampton, "Selflessness and the Loss of Self," *Social Philosophy and Policy* 10(1) (1993): 135–65. It is worth pointing out, however, that the self-abnegation Hampton and I both reject might well be more positively valued within certain religious traditions. Here, as elsewhere, the decision to conduct moral analysis within a specific philosophical frame carries with it assumptions (typically tacit and even invisible) concerning the weight properly accorded to the self.
6. Thomas Nagel, *The View from Nowhere* (New York: Oxford University Press, 1986), pp. 159–62. Nagel's point is not that empathetic identification with the interests of others necessarily depends on the construction of a rational argument, but rather that certain kinds of self-preference with regard to certain interests are self-contradictory. Once subjected to challenge, Nagel claims, exclusive self-preference concerning (say) pain cannot be maintained as a rational moral stance.
7. *The View from Nowhere*, pp. 166–8. The argument Nagel discusses is advanced in T. M. Scanlon, "Preference and Urgency," *Journal of Philosophy*, 72 (1975): 655–69.
8. Christine M. Korsgaard, "The Reasons We Can Share: An Attack on the Distinction between Agent-Relative and Agent-Neutral Values," *Social Philosophy and Policy* 10 (1) (1993): 24–51
9. See especially Lawrence A. Blum, *Friendship, Altruism, and Morality* (London: Routledge & Kegan Paul, 1980).
10. See especially, Thomas Nagel, *The Possibility of Altruism* (Oxford: Clarendon Press, 1970).
11. Monroe et al., "Altruism and the Theory of Rational Action," p. 119.
12. James D. Watson, *The Double Helix: A Personal Account of the Discovery of the Structure of DNA* (New York: Atheneum, 1968).
13. In this notorious New York City incident, Genovese was assaulted within earshot of dozens of people living in a nearby apartment building. No one

came to her assistance, including individuals who were not only hearing but actually witnessing the assault. For an extended period, no one even bothered to call the police!

14. Richard Rorty, *Contingency, Irony, and Solidarity* (Cambridge: Cambridge University Press, 1989), p. 192.

15. Isaiah Berlin, *Four Essays on Liberty* (London: Oxford University Press, 1969), p. 169.

16. Susan Wolf, "Moral Saints," *The Journal of Philosophy*, 79 (8) (August 1982): 419–40.

17. "Several rescuers had to go against critical loved ones in order to rescue Jews" (Monroe et al., "Altruism and the Theory of Rational Action," p. 113). In more than one case, rescuers hid their activities from relatives and spouses, who were nonetheless implicated and paid with their lives (pp. 113 n30, 115).

18. Monroe, "John Donne's People," pp. 423–4: "Most rescuers shrugged off their rescue actions as 'no big deal'."

19. Monroe et al., "Altruism and the Theory of Rational Action," p. 109: "The honors or thanks the rescuers received were not sought and were as often as not a source of embarrassment as one of pride.... [For example,] Leonie refused the Yad Vashem award, saying she had not really done enough to deserve it."

20. Badhwar is quite right to emphasize the great confidence rescuers displayed in their own judgment, intelligence, courage, and endurance – in themselves as independent actors ("Altruism Versus Self-Interest"). But I do not believe (as she does) that Monroe et al. meant to deny this. The point is rather that the rescuers' capacity to identify with humanity as a whole gave them the inner resources to resist the pressure of family, neighbors, and the political community. This might be taken as an instance of the more general hypothesis that the ability to resist social pressure, to develop and display true individuality, must somehow be rooted in potent countervailing forces.

PART III

# POLITICS, MARKETS, AND CIVIC LIFE IN
# LIBERAL PLURALIST SOCIETIES

# 7

# The Public and Its Problems

## 1 INTRODUCTION

One may wonder how a philosophical approach to politics built on the
three pillars of value pluralism, political pluralism, and expressive liberty could yield anything close to a determinate picture of a good society. In key respects it cannot: Pluralists cannot embrace Plato's republic,
Rousseau's social contract, or even Rawls's two principles of justice as
the picture of the one best form of political organization under the most
fortunate circumstances. Pluralists will insist, rather, on two propositions.
First, every acceptable polity will fulfill the conditions of minimum decency – that is, it will organize itself so as to minimize the great evils of the
human condition. Second, polities that meet the condition of minimum
decency can build on that foundation in a wide variety of ways, all of
which are legitimate, and there may be no way of judging that, all things
considered, decent polity A has a better form of organization than does
decent polity B. (A may do better along some dimensions, B along others,
with no way of reducing qualitatively different dimensions to a common
measure of value.)

A pluralist philosophy, therefore, will leave a wide scope for politics –
that is, for public determination of most fundamental political questions.
For example, a constitution represents an authoritative partial ordering
of public values. It selects a subset of worthy values, brings them to the
fore, and subordinates others to them. Within the pluralist understanding, there is no single constitutional ordering that is rationally preferable
to all others – certainly not across boundaries of space, time, and culture.
Nonetheless, the worth of a constitution can be assessed along three

dimensions – call them realism, coherence, and congruence. A constitution is realistic if the demands it places on citizens are not too heavy for them to bear. A constitution is coherent if the ensemble of values it represents can coexist. A constitution is congruent if its broad outlines correspond to the main current of the community's public culture and to the situation that community confronts.[1]

In this chapter, I will explore the circumstances that should shape constitutional discussion in the United States and, in some respects, throughout advanced industrialized nations. I will focus on three broad categories of situational constraints on constitutional arrangements: public culture, socioeconomics, and path dependency – that is, the necessity of acting from where one already is. I begin with some reflections on the concept of public philosophy.

## 1.1 The Concept of Public Philosophy

Public philosophy should be understood in contradistinction to the classical conception of a universal or perennial philosophy that is addressed to all human beings at all times. First, a public philosophy is rooted in, and addressed to, a particular public in a specific historical situation. A public philosophy may include some universalizable claims, as did – for example – Abraham Lincoln's Gettysburg Address. But that speech was addressed principally to citizens of the United States, who found themselves in the midst of a great war fraught with contested moral significance. The validity of Lincoln's assertions for other political communities raises a different set of issues altogether.

Second, every political community possesses a distinctive public culture, rooted in its specific history and circumstances. This culture provides an ensemble of principles and goods from which visions of good political orders can be fashioned and refashioned. Each of these visions – a public philosophy – represents a particular selection, ordering, or weighting of the elements of this ensemble. A community's public philosophy shifts when previously ignored or secondary principles are brought to the fore – for example, when Franklin D. Roosevelt revitalized the dormant Hamiltonian tradition of vigorous executive power pursuing the general welfare.

From a liberal pluralist perspective, many different public cultures, and public philosophies drawn from them, are regarded as legitimate so long as the components of these public cultures are genuine goods and each culture meets the condition of minimum decency. Assuming that a public culture satisfies these threshold criteria, contests among contending public philosophies within the culture revolve around claims rooted in the circumstances that the particular community faces at a particular moment in its history.

Third, a public philosophy consists in more than fundamental moral propositions such as "All men are created equal." Public philosophy links such abstract propositions with specific conceptions of socio-political institutions. In the U.S. context, this institutional specification takes the form of liberal-constitutional democracy, which encompasses at least the following familiar elements:

- a system of rights, fully and equally enjoyed by every individual, spelled out and secured against invasion by other individuals, social groups, and public authorities;
- a boundary, ever shifting and contestable to be sure, between matters legitimately subject to public determination and those that are private;
- freedom of religion, expressed institutionally as non-establishment and socially as a pluralism of faiths practiced without impediment;
- a market economy in which the influence of public command-and-control decisions is relatively confined;
- a zone, neither market nor state, in which individuals may freely belong to, enter, and leave a range of diverse groups and associations to pursue common purposes and express shared values;
- a society of "careers open to talents" in which every individual enjoys an equal opportunity to develop and use talents and in which none is subject to discrimination;
- a government in which all legitimate authority is derived from the people and in which institutions of popular representation and direct participation are combined in a manner and proportion determined by the people; and
- the rule of law through settled and promulgated procedures rather than arbitrary whim or irregular decree.

In the United States, then, discussions of public philosophy can address two quite different kinds of questions: whether changing circumstances make it necessary to alter the manner in which we seek to realize these core elements of liberal-constitutional democracy; or whether liberal-constitutional democracy is itself adequate to achieve central public purposes.

Fourth, public philosophy goes beyond principles and institutions to specify general directions for public policy within a basic understanding of how the world works. (Neo-classical economics is one example of such an understanding; the *Federalist*'s emphasis on the scarcity and unreliability of civic virtue is another.)

Finally, a public philosophy represents an effort to solve specific public problems. In the United States, one of the most creative periods for public philosophy occurred between 1890 and 1920, as intellectuals and political leaders grappled with the challenges of an economy shifting from a agriculture/craft base to industrial corporations, a society in rapid transition from rural small towns to the large cities, a diversifying population swelled by unprecedented waves of immigration, and an increasingly corrupt and unresponsive political system. This period of intellectual development spawned the era of Progressive reform and culminated in the public philosophy of the New Deal, which dominated the U.S. political landscape from the 1930s through the early 1970s.

## 2 THE PUBLIC AND ITS PROBLEMS

Over the past three decades, the basic principles of the New Deal approach have been called into question. Conservatives have challenged the presumption in favor of national government solutions to social problems, while a new generation of public intellectuals has sought progressive alternatives to an increasingly sclerotic bureaucratic-regulatory state.

These developments have been sparked by new conditions. I single out three: the *economic anxiety* produced by the shift from a hegemonic national industrial economy to a global information economy; the *social dislocation* associated with the decay of traditional sources of stability and meaning such as nuclear families, neighborhoods, and voluntary associations, and with the rise of a social understanding focused increasingly on individual rights and choice; and the *political dysfunction* that accompanies the decline of traditional parties and the rise of a politics dominated by the media and concentrated economic power. (The United States' dominance as the world's sole remaining superpower, coupled with the emergence of new threats to that dominance, calls for another dimension of public philosophy that I cannot develop here.)

Beyond these key features of the American landscape, there are problems common to virtually all the Western democracies: an emerging imbalance between the social promises of the welfare state and the resources that governments can mobilize to meet those promises; an increasing orientation toward present consumption at the expense of investments for future needs; increasing tension between the requirements of national unity and the centrifugal tugs of subnational identity groups based on region, ethnicity, or religion; an escalating citizen mistrust of government and established institutions in general; and a weakening of the voluntary associations of civil society that should discharge many of the functions that governments do not.

Let me now return, somewhat more systematically, to public problems as seen from the specific vantage point of the United States.

### 3 THE ECONOMY

As recently as two decades ago, economists and political candidates debated the prospects for the industrial economy. Today, most would agree that we are in the midst of a great transformation from an economy based on industrial mass production to one revolving around knowledge, information, and technological innovation. This transformation is every bit as sweeping as the shift a century ago from agriculture to industry as the basis of national wealth, from rural life to urban life, and from individual artisanship to the giant corporation. And it is generating significant new problems not yet adequately addressed through public policy.

1. At the peak of the industrial economy in the quarter century after World War II, the fruits of economic growth were widely shared, and gross disparities of income and wealth tended to diminish. But for much of the past quarter-century, those best able to function in the emerging information economy (a relatively small fraction of the workforce) have reaped the lion's share the gains from growth while the incomes of others have stagnated or actually fallen. This is more than a statistical issue; it raises social and normative questions.

2. The new economy is also shattering expectations. A generation or two ago, it was not unusual for workers (both blue-collar and managerial) to spend their entire working lives within a single large corporation. Unemployment tended to be cyclical and temporary. Individuals enjoyed a substantial measure of job continuity, and employers gradually increased their contributions to health and pension plans. Today, insecurity is the watchword. Technology is replacing blue-collars jobs. Waves of corporate downsizing have thinned the ranks of middle managers. Employers are reducing health care and pensions, and they are resorting more and more to temporary contractual relations that free them from these responsibilities altogether.

3. In addressing these and other problems, citizens and public leaders must now operate in a world in which individual nations have lost a substantial measure of control over their own economic destiny. Multinational corporations, technological diffusion, and unchecked capital flows have reduced the efficacy of traditional instruments of macroeconomic management. The restoration of the largely closed national economies in which these tools once operated is unlikely at best. If a global race to the bottom is to be averted, many believe that new transnational norms and institutions will have to be constructed. But this strategy will encounter – indeed, has already triggered – anxiety verging on paranoia about the further loss of national sovereignty, especially among those who feel most threatened by the new economy.

### 4  CIVIL SOCIETY

A vigorous network of nonstate, nonmarket associations ("civil society") has long been seen as a distinctive strength of American liberal democracy. They are widely regarded as the arenas within which we learn to trust and work with one another, accommodate rather than demonize differences, develop the rudiments of a shared civic culture across those differences, and cultivate the dispositions and traits of character a healthy liberal democracy requires. Some theorists, of whom I am one, also see civil associations as bastions of resistance against totalizing state power and as arenas within which a variety of conceptions of the good – including many that deviate widely from the beliefs of the mainstream majority – may be freely enacted.

Not surprisingly, signs of decay in civil society – weaker families, fraying neighborhoods, a decline of voluntary associations, increased dependency and diminished regard for law, among others – have sparked widespread anxiety. We can argue about whether the dramatic increase in mistrust of government over the past three decades is warranted or unwarranted, good or bad. (I believe that this development has pushed a classic American tendency well beyond reasonable and productive bounds.) But it should be difficult for anyone to view with equanimity the significant decline in our propensity to trust one another, as fellow citizens.

As one might expect, these phenomena have evoked a range of explanations. Many conservatives argue that civil society has become weak because government, especially the national government, has grown too strong. Many liberals (joined by some conservatives) counter that the dynamics of global economic competition are at war with stable and healthy social relations. Across the political spectrum, it is widely thought that television is also part of the explanation, because it reduces family solidarity, promotes consumption over civic engagement, and fosters a comprehensive, home-based privatism ("cocooning"). The expansion of rights-based individualism may corrode associational motives and capacities. The rise of "identity politics" based on characteristics such as race, ethnicity, and gender may diminish trust across these lines of division and multiply barriers to certain kinds of associational life. Whatever the causes, the status of civil society is clearly one of the central public concerns of liberal democracy in America at the beginning of the twenty-first century.

## 5 GOVERNANCE

Starting with the rise of the Progressive movement, and accelerating during the New Deal, a novel conception of liberal democratic governance took hold in America. Its basic elements included expanded functions for public institutions, political centralization at the national level to carry out these functions, bureaucracy as a key institution for command and control, and detailed regulation as a key means of control involving the restriction of administrative and local discretion. Today, the Progressive/ New Deal model of governance is under attack, and not just by conservatives. Many wonder whether government can possibly carry out all the tasks it has assumed during the past century, whether centralization has usurped responsibilities better discharged by states and localities, whether multilayered bureaucratic hierarchy is really effective in the information age, and whether the endless multiplication of regulations accomplishes public purposes efficiently and effectively. The federal budget has become the vehicle for questioning long-established institutions and programs.

These difficulties illustrate the contemporary vicissitudes of the rule of law. The core idea is compelling: equal concern for, and fair treatment of, every individual within a system of legislation and adjudication authorized by the people. No prejudice, no favoritism, no special exemptions; only the evenhanded application of the rules in accordance with a publicly recognized truth. But since the New Deal, this idea has been expanded to the presumption that every aspect of life should be governed by law and administrative regulation.

Two difficulties arise. First: As law expands, the scope for discretion and judgment contracts, and decisions that are best made informally are enveloped in cumbersome rules. Second: If everything is to be subject to public law, then the classic liberal distinction between public and private collapses. It is one thing for law to define the boundary between public and private, or even a general framework within which private decisions must be made; quite another for law to determine, or review, the content of those decisions. The rectification of private unfairness frequently requires, and must be balanced against, the restriction of personal liberty. The mistrust of government we see today can be traced in part to a widespread sense that this balance has been poorly struck.

Other unattractive features of contemporary governance exacerbate this mistrust. Let me mention just three. The political reach of special interests – organized lobbies and concentrated wealth – expands inexorably at the expense of average citizens and the common good. Existing mechanisms of communication and decision-making do not encourage public education and deliberation, turning our politics into a battle of dueling slogans and sound bites. And the terms of political combat tend to drive the established political parties toward extreme positions and uncivil discourse rather than sensible problem solving built on common ground. The result: Many Americans feel shut out, ill-informed, unrepresented, manipulated, and politically homeless.

## 6 SOCIALISM, MARKETS, AND LIBERAL DEMOCRACY

Possible responses to these public problems are constrained by the near-disappearance of what was until recently the principal secular alternative to market democracy. Clearly we live in a post-socialist age. I do not mean to suggest that libertarianism, or even what Europeans call "neo-liberalism," has triumphed; social democracy and the welfare state are alive if not altogether well through advanced industrialized societies. I refer, rather, to the fact that the undemocratic form of "actually existing socialism" known as communism has collapsed virtually everywhere, and that in democratic polities, core socialist tenets such as the public ownership of the means of production have been watered down or discarded altogether. We cannot address the question, "What next?" without some understanding of why socialism, so understood, has all but disappeared. There were, I believe, three principal causes for this historic development.

1. As Friedrich Hayek had predicted as early as the 1940s, command economies proved incapable of processing the vast amount of

multivariate information needed to coordinate the needs and preferences of producers and consumers. To the extent that central planning was defended as an alternative path to economic growth and a consumer society, this flaw was a fatal objection.[2]

2. Socialist demands for motivational devotion to the collectivity clashed with the ineradicable self-interest of individuals. As revolutionary zeal faded and charismatic leadership became institutionalized in bureaucratic one-party states, those who enjoyed a monopoly of political power used it to entrench corruption and grasp material advantages unavailable to the mass of citizens.[3] The ensuing gap between officials' norms and observed conduct undermined both public policy and public confidence.

3. In practice, socialism – especially in its most undemocratic and totalistic forms – proved to be incompatible with rising demands for individual and collective self-determination. Information technology brought images of freedom and democracy to those who lacked either, undermining the credibility of socialist claims. In the democratic West, the growing credibility of reports about the use of state terror, gulags, and the like weakened support for socialism, even among left-leaning intellectuals.

Given these three points, we are entitled to draw the following conclusion: A viable post-socialist public order must be compatible with economic systems that yield sustained growth whose fruits are widely shared; it must rest on a realistic assessment of human motivation and conduct; and it must guarantee basic individual liberties and some form of democratic self-government.

The evidence of the postwar years suggests that a market economy is a necessary though not sufficient condition for liberal democracy. I say necessary but not sufficient because market authoritarianism is a real possibility; Pinochet's Chile is a standard example, one that Putin's Russia may well be in the process of emulating. Still, the relationship between liberal democracy and markets is more than contingent. Market economies are more conducive to economic growth than are other forms of economic organization. There is, in turn, a tendency for economic growth to enlarge the middle class, which typically leads to an increase in demands for individual liberty and collective self-government. (The apparent victory of the pro-democracy movement in previously market-authoritarian South Korea is a good example of this process.) In addition, there is evidence that economic growth produces generalized "affluence effects" – cultural shifts that promote the desires for individual choice and for governments that respect individual liberty.[4]

To the extent that the market produces some losers, the existence of democratic institutions guarantees a sympathetic hearing for efforts to create buffers or compensations. Uncompensated market losses can be enforced only with difficulty (if at all) in the absence of authoritarian government. That is one reason – not the only one, to be sure – why Pinochet's Chile could impose free-market policies that have proved unsustainable in democratic Argentina. So all liberal, democratic market societies are going to have mixed economies of one sort or another, with considerable national variation.[5]

This is one of several reasons why the collapse of socialism neither produces nor validates the pure unregulated market. As the republics of the former Soviet Union have discovered, effective markets have institutional and cultural preconditions. Four decades ago, Milton Friedman pointed out that every form of social organization – including markets – relies on a framework of generally accepted rules, and that "no set of rules can prevail unless most participants most of the time conform to them without external sanctions."[6] Not only must participants internalize rules, they must develop certain traits of character. These traits are especially demanding in systems of liberty: Freedom can be preserved "only for people who are willing to practice self-denial, for otherwise freedom degenerates into license and irresponsibility."[7] It follows from this that believers in free institutions must be attentive to the conditions that help develop citizens' capacity to follow rules and restrain their raw instincts. It would be reckless to assume that an invisible civic hand will do the job.[8]

To these considerations against the unregulated market, we may add others, even more familiar. First: While "political failures" are endemic, so are market failures (for example, those produced by the existence of externalities). Second: There are legitimate purposes that individuals can only pursue through mechanisms of collective decision-making backed by coercion (for example, in circumstances in which free-rider problems would undermine systems of voluntary cooperation). Finally: There is no guarantee that the unchecked operation of the modern market will produce distributive outcomes that meet even minimal moral requirements; indeed, there is evidence that deregulation of markets tends to widen inequalities of income and wealth in ways that undermine social solidarity and public-spirited governance.

## Notes

1. For more on pluralist constitutionism, see my *Liberal Pluralism: The Implications of Value Pluralism for Political Theory and Practice* (Cambridge: Cambridge University Press, 2002), pp. 66–9.

2. See, *inter alia*, F. A. Hayek, *The Road to Serfdom* (London: Routledge, 1944); and *The Fatal Conceit: The Errors of Socialism* (Chicago: University of Chicago Press, 1989).

3. I refer here to the theory of the "routinization of charisma" first (and presciently) advanced by Max Weber. (See *From Max Weber: Essays in Sociology*, H. H. Gerth and C. Wright Mills, eds. [New York: Oxford, 1958], p. 297.) The Soviet Union and the People's Republic of China offer classic examples of this process, through which revolutionary asceticism yields to the self-interest of the ruling party.

4. See especially Daniel Yankelovich, "How Changes in the Economy Are Reshaping American Values," in *Values and Public Policy*, Henry J. Aaron, Thomas E. Mann, and Timothy Taylor eds. (Washington, DC: Brookings Institution, 1994), pp. 16–53.

5. For the best discussion of this point that I know, see Robert A. Dahl, "Why All Democratic Countries Have Mixed Economies," in *NOMOS XXXV: Democratic Community*, John W. Chapman and Ian Shapiro, eds. (New York: New York University Press, 1993), pp. 259–82.

6. Milton Friedman, *Capitalism and Freedom* (Chicago: University of Chicago Press, 1962), p. 25.

7. Friedman, *Capitalism and Freedom*, p. 18.

8. These preconditions include well-functioning families, which (*pace* Gary Becker) neither do nor should organize themselves on purely self-interested principles. For two discussions of this matter from very different points of view, see Jennifer Roback Morse, *Love and Economics: Why the Laissez-Faire Family Doesn't Work* (Dallas, TX: Spence, 2001); and Carl E. Schneider, "Law and the Stability of Marriage," in *Promises to Keep: Decline and Renewal of Marriage in America*, David Popenoe, Jean Bethke Elshtain, and David Blankenhorn, eds. (Lanham, MD: Rowman and Littlefield, 1996).

# 8

## The Effects of Modern Markets on Civic Life

### 1 INTRODUCTION

My theme in this chapter is the effect of modern markets on civic life. That is a very broad topic. To define it more precisely, let me offer some preliminary distinctions.

**1.** While there are examples of nondemocratic market societies, I will focus on the dominant phenomenon of liberal democratic market societies and on civic life within such societies. By "civic life" I mean, not only official politics, but also the unofficial or voluntary associations and processes through which aims are pursued collectively.

As Peter Berger and many others have observed, there are no examples of liberal democratic polities without market economies. As far as we know, a relatively free market is a necessary though not sufficient condition of democratic political institutions.[1] One plausible explanation for this link is that while liberal democracy is a form of limited government, democratic institutions (like all other political institutions) have a tendency to breach their limits and aggrandize power unless confronted by sources of institutionalized resistance, of which a relatively autonomous market is among the most important.[2] The analysis in this chapter will presuppose, without further discussion, this crucial positive impact of free markets on free government. My focus will be on the ways in which the market impact is more ambiguous, perhaps even negative for liberal democracy.

**2.** By "modern markets" I mean economic systems strongly affected by globalization, technological innovation, and the expansion of knowledge. Such systems embody distinctive patterns of production as well as consumption. Much recent social analysis has focused on the consequences of consumption while neglecting production; I hope to redress that imbalance to some extent.

**3.** I want to distinguish between market *systems* and market *mechanisms*. During the past decade, a growing body of thought has explored the ways in which public sector institutions can make effective use of strategies that increase competition and choice and that focus on the management of outputs rather than inputs. New Democrat theorists in the United States and New Labour theorists in the UK have been at the forefront of this movement. The guiding idea is that in contemporary circumstances, an active government remains necessary, but the form of its activity must change. While the operation of the public sector has become less efficient and effective, the argument goes, the operation of the private sector has become more so. This suggests that government has much to learn from business, but it can and must absorb the lessons of reform without abandoning its traditional concerns and objectives.

I believe that this effect of modern market mechanisms on liberal democratic civic life is here to stay. My main topic, however, is the impact of markets understood as semi-autonomous systems of organization and endeavor.

**4.** I say "semi-autonomous" rather than "independent" because the relationship between markets and liberal democratic civic life is strongly reciprocal. The political order defines and enforces the rules of the market, regulates processes of production to protect workers and the environment, delimits the terms and conditions of employment and of bargaining between employers and employees, directs public investment, and intervenes in market-produced patterns of income and wealth in order to serve various social objectives. The *content* of state action in each of these areas is highly contested, both in theory and in practice, but the *fact* of such action is not. For the purposes of this chapter, I want to note (as the lawyers would say, "stipulate") this large area of analysis, and move on.

My strategy is straightforward. I state, as directly as I can, the concerns that animate recent explorations of the impact of market systems on civic life. I then identify and distinguish a number of hypotheses about this causal relationship, singling out a handful for more detailed analysis. I conclude with some brief speculations about the reforms of civic life that might ameliorate some of the problems.

The question before us has been debated by political and social theorists for centuries, but it cannot be resolved on the basis of theoretical considerations alone. In the course of this chapter, I bring a range of empirical data and research to bear on various causal assertions. As we will see, however, the available evidence does not always allow us to reach firm, or even probable, conclusions about the impact of modern markets on civic life. My hope is that the reader will at least come away with a clearer sense of the issues is dispute, and of the kinds of evidence that would be needed to resolve them.

## 2  CIVIC LIFE IN MODERN MARKET SYSTEMS: SIX HYPOTHESES

As a general matter, civic life in contemporary liberal democratic market societies is stable and tranquil, judged by historical standards. Most citizens obey the law most of the time; the level of dissent is low; and governments enjoy basic legitimacy. At the same time, there is a widespread anxiety about what is seen as a weakening of civic life. Political participation is declining, as is trust and confidence in government. Fewer and fewer young people regard public service as a desirable way to spend their lives. Special interest groups are proliferating, and the bonds of social solidarity are fraying. Led by Robert Putnam, a number of scholars argue that nonpolitical forms of civic affiliation and engagement are also in decline, at least in the United States, and perhaps elsewhere as well.[3]

Many analysts suggest that the modern market has something to do with these adverse trends. At the core of their concern is the sense that political activity differs qualitatively from market activity and that modern markets threaten to erode the distinctiveness of politics. The arguments are familiar: Markets rely on self-interest, while politics requires at least some devotion to the common good. Markets foster hyper-individualism, while politics requires at least some forms of solidarity and common action. Markets engage in a ceaseless process of creative destruction, while politics requires at least some stability and tradition. Market actors calculate, while citizens must deliberate.

There are various versions of the claim that modern markets tend to weaken liberal democratic institutions. These versions are not always clearly distinguished from one another and point in different directions, theoretically and practically. Let me try to disentangle them.

### 2.1  The Displacement Hypothesis

As the market becomes more pervasive, expanding to fill social space once occupied by collective endeavors, it seduces people away from public life.

People fly to the marketplace rather than the assembly, and private acquisition replaces public deliberation and decision as the focus of existence.

## 2.2 The Devaluation Hypothesis

In classical political thought, market activities were seen as inferior, or at best ministerial, to politics. Modern market ideology (as expressed in libertarian and public-choice literature, for example) inverts this hierarchy: Entrepreneurs and workers create wealth and opportunity, while politicians are said to meddle destructively, through redistribution and "rent-seeking." Public officials' professions that they act for the common good are bogus; they are no less self-interested than are market actors, but the results of their actions are far less beneficial for others.

## 2.3 The Division Hypothesis

Political life cannot be vigorous and healthy unless citizens develop a sense of fellow-feeling and shared fate. But the operation of the modern market pulls in the other direction. In economies marked by knowledge-intensity, technology, and global competition, economic growth intensifies the gulf among classes. Instead of a dominant middle class, those who possess scarce knowledge and skills become an upper-middle-class stratum, lower skill and manufacturing workers experience downward mobility, and the middle class forms a decreasing share of the population. The result: Both the winners and the losers are dropping out of civic life – the winners because they believe they no longer need it, the losers because they believe they can no longer influence it.

## 2.4 The Discomfort Hypothesis

In the civic republican tradition, political participation is seen as an intrinsic good and as a source of personal development and fulfillment for citizens. But real-world politics does not conform to this ideal. Most individuals do not experience political activity as an intrinsic good. They regard it as at best an instrumental good, and judged by that standard it often falls short. Collective action demands considerable time and effort, involves conflict that most individuals find distasteful, and often fails to achieve collective goods, even when it enjoys majority support. By contrast, market transactions allow individuals to attain their ends far more efficiently and reliably, with less conflict, and to experience a sense of control over their environment that is a highly prized psychological good. From an economic standpoint, moreover, rising affluence increases the opportunity costs of nonmarket endeavors, including public life. (This affluence effect also could help explain the astonishing drop in fertility rates in the wealthiest nations, which offer the highest levels of education and employment for women.)

## 2.5 The Efficacy Hypothesis

Individuals of modest means and skills need collective action to attain their aims. (This is not to say that such individuals will necessarily have the skills, motivation, or opportunity to achieve effective collective action.) Without unions and union-influenced political parties, manufacturing workers could not have improved the condition of the lives as they did in the heyday of the industrial economy. By contrast, today's upper-middle-class knowledge workers can use their individual skills and resources to get what they want without resorting to collective action. If they are dissatisfied with their physical security, they can buy private guards and retreat into gated communities. If they are dissatisfied with their children's public schools, they can send them to private schools. The result is the retreat of the successful from civic life, except when they are forced to use political means to defend themselves against political threats (changes in zoning or professional regulation, for example).

## 2.6 The Entertainment Hypothesis

Through the nineteenth century and the early decades of the twentieth, political events (along with holidays and sports) served as central sources of entertainment for local communities. Citizens came for the food, liquor, and social interchange, and stayed for the speeches and debates. As a consequence of market-driven innovation, the development of modern communications technology – especially television – has provided new, more privatized modes of entertainment that have displaced preexisting communal forms. Because politics is increasingly experienced through television, it is judged by the standards of television entertainment and found wanting, except for the moments of political scandal and crime to which the public is irresistibly drawn. The result is a broad withdrawal from political events, with occasional scandal-driven attention "spikes."

Reviewing the empirical evidence bearing on these hypotheses would take a very large book. For my purposes here, the best I can do is offer a summary judgment: I believe that each of these hypotheses has merit and must be taken seriously as part of a comprehensive analysis of civic life in contemporary liberal democratic societies. As can be seen, many of these causal processes go very deep and will be hard to address through standard political mechanisms. For example, I do not believe that the retreat of economically successful individuals from civic affairs can be adequately addressed through measures that appeal to self-interest, however understood. It is true that their lives would improve if there were less urban crime and better schools. But to the extent that the perceived costs of effecting these changes is high, they will continue to prefer the strategy of separation to that of engagement. Re-engaging the successful will require an overtly civic and moral appeal: "You may be able to insulate yourself from public ills, but the less fortunate you leave behind cannot. From those to whom much is given, much is expected." This may sound naive if not utopian, but I believe that it is actually the counsel of realism.

### 3 CIVIC LIFE IN MODERN MARKET SOCIETIES: THREE GRAND THEORIES

#### 3.1 The De Tocqueville Hypothesis: The Rise of Individualism

In *Democracy in America,* Alexis de Tocqueville describes a new phenomenon, which he calls "individualism" – a "calm and considered feeling which disposes each citizen to isolate himself from the mass of his fellows and withdraw into the circle of family and friends." Initially, he links individualism to democracy, but as the discussion proceeds, it becomes clear that the more precise analysis traces individualism to social mobility, rooted in the operation of the modern market economy. Social mobility blurs class distinctions and erodes communal loyalties. As social equality spreads, he continues,

There are more and more people who, though neither rich nor powerful enough to have much hold over others, have gained or kept enough wealth and enough understanding to look after their own needs. Such folk owe no man anything and hardly expect anything from anybody. They form the habit of thinking of themselves in isolation and imagine that their whole destiny is in their hands...

Each man is forever thrown back on himself alone, and there is danger that he may be shut up in the solitude of his own heart.[4]

Social isolation is hospitable to despotism, not democracy. How then did nineteenth century American democracy check and tame individualism? The answer: through federalism, which not only devolved authority to localities but compelled individual citizens to take responsibility for local affairs:

> Citizens who are bound to take part in public affairs must turn from the private interests and occasionally take a look at something other than themselves. As soon as common affairs are treated in common, each man notices that he is not as independent of his fellows as he used to suppose and that to get their help he must often offer his aid to them.[5]

The point is not that responsibility for local affairs leads to altruism or civic sacrifice, but rather that unlike national issues, local affairs make it easy to see the relationship between individual self-interest and communal concerns:

> It is difficult to force a man out of himself and get him to take an interest in the affairs of the whole state, for he has little understanding of the way in which the fate of the state can influence his own lot. But if it is a question of taking a road past his property, he sees at once that this small public matter has a bearing on his greatest private interests... Thus far more may be done by entrusting citizens with the management of minor affairs than by handing over control of great matters, toward interesting them in the public welfare and convincing them that they constantly stand in need of one another in order to provide for it.[6]

From this perspective, a modern-day de Tocqueville would conjecture that all other things being equal, the nationalization of American politics during the twentieth century, the drift toward restricting the authority and responsibility of local communities, was bound to weaken civic engagement and intensify the drift toward extreme individualism.

This is not to say that the story of twentieth-century America was one of steady civic decline, because other things were not almost equal. Robert Putnam describes a highly engaged "civic generation" defined by the shared experience of the Great Depression and World War II.[7] This suggests that unusual events at the national level can serve as functional substitutes for local responsibilities. The Depression fortified a sense of a common fate, and the military draft threw million of citizens together in circumstances of obvious and undeniable mutual dependence. But in the absence of such events, the nationalization of politics removes a key bulwark against the rise of individualism. Today, with the exception of the occasional summons to jury duty, there are no mandatory civic experiences. The draft was abolished a generation ago, and nothing has taken its place in the lives of young people. De Tocqueville would not be surprised at the consequences and, if his hypothesis is correct, we should not be either.

There is considerable evidence, quantitative as well as qualitative, that supports de Tocqueville's hypothesis. Transnational social surveys have traced the rise of "post-material" values, with the preference for individual autonomy and choice at their core.[8] Most competent observers of the U.S. scene agree that the norm of individual choice, expression, and self-sufficiency is far more central to our culture than it was even a generation ago.[9] Here are two of my favorite anecdotes, each drawn from the world of advertising:

When I was a boy, one of the largest U.S. insurance companies had as its slogan "Prudential: solid as a rock," which, along with its Rock of Gibraltar icon, festooned billboards along our roads. The message was clear: You can rely on us for your security. A few years ago, Prudential changed its slogan to read: "Be your own rock." The new message was equally clear: You must rely on yourself, and we can help you do that if you choose wisely.

A second example: For many years, the U.S. Army recruited young volunteers with the slogan, "Be all that you can be." The idea, backed by well-edited film clips, was that by participating in demanding activities requiring teamwork and mutual reliance, individuals would develop traits of mind and character that would serve them well in their future endeavors, whatever those might be. Not long ago, after what was widely reported as extensive and expensive market research, the Army changed its tune. It now reaches out to young Americans with an extraordinary (I would say, based on my military years, oxymoronic) new slogan: "An Army of one." The message is that participating in a group will not jeopardize one's individuality or capacity for self-direction. The point I want to stress is that one of the largest, experienced, and most tightly organized institutions in our country concluded that the new cultural climate compelled it to move in this direction.

Market life goes with the grain of modern individualism to a greater extent than does civic life, and so it expands its influence at the expense of politics. As this happens, a vicious circle develops: individuals' withdrawal further weakens the ability of the political system to work effectively, and the increased distance between the government and the governed diminishes trust. The result: Many citizens come to believe that they can achieve their purposes more efficiently, and with less chance of encountering dishonesty and manipulation, in the market sphere explicitly governed by self-interest rather than in the sphere purportedly motivated by concern for the public interest.

There are those who are untroubled by these developments. Some political scientists argue that there is no linear relationship between the amount or intensity of civic engagement and the health of political systems. Indeed, they suggest, high levels of participation can be a sign of passionate divisions that do not bode well for the maintenance of political stability. For their part, pro-market advocates regard rising mistrust of politics as a long-overdue unmasking of politicians' bogus claims about promoting the common good, and withdrawal from political engagement as a redirection of intellect and energy toward enterprises that produce real wealth rather than redistributing it or skimming it off as undeserved "rent."[10]

Others (and I include myself) are no more persuaded by this indifference (or hostility) toward civic engagement as we are by civic republicans' insistence on it as the highest form of human life. At some point, we believe – the location of that point is hard to determine – civic withdrawal weakens the capacity of societies to carry out essential tasks and to respond effectively to crises. Like other aspects of existence, collective action is a capacity that can wither from disuse. For us, it is essential to reflect on strategies that might halt and even reverse this adverse trend. One kind of strategy would explore ways of reorganizing civic life to render it more compatible with individualism. But while this may produce modest improvements, I am skeptical that it could get the job done. I believe that there is no alternative to strategies that can limit the sway of individualism. One possibility is to build institutional barriers against it, the sorts of devices Michael Walzer calls "blocked exchanges" – areas in which the power of money is not allowed to operate (buying votes, bribing judges, distorting decision making in response to campaign contributions).[11] Another complementary strategy is to bolster formative processes in schools and workplaces, for example – that over time can shift the balance of motivations of a fair number of citizens in advanced societies.

### 3.2 Spillover Effects of the Modern Market on Civic Life

These proposals raise a key empirical issue about the extent of spillover across spheres: Is market behavior a partial "role morality" that individuals engaged in market activities can set aside when they shift to other kinds of activities in families, communities, and public life? Or is it a way of thinking and acting that permeates, willy-nilly, the rest of human existence? If so, how should we evaluate the consequences?

I should note at the outset that the force of these questions depends crucially on one's understanding of the non-economic spheres. If one believes (as do those who propound "economic theories of democracy") that civic life does not differ, qualitatively and in principle, from market life, then the possible spillover from the latter to the former loses much of its significance. (Similarly, if one believes that family life is always structured by agreements and decisions based on self-interest, then the impact of the market on intimate relations will not appear particularly threatening.[12]) If one believes, on the other hand, that there is a difference between self-regarding and public-regarding behavior, between calculation and deliberation, between satisfying preferences and reflecting on them, then the possibility of a spillover becomes consequential indeed.

There is a classic philosophical tradition that suggests that involvement in market activities produces a specific social outlook, motivation, and behavior. Consider, for example, the thesis offered by Montesquieu:

The spirit of commerce produces in men a certain sentiment of exact justice, opposed on the one hand to brigandage – but opposed as well to those moral virtues which restrain one from always pressing one's interests with rigidity, and which enable one to neglect one's interests for the sake of the interests of others.[13]

So understood, commercial republics can embody the norm of reciprocity based on mutual advantage but are incompatible with the more stringent, sacrificial demands of the civic republic. In addition, Montesquieu claims, it is impossible to participate effectively in commercial life without developing and exercising certain distinctive traits of character: "The spirit of commerce carries in its train the spirit of frugality, economy, moderation, work, prudence, tranquility, order, and regulation."[14] If so, the denizens of commercial republics will have the capacity to internalize the social rules that sustain a peaceful social order over time. (Note that Montesquieu focuses on the effects of productive market activities rather than on consumption.)

In their capacity as social observers, many literary figures of the industrial age concluded that spillover effects were real, and even less benign than Montesquieu had suggested. Charles Dickens' Ebenezer Scrooge is a memorable portrait of a man whose crabbed market mentality came to dominate his entire life, with devastating effects on all those around him (and eventually on his own soul).

Another possibility is the political psychology of role morality – the ability of individuals to internalize the qualitative differences among spheres of life and to alter their conduct accordingly. Robert Lane finds evidence that internal psychological "walls" separate family and personal life from markets. The idea of spheres or domains is not just an analytical or theoretical category, he concludes, but has real resonance in the lives of individuals.[15] Indeed, the structure of domains protects personal life from markets, and vice versa.[16] But Lane also catalogues social scientific evidence indicating that what is learned in the market does affect other domains. Countering John Rawls's conjecture, Lane finds no evidence that the exercise of rights and political participation increases self-esteem. If anything, the causal arrow points in the opposite direction: Those who develop self-esteem elsewhere are more likely to become actively engaged.[17] There is evidence, however, that the exercise of discretion on the job does increase self-esteem and spills over into political participation.[18] The work experience shapes worldviews as competitive or cooperative, and the cognitive complexity or lack of complexity of jobs affects broader outlooks and behavior, including a sense of individual moral responsibility and the affinity for liberal democratic as opposed to authoritarian values.[19]

For the most part, Lane suggests, workplace learning cannot be replicated in the consumer market.[20] Unfortunately, the dynamics of modern market economies will inevitably give priority to consumer interests (such as lower prices and better products) over producer interests (the formative effects of the work experience itself) unless workers are willing to sacrifice some income to improve the quality of their work life.[21]

Drawing on a relatively small number of qualitative interviews, not necessarily representative of the entire workforce, Richard Sennett reaches somewhat different conclusions.[22] He focuses his analysis on the transition from the Old Economy of large industrial structures and mass production to the New Economy based on knowledge, technological innovation, and global competition. The following is a summary of his argument.

The greater mobility and instability in the New Economy workplace is part of its normal functioning, not a sign of crisis. The resulting erosion of long-term relationships between workers and employers corrodes trust, loyalty, and mutual commitment. In addition, the horizontal networks and ideology of teamwork in the modern workplace undermine parental authority when brought home. The challenge is to protect family relations from New Economy values. More broadly, these market-generated values may make it more difficult for human beings to develop a stable sense of self, a coherent narrative of life. Rhythms and routines aren't necessarily deadening but can contribute to a sense of inner order and meaning. Workplace "flexibility" doesn't necessarily empower workers but may divide them and transfer power to employers. The consequences of flexibility – the capacity to let go of one's past, the confidence to accept fragmentation and disjunction – work better for those at the top than for those down the hierarchy. High-tech workplaces can diminish workers' understanding of production processes as well as their sense of control and identity. The new imperative of constant risk-taking can increase the sense of vulnerability and even depression; we tend to care more about losses than gains. Risk-taking has become a test of character in the new economy, with negative results. Again, risk-taking works better psychologically and materially for those at the top. And the new market tends to value youth over age, daring over experience. In fact, it devalues experience. In the modern workplace, delay of gratification is no longer encouraged, and the emphasis on teamwork obscures the reality of hierarchical authority and promotes ironic superficiality. Economic insecurity tends to replace the old-market notion of a career with new-market forms of life based on discontinuity and pastiche; rather than pursuing coherent "life-plans," we tend to piece our lives together. Organizations that emphasize independence and self-reliance arouse a sense of vulnerability, increase the difficulty of acknowledging mutual dependence, and undermine trust. Taken as a whole, these experiences of middle-class insecurity and displacement have diminished interest in civic affairs while stimulating religious participation; the denizens of the new market are turning inward.

Sennett is aware that his argument risks shading over into nostalgia for a vanishing industrial economy whose effects on workers and families were by no means wholly benign. Moreover, it turns out that the children of Old Economy parents don't want to go back to the old economy, or for that matter the industrial-era family. Though not negligible, the constituency favoring the renewal of social stability based on hierarchy, ascribed status, and limited mobility is far short of a majority. Like other observers, Sennett finds most Americans torn between the desire to retain the advantages of enhanced individualism and choice and a growing awareness of what they have sacrificed to attain these advantages. Indeed, as European economies continue to shift away from traditional mass production toward knowledge, flexible specialization, and technological innovation, this tension may come to be a central reality in the lives of citizens of all post-industrial societies.

Via a different route, Michael Sandel reaches parallel conclusions. His focus is on the rise of the "voluntarist ideal" and its consequences for civic life. Politically, voluntarism is expressed through individual rights and entitlements. The problem is this: As rights and entitlements expand, citizens' sense of control over the forces that govern their lives contracts. The ideology of individual voluntarism and choice is at odds with the actual condition of our lives, in which we are enmeshed in a network of dependencies we do not choose. This contradiction leads to a severe difficulty in the lived experience of today's citizens: "Two fears – for loss of self-government and the erosion of community – define the anxiety of our age."[23] This discontent, Sandel suggests, reflects the power of a latent counter-ideal–civic republican freedom understood as sharing in the governance of a political community that controls its own fate. It is not clear that this civic ideal can be realized in an era of globalization. But individualistic voluntarism surrenders without firing a shot.

We must ask, Sandel concludes, what economic arrangements are hospitable to meaningful self-government under modern circumstances and how a pluralist society can encourage the "expansive self-understandings" that civic engagement requires. The issue is not just structures of civic opportunity, but also citizens' civic motivation. These concerns require us to revive an older discussion about the "political economy of citizenship,"[24] which Sandel argues was a staple of American political discourse from the Founding until the rise of consumerism and Keynesian economics in the twentieth century.

The story goes as follows: The U.S. debate over the political economy of citizenship begins with the agrarian ideal – the yeoman farmer as the bastion of republican government – and with the debate between Jeffersonians and Hamiltonians over the relative civic merits of agriculture and manufacturing, small towns and urban centers. During the early decades of the nineteenth century, the class of individual craftsmen and entrepreneurs expanded. Abraham Lincoln defended this as "free labor" – the opportunity to own productive property and work for oneself. As the agrarian ideal faded, craft self-employment was thought to be the form of economic organization most conducive to democratic self-government.

Toward the end of the nineteenth century, two trends threatened self-government – the rise of the giant corporation and the displacement of local communities. The Progressive response included urban planning designed to foster self-government, and a rear-guard effort, led intellectually by Louis D. Brandeis, to promote economic decentralization and worker participation in industrial management. Brandeis and his followers made a civic republican case against industrial oligopolies and national retail chain stores. Many early anti-trusters understood preserving competition among many small producers and retailers in formative as well as economic terms. Limits on competition, including price-setting, could be defended on civic grounds as enabling small producers and merchants to survive.

Economic decentralization was not the only Progressive response to industrialization. The "New Nationalism" of Theodore Roosevelt and Herbert Croly accepted a substantial measure of economic concentration as inevitable, but tried to revitalize civic formation through national rather than local or decentralized processes. A few brave dissenters argued the case for large corporations on civic grounds: Individual workers in corporations enjoyed more security, and therefore real civic independence, than did vulnerable small entrepreneurs and the handful of workers they employed.

Finally, some Progressives initiated the fateful shift of emphasis from production to consumption. In the republican tradition, citizens' identities as producers mattered more, and consumption was to be disciplined and restrained. The shift to consumerism reflected a larger shift from shaping wants to satisfying them, as did the rise of Keynesian economics. From Jefferson to Brandeis, Sandel argues,

Republicans worried more about conditions of production than about conditions of consumption because they viewed the world of work as the arena in which, for better or worse, the character of citizens was formed. The activity of consumption was not decisive for self-government in the same way.[25]

After World War II, these trends culminated in a cultural shift that can be characterized as a triple revolution: from production to consumption (the consumer movement); from civic formation to want-satisfaction (Keynesian economics); and from civic liberty to individual autonomy. Of the three elements of this revolution, the third went deepest, Sandel argues:

Americans of the postwar years found their way to a new understanding of freedom. According to this conception, our liberty depends not on our capacity as citizens to shape the forces that govern our collective destiny but rather on our capacity as persons to choose our values and ends for ourselves.[26]

This new conception of freedom as individual voluntarism held out a promise of agency "that could seemingly be realized even under conditions of concentrated power."[27] It did not work out as planned, in part because large impersonal structures resisted individual choice, but also because liberty understood in exclusively individualistic terms proved unable to inspire the moral and civic engagement that self-government requires.

Starting in the 1960s, thinkers and political leaders began responding in different ways to a growing if inchoate discontent with the voluntarist ideal and with the government structures that structured and expressed it. These responses included political decentralization, championed by Robert F. Kennedy in the months before his death in 1968; a growing emphasis on civil society, starting in the 1970s; and the conservative/communalist critique of the rights revolution and big government (though not big business). Meanwhile, liberal Democrats defended a national state that provided "welfare" but did not speak to the anxieties of the age.

All of these responses were flawed, Sandel concludes, by their inattention to the interaction between economic organization and civic life. It is preferable to restore dialogue about the political economy of citizenship, about new modes of economic activity that might help revitalize civic spirit. This response might include: a critique of excessive inequality on grounds of civic division rather than "fairness"; efforts to the fortify the public programs and public spaces that bring people together and reduce the power of money; and a strategy to strengthen community development corporations and other locally based economic entities over which individual workers and citizens can exercise a measure of control. If bolstered by other pro-civic initiatives such as serious civic education and the aggressive use of federalism to promote decentralization and local political responsibility, the United States might be able to restore a portion of the lost connection between the people and their government.

Sandel recognizes that to the extent that economic globalization is a reality, the efficacy of these strategies is likely to be limited. Transnational commerce and capital flows reduce the power of even powerful national governments. There is a growing mismatch between the scale of economic and political organizations with which citizens can identify and those much larger institutions that would be needed to bring global economic activity under greater collective control. Even if undertaken in the name of classic civic ideals, Sandel concludes, any move toward transnational governance could end by further weakening civic life.

## 3.3 Fouling the Nest: Unintended Externalities of the Market

It is generally acknowledged that successful market economies draw on certain individual habits and traits of character. No market system has the capacity to operate on the basis of external enforcement mechanisms alone; each system presupposes that most market actors have internalized basic norms such as honesty, promise-keeping, and responsibility to employers and stakeholders.

There is less agreement as to the source of the internal norms on which markets depend. A minority view is that they evolve and persist spontaneously, through the working of the market itself. For example, the Hayek scholar Norman Barry insists that

> [t]he practice of trade itself generates those capacities of honesty and trust that the market needs ... It is true that we inherit rules that we did not choose ... But we accept them and we follow them precisely because they have utilitarian value.[28]

A more widely accepted view is that successful markets draw on reserves of cultural and moral capital generated by institutions and processes outside the market, such as families, civil associations, and religion. This view is endorsed by most neoconservatives and by many liberals as well. Notably, even Friedrich Hayek came around to a version of it toward the end of his long and distinguished career: Free markets, he concluded, rest on traditional moral restraints, which cannot be maintained in the absence of religion.[29]

Clearly it makes a big difference which of these theories about the sources of necessary market norms is closer to the truth. If the "internal" view is correct, then we have a virtuous circle: The market creates what it needs, in a continuously self-reinforcing process. But if the "external" view prevails, then matters are not so simple. For example, if certain kinds of family life are vital to the reproduction of market norms, then it is at least possible that by weakening families, the market over time weakens itself. As Jonathan Sacks puts it:

> When everything that matters can be bought and sold, when commitments can be broken because they are no longer to our advantage, when shopping becomes salvation and advertising slogans become our litany, when our worth is measured by how much we earn and spend, then the market is destroying the very virtues on which in the long run it depends.[30]

The question is not only the effect of the market on itself but (most pertinently for our purposes) its political externalities. The Catholic thinker Michael Novak has argued that it is a mistake to think of economic systems as merely instrumental: "They carry some moral imperatives of their own, and these are often rather different from those which prevail in the moral-cultural institutions to which they are joined."[31] Novak is confident that the moral imperatives of the modern market are consistent with – indeed, coincide with – those of liberal democracy: Far from ideological mystification, "democratic capitalism" denotes a deep sociological reality.[32]

Others are not so sure. The market is an enormously powerful and seductive machine that tends to homogenize different spheres of human existence into expressions of the market ethos. The result is to distort and degrade our social and civic life. To quote Jonathan Sacks once more:

If products can be bought and sold, why not health or education or art or confidential information or reputations or relationships? Why not see marriage as a commercial contract for mutual advantage? Why not see children as commodities to be designed by genetic engineers and produced or terminated at will? Why not see all values as reducible to profit?[33]

Sacks speaks, not as an enemy of the market, but as its proponent and friend. His defense rests, however, on the hope – which may prove contrary to fact, even in the best case – that its effects can be contained within its own sphere.

The issue is this: If democratic politics and capitalist economies are not qualitatively and morally distinct from one another but rather draw from, and function according to, similar norms, then there is no reason to fear the impact of market externalities on free political institutions. But if market and political norms are in important respects different, then there is at least as much reason to fear the impact of a pervasive market mentality on democracy as there is to fear the impact of democratic politics on markets.

As the discerning reader will have guessed, I incline toward the latter view. Politics *is* different. It is a mistake to believe that individual exit is always an adequate substitute for collective voice, or that calculation concerning means can wholly replace debate concerning principles and ultimate ends. It is wrong to buy votes, or to sell candidates like soap, or to adjust one's political product merely to increase market share. It degrades politics to turn it into another form of passive entertainment, a spectacle judged by its capacity to amuse. Rightly understood, citizens are neither spectators nor consumers. A culture dominated by tabloids, MTV, and shopping malls encourages us – and worse, our children – to forget the difference.

## 4 CONCLUSION

While this discussion has been exploratory, let me summarize some of the tentative conclusions to which we have been led.

**1.** There is evidence that civic life in contemporary liberal democratic societies is weakening – certainly in the United States, probably in the UK, and arguably throughout Europe as well.[34] For a range of reasons, practical and normative, it is difficult to agree with the political scientists and market theorists who view this trend with equanimity.

**2.** There is evidence – qualitative, quantitative, and historical – that the operation of the modern market is implicated in this trend, through a wide variety of causal mechanisms and effects. Despite the complex differentiation of roles and spheres in contemporary society, the market cannot be sealed off from the rest of social life, but rather spills over into it.

**3.** In considering the civic consequences of modern markets, it is important to explore the effects of modes of production as well as patterns of consumption. The scale and structure of productive systems create workplace experiences that have formative effects.

**4.** The market/civic nexus must be understood within the larger context of the rise of individualism, voluntarism, and choice as both facts and norms within modern and modernizing societies. This context suggests the complexity of any efforts to intervene in the market/civic relationship: While troubled by many of the collective consequences of hyper-individualism, the inhabitants of contemporary societies prize its consequences for individuals. While outbursts of nativism and fundamentalism indicate a desire in some quarters for more stable and predictable societies, most would not willingly return to an older order of limited mobility and fixed ascribed identities. Efforts to revive civic life in liberal democratic market societies must be broadly compatible with the perceived gains of individualism.

### Notes

1. Peter Berger, *The Capitalist Revolution* (New York: Basic Books, 1986), pp. 76, 81.
2. Berger, *The Capitalist Revolution*, p. 79. For a broad examination of empirical linkages between political democracy and various kinds of economic institutions, see Robert A. Dahl, "Why All Democratic Countries Have Mixed Economies," in *Democratic Community: NOMOS XXXV*, John W. Chapman and Ian Shapiro, eds. (New York: New York University Press, 1993). For an account

of civil society as another semi-autonomous restraint on the power of the democratic state, see my "Civil Society and the 'Art of Association'," *Journal of Democracy* 11 (1) (2000): 64–70.

3. See Robert D. Putnam, *Bowling Alone: The Collapse and Revival of American Community* (New York: Simon & Schuster, 2000).

4. Alexis de Tocqueville, *Democracy in America*, trans. George Lawrence, ed. J. P. Mayer (Garden City, NY: Doubleday, 1969), p. 508.

5. de Tocqueville, *Democracy in America*, p. 510.

6. de Tocqueville, *Democracy in America*, p. 510.

7. Putnam, *Bowling Alone*, pp. 254–5.

8. See Ronald Inglehart, *Culture Shift in Advanced Industrial Society* (Princeton: Princeton University Press, 1990); also Ronald Inglehart, *Modernization and Postmodernization: Cultural, Economic, and Political Change in 43 Societies* (Princeton: Princeton University Press, 1997).

9. For example, see Daniel Yankelovich, "How Changes in the Economy Are Reshaping American Values," in *Values and Public Policy*, Henry J. Aaron, Thomas E. Mann, and Timothy Taylor, eds. (Washington, DC: Brookings, 1994).

10. For a discussion of the latter group, see Robert Kuttner, *Everything for Sale: The Virtues and Limits of Markets* (New York: Knopf, 1997), pp. 333–42.

11. Michael Walzer, *Spheres of Justice: A Defense of Pluralism and Equality* (New York: Basic Books, 1983), pp. 100–3.

12. For the canonical statement of this thesis about family life, see Gary S. Becker, *A Treatise on the Family* (Cambridge, MA: Harvard University Press, 1991).

13. Quoted and discussed in Thomas L. Pangle, *The Spirit of Modern Republicanism: The Moral Vision of the American Founders and the Philosophy of Locke* (Chicago: University of Chicago Press, 1988), p. 68.

14. Quoted in Pangle, *The Spirit of Modern Republicanism*, p. 68.

15. Robert E. Lane, *The Market Experience* (Cambridge: Cambridge University Press, 1991), p. 451.

16. Lane, *The Market Experience*, p. 519.

17. Lane, *The Market Experience*, p. 197.

18. Lane, *The Market Experience*, pp. 198–9.

19. Lane, *The Market Experience*, pp. 239–42.

20. Lane, *The Market Experience*, p. 259.

21. Lane, *The Market Experience*, p. 336.

22. Richard Sennett, *The Corrosion of Character: The Personal Consequences of Work in the New Capitalism* (New York: Norton, 1998).

23. Michael L. Sandel, *Democracy's Discontent: America in Search of a Public Philosophy* (Cambridge, MA: Harvard University Press, 1996), p. 294.

24. Sandel, *Democracy's Discontent*, pp. 201–3.

25. Sandel, *Democracy's Discontent*, p. 268.

26. Sandel, *Democracy's Discontent*, p. 275.

27. Sandel, *Democracy's Discontent*, p. 278.

28. Norman Barry, "The Market Still Inadequate?" in Jonathan Sacks, *Morals and Markets* (London: Institute of Economic Affairs, 1999), pp. 32–3.

29. For a noteworthy discussion, see Sacks, *Morals and Markets*, pp. 10–11, 56. (Sacks is not only a distinguished philosopher but also Chief Rabbi of the United Hebrew Congregations of the British Commonwealth.)

30. Sacks, *Morals and Markets*, p. 24.

31. Michael Novak, *Three in One: Essays on Democratic Capitalism, 1976–2000*, Edward W. Younkins, ed. (Lanham, MD: Rowman & Littlefield, 2001), p. 27.

32. Novak, *Three in One*, p. 37.

33. Sacks, *Moral and Markets*, p. 53.

34. For much more on this topic, see my "Civic Knowledge, Civic Education, and Civic Engagement: A Summary of Recent Research," in *Constructing Civic Virtue: A Symposium on the State of American Citizenship* (Syracuse, NY: The Maxwell School, 2003).

# 9

## The Politics of Reciprocity

### *The Theory and Practice of Mutualism*

The aim of this chapter is to offer an account of governance that is consistent with both liberal pluralist theory and some significant facts of human life under modern conditions. While in the abstract, liberal pluralism is consistent with a wide range of regime forms, practical circumstances in a given time and place are likely to narrow that range considerably. We have already encountered some of these circumstances – among them, declining political engagement, an active but ambiguous associational life, and a pervasive market. I turn now to other significant facts that delimit modern conditions, and then to their implications for governance.

### 1  THREE BUILDING BLOCKS FOR AN ACCOUNT OF GOVERNANCE

In this section, I want to develop what I regard as three building blocks for an account of governance. The first of these is individualism, understood as an ineliminable feature of modern societies. The second is an account of human motivation that asserts the reality of moderate self-interest – that is, of the capacity of normal human beings to act in ways that do not always reflect naked self-interest. The third is a moral framework that emphasizes the reciprocity and mutual responsibility stemming from political arrangements founded on choice and contract.

### 1.1  The Rise of Individualism

The legal scholar Lawrence Friedman argues that the United States is becoming what he calls a "republic of choice." In this new age of individualism,

The state, the legal system, and organized society in general . . . seem more and more dedicated to one fundamental goal: to permit, foster, and protect the self, the person, and the individual. A basic social creed justifies this aim: each person is unique, each person is or ought to be free, each of us has or ought to have the right to create or build up a way of life for ourselves, and to do it through free, open, and untrammeled choice. These are the unspoken premises of popular culture. They find their way into policy not because of some direct, conscious command or decision of the rulers, but because of global, powerful forces . . .[1]

This development may have gone farther in the United States than elsewhere, but it is hardly confined to one country. Indeed, Friedman points out, individualism and individual choice are central themes in the work of "most theorists who have tried to distill the essence of modernization."[2] These theorists depict human beings in nonmodern societies as prisoners of status, locked in the iron cage of custom and family/group ties. A modern society, by contrast,

is one that emphasizes the individual rather than the group; . . . allows free – wheeling choice among options; . . . structures relationships contractually, rather than through time-honored customs and mores; . . . does not force people into fixed roles, decreed by sacred tradition and inexorable at the moment of birth, or at set stages of life; it turns its back on inheritance and ascription, and opens the door to freedom, mobility, and choice.[3]

In a similar vein, the sociologist Anthony Giddens warns against the tendency, pronounced among thinkers on the left, to reduce individualism to selfishness and consumerism. There is a connection between these concepts, but individualism involves more than this and goes deeper:

Individualism is a structural phenomenon in societies free from the hold of tradition and custom, a transition that is again taking place on a widespread basis. We live our lives in a more open, reflective way than was the case in the past. Among the areas . . . where individualism has made itself felt are the family and in gender relations. Women no longer are inevitably "fated" to lives of domesticity and the rearing of children.[4]

The social theorist Ralf Dahrendorf suggests that our lives are a function of options (or choices) and linkages (or bonds). The shifting balance between these two primary social forces defines the basic nature of society, and of the life-chances that denizens of different societies can enjoy. And while their relationship is not strictly zero-sum, there is a tendency for societies high along one dimension to be low along the other, a tendency that finds expression in processes of modernization.

Pre-modern societies with their overpowering forces of family, estate or caste, tribe, church, slavery or feudal dependence, were in some ways all linkage and no choice. The social bonds of inescapable statuses dominated most people's lives.[5]

Modernization, by contrast, means the extension and expansion of choice.

But modernization provides choices as often as not by the disruption of linkages. Mobility has come to mean that the family or the village are no longer communities of fate, but increasingly become communities of choice. The money economy generalizes social relations in a way that implies the abandonment of many specific bonds.[6]

Applied to our current topic, these theories play out roughly as follows. As recently as 1960, Western societies were a complex mix of modernity and tradition. Some aspects of social life, for some groups or classes, embodied principles of choice, while others reflected ascribed status or customary relations. Civic life drew on tradition as well as choice, in ways that both energized and disfigured politics. More recently, the social balance has shifted sharply toward choice. Rather than being forced either to endure, or to create collective protests against, unpalatable circumstances, more and more individuals have the liberty and the wherewithal to walk away from them. In economist and social theorist Albert Hirschman's terms, the rise of choice means more "exit" but less "voice."[7] The result is that politics is on the whole more tranquil but less vigorous. The same processes that allow individuals to opt out of traditional ties also allow them to opt out of active political engagement, and many are taking advantage of their opportunity to do so.

In *Democracy in America*, as we have seen, Alexis de Tocqueville described a new phenomenon, which he was the first to call individualism – namely, a "calm and considered feeling which disposes each citizen to isolate himself from the mass of his fellows and withdraw into the circle of family and friends."[8] The problem with individualism thus understood is three-fold. First, it can lead to isolation that contradicts the basic human need for social relations. Second, it can induce individuals to fool themselves about the extent of their actual dependence on others for the attainment of their aims. And third, it can weaken the ability of individuals to engage in needed collective action, whether through public institutions or civil society.

Nonetheless, individualism understood as individual choice and self-determination is here to stay; its attractions and advantages loom too large to be put aside. The task of modern politics is not to engage in a quixotic campaign against the spirit of individualism, but rather to devise principles and forms of vigorous public life that are consistent with it.

## 1.2 Moderate Self-Interest, Regard for Others, and Internalized Norms

The evidence of observation and social science argues against the hypothesis of motivational purity, of whatever kind. Most individuals are incapable of anything approaching sustained devotion to the common good, the motive that writers in the civic republican tradition invoke as an effective antidote for the inevitable tendencies toward privatism and selfishness. Nonetheless, to varying degrees, individuals are capable of behavior that diverges from narrow self-interest. Economic theories resting on the hypothesis of consistent self-interest are as unrealistic as civic republicanism.

The framers of the U.S. Constitution understood human beings as motivationally mixed in just this way. On the one hand, they argued, devotion to principle and the common good was bound to be in short supply, and institutions that counted too heavily on it were bound to fail. For this reason, James Madison concluded that virtue stood in need of assistance, in the form of suitably designed institutions:

Ambition must be made to counteract ambition. The interest of the man must be connected with the constitutional rights of the place. It may be a reflection on human nature that such devices should be necessary to control the abuses of government. But what is government itself but the greatest of all reflections on human nature? (*Federalist* 51)

At the same time, Madison insisted that human beings had some capacity for good, in their public as well as private lives:

As there is a degree of depravity in mankind, which requires a certain degree of circumspection and distrust, so there are other qualities in human nature, which justify a certain portion of esteem and confidence. *Republican government presupposes the existence of these qualities in a higher degree than any other form.* Were the pictures, which have been drawn by the political jealousy of some among us faithful likenesses of the human character, the inference would be that there is not sufficient virtue among men for self-government. (*Federalist* 55; emphasis added)

I would suggest, as have many before me, that the endurance of the U.S. Constitution rests in no small measure on this complex psychological realism, which stands opposed to both idealism and cynicism and furnishes a more secure basis for liberty than do either of the simplifications.

We must then pose the next question: What kinds of alternatives to pure self-interest do we observe in human conduct, and how far do they go? I offer the following as a brief catalogue of behaviors for which there is substantial empirical evidence. They represent, not heroic or supererogatory virtue, but activities within the reach of most people at least some of the time:

- *Intra-family sacrifice*: People regularly sacrifice their own well-being for that of their children and parents, a fact of no small significance in policy arenas such as education and health care.
- *Limited empathy with strangers, if the costs of assistance are not excessive*: For example, skilled swimmers not employed as lifeguards regularly intervene to rescue potential drowning victims. We would think it odd, even culpable, if someone could prevent harm to another by making a brief local telephone call but failed to do so. On the other hand, few feel impelled to treat strangers as they do family members or themselves, and this kind of impartiality is not often expected.[9]
- *The capacity for promise-keeping and more broadly, for internalizing and acting on self-limiting norms*: The point of a promise is to bind oneself to specified future conduct, even if fulfilling the promise at that time would be contrary to immediate self-interest. The promise may well be undertaken with the expectation that it will promote one's self-interest, but matters may not turn out that way. The upsetting of self-interested expectations does not nullify the moral force of promises, and in practice individuals are capable of adhering to them, even when the costs are substantial. Promise-keeping is an instance of a large class of self-limiting norms that many (not all) human beings are capable of internalizing and honoring, some if not all the time.

- *Some capacity to identify one's own well-being with that of a collectivity to which one belongs*: Individuals can come to believe strongly that their well-being is linked, even identical, to that of a larger group – ethnic, religious, or political. Under such circumstances, which are not rare, individuals are willing to sacrifice their own self-interest as ordinarily understood (perhaps even their lives) to advance group interests. To be sure, such individuals are often motivated by some expectation of long-term payoff for their sacrifice – as, for example, when terror bombers are promised eternal bliss in Paradise as a reward for suicidal attacks on their group's enemies. But we also observe self-sacrificing group-oriented behavior not obviously linked to anticipated individual rewards.
- *The capacity to perform public duties*: It is a perennial conundrum of voting studies, not that turnout falls short of universality, but rather that anyone at all votes in mass democracies. Voting is somewhat costly, as measured in time and effort, and there is a vanishingly small chance that anyone's single vote will turn out to make a difference. (Nor is it the case that most voters are deluded about this.) The most persuasive explanation for why people vote is that they do so because they have come to believe that it is what citizens ought to do. There is no reason to think that voting is the only public act motivated in this way.
- *An intuitive sense of fairness or fair play*: While the self-interested rationale for free-riding is well-established and powerful in many situations, in practice it turns out that not everyone will be a free rider, even when effective enforcement of individuals' fair-share contributions is lacking and fear of social disapproval is not the operative motive for individual conduct. No one wants to be a sucker, but many individuals will do what they take to be their fair share unless they are confronted with evidence that most others are shirking.
- *The capacity to identify with and adhere to rules that one has a hand in establishing*: Evidence from controlled experiments shows that individuals in groups that are empowered to establish their own rules for distributing economic rewards are capable of honoring those rules even when they work to one's disadvantage. When the identical rules are imposed from outside, the motivation to obey weakens substantially.[10]
- *Intrinsic motivation toward excellence in performance*: There is evidence that creativity and innovation in markets flow more from intrinsic than

extrinsic payoffs. According to studies summarized and discussed by political scientist Robert Lane, innovation comes from self-direction, which is expressed in jobs where contingent rewards are not controlling. The principal fruits of modern markets – efficiency, growth, and progress – substantially depend on nonmarket motivations.[11] This conclusion applies a fortiori to social and political life, where substantial numbers of people are motivated by the desire to carry out their roles and tasks at a high level of performance.

If these points are tolerably accurate, it follows that we must reject the pure "economic theory of democracy" – the thesis that self-interest furnishes an adequate basis either for understanding political behavior or for constructing political institutions. Madison was right: We need a fuller, more complex, more balanced view of human nature and motives.

## 1.3 A Normative Framework for Contemporary Political Community

In this section, I offer a brief sketch of a normative framework for liberal pluralist political communities. I see a complementary relationship between norms and empirical findings. As a threshold requirement, this framework (or any alternative to it) must comport with what we have learned about individual motivation, personal and civic liberty, the functioning of markets, and the relationship between economic systems and political regimes. I divide my proposed framework into four parts: moral theory, political theory, individual responsibilities, and social responsibilities.

*1.3.1 Moral Theory.* As I have argued throughout this book and elsewhere, value pluralism offers the most secure foundation for a politics of liberty.[12] To recall, briefly: For value pluralists, the distinction between good and bad is objective, but goods are heterogeneous, there is no single dominant good for all purposes, and there is no way of life that is preferable to all others for all individuals. Applied to the conditions of human life, value pluralism yields a threshold of basic goods common to all decent lives, with a wide range of legitimate ways of life above the baseline of common decency.

Because pluralism rejects the idea that any way of life above the baseline is demonstrably inferior to the others, it implies a general presumption against the kind of paternalism based on assumptions of such inferiority.

In particular, it implies the rejection of "political perfectionism" as a general norm. A way of life can be good for an individual even if it is conducted in substantial isolation from public life. (I say "substantial" rather than "full" isolation because, as I argue later, membership in a political community does carry with it some basic obligations.) The fact that man is a *social* animal – a being who needs the regular company of other members of the species – does not imply that man is a *political* animal, at least not in the same way. Human sociability is an intrinsic good, needed for any choiceworthy life; political engagement is not.

*1.3.2  Political Theory.* To be legitimate, coercive public authority must be publicly authorized, actually rather than hypothetically. (There is room for reasonable debate as to what constitutes actual authorization.) Top-down claims to authority (for example, those that spring from the divine right of kings or its modern equivalents) are rejected; "vanguard parties" claiming, without actual authorization, the right to speak and act in the people's name are illegitimate on their face.

However they may originate historically, political communities are understood to be systems of cooperation for the mutual advantage of their members. Moral theory provides some guidance concerning what counts as mutual advantage. For example, unless there is clear evidence that some individuals in a community voluntarily forego basic goods, or that these goods are too scarce to permit universal provision, the existence of groups deprived of access to such goods strongly suggests that the conditions of mutuality have been violated and that some have accepted the terms of social cooperation under duress. Mutual advantage does not presuppose perfect equality of power among members of the community, but it does rule out "desperate bargains" made in circumstances in which the only alternative to disadvantage is disaster.

It is possible to imagine a variety of terms of cooperation consistent with the basic requirements of mutuality. I assume that in modern circumstances, anyway, preferred systems of cooperation will involve a substantial range of individual liberties (civil, social, and economic), some form of democratic self-government, a robust though not wholly unregulated market, and respect for the imperatives of individualism. This last element implies a wide range of individual choice, consistent with the maintenance of basic order, in areas such as the family, employment, and personal lifestyle. It also implies a presumption against public policies based on fixed or ascribed identities. Individuals may choose to take on various identities, but political authorities under normal circumstances will not dictate those identities to individuals.

1.3.2a COMMUNITY. Adapting Aristotle, I think of community as a sharing association involving two or more human beings. This simple definition directs our attention to some key dimensions of analysis. Communities will reflect what it is that their members actually share – often shared purposes or aspirations, but in other cases something different. There are important distinctions concerning how something is shared. Sharing can take the form of participation in a good that is collectively produced, such as national defense. Alternatively, sharing can take the form of participation in a common activity that would be diminished without the co-participation of others. The simplest example of this would be the telling of a joke. Telling a joke to oneself is not the same (and hardly ever as good) as telling it to others – particularly if they laugh. But regardless of the response, the presence of others generates a qualitatively different experience.

This distinction between collective production and sharing in a common activity reflects the classical Aristotelian distinction between *poeisis* and *praxis* – making and doing. There are communities of making, and also communities of doing. I do not mean to suggest that one is more primary or important than the other, but only that they represent different forms of community.

Based on this general definition of sharing association, we can see that communities range from the small to the very large: friendships, families, neighborhoods, voluntary associations, religious institutions, cities, regions, national political communities. There are even transnational communities – for example, the international community of scientists with its own membership, rules, and purposes. This underscores the broader point that it is meaningful to talk about individuals separated by vast distances who nonetheless share things important enough to constitute communities in the full and proper sense.

Many communities are brought together and held together by shared purposes. Instances of this include sports teams, political campaigns, scientific laboratories, and orchestras. These examples, among many others that might be offered, have some common characteristics. They have tolerably clear goals (which is not to say that they are lacking in complexity). These goals structure a range of debates over appropriate strategies and tactics for carrying them out. They orient common enterprises that do not in any way entail uniformity – the absence of differentiation or individuality among their members – but are consistent with a wide range of individual goals and expression and do not require the subordination of individuality to collective purposes.

In groups so constituted, there is a place for legitimate self-interest and even intragroup competition. There is a tolerable midpoint in all these groups between self-effacement on the one hand and what in sports is called hot-dogging on the other. There is a certain point of self-promotion and self-display beyond which members of communities of shared purposes are expected not to go, and are subject to disapproval if they do. Nonetheless, up to a point the display of individual distinctiveness and excellence is fully consistent with the pursuit of the shared purposes of the group.

The final point about community, so understood, is that the shared purposes constitute a basis for defining the common good. The common good is not some theoretical notion floating in moral hyperspace. It is a practical reality. It is what the members of the groups accept and pursue in common.

I do not want to suggest that shared purposes or overlapping interests are sufficient to define a community; if they were, a wide range of commercial relationships and transactions would qualify. There must also be some ingredient of what Aristotle called fellow-feeling, a kind of emotion connecting the different members of the community. There must be some special moral weight accorded to the particular family or party or country to which one is affirming a connection. And finally, there must be a sense of shared fate with the other members of the group. This can take a number of forms: the sense that we are all in it together, that what happens to the person across the street in a sense happens to me as well; or a kind of sympathetic identification, of being able to say about misfortunes befalling other members of the community, "There but for the grace of God go I." These reflections in turn lead to the idea of what might be called "nonpurposive" sharing as an alternative (in some cases) and an adjunct (in others) to the idea of shared purposes. This second kind of sharing can involve history or myth, ethnicity or race, religion or faith, even strongly held sentiments or feelings.

Whatever their other features may be, communities also require some stability of attachment over time – that is, some continuity. That suggests that processes of very rapid change – economic, social, or moral – stand in tension with the maintenance of community, however constituted and understood.

Community is among other things a cooperative endeavor. Membership in a community therefore entails the willingness to accept the burdens as well as the benefits of that cooperation. More generally, it embodies the principle of reciprocity, the willingness to do one's fair share to promote the community's purposes and uphold its institutions provided most others do so as well. (The fact that John Rawls advanced versions of these propositions is evidence that the phrase "liberal community" is not a contradiction in terms.)

From this perspective, two points must be stressed. First, if one views community as a cooperative endeavor to produce a joint product, then one's willingness to participate in that process of production affects the claims one can make on the community. One is not free to say, as in Woody Allen's famous quip, that ninety percent of life is just showing up. You have to do something; if you do not, your legitimate claim on the community is thereby diminished. So Rawls's notion that individuals are sources of valid claims at least must be modified to include the dimension of relevant performance as well as bare existence.

Second, the idea of reciprocity itself rests on an underlying sense of solidarity with other members of the community. It is this more primordial identification that makes it possible to accept and discharge the responsibilities of reciprocity.

1.3.2b CONSTITUTIONALISM. Constitutions help mediate between the public purposes that constitute communities, on the one hand, and specific institutions and policies and specific understandings of citizenship and of relevant virtues, on the other.

Consider the Preamble to the U.S. Constitution. The Constitution is admirably terse in every respect. The Preamble could simply have said, "We the people of the United States do ordain and establish this constitution of the United States." But it says more than that: "We the people of the United States, *in order to*" – and following those words "in order to" is a long list of shared purposes that give the constitutional institutions their point. The U.S. constitution is the model of a community based on broad shared purposes that are not so general as to be devoid of meaning or as to fail to distinguish liberal democratic community from other forms of community.

The constitutionalism of the U.S. community interprets public institutions and policies through the constitutional purposes established in the Preamble. From this perspective, when Franklin D. Roosevelt interpreted the powers and responsibilities of his presidency in light of the need to preserve domestic tranquility and promote the general welfare, he was operating appropriately and not, as many conservatives allege, in a paraconstitutional manner. (This is not to say that all the tactics he employed in pursuit of this understanding were themselves legitimate.)

*1.3.3 Individual Responsibilities.* Taken together, classical political theory and modern individualism point toward a range of basic responsibilities for individual members of political communities. To begin, a society's public institutions do not just drop like manna from heaven. It takes effort to create and sustain them, effort from which all benefit. So a principal responsibility of each community member is doing one's fair share to sustain institutions that meet the test of mutual advantage. This involves not only internalizing and acting on norms of obedience to law, but also serving on juries, participating in civic associations and activities, and answering the call of national defense.

Public authorities are justified in enforcing some of these responsibilities – obeying the law and serving on juries, for example. On the other hand, participation in civic associations is inherently voluntary; public leaders may encourage this behavior but cannot compel it.[13]

The material resources needed to sustain decent lives under modern circumstances do not drop from heaven either; they must be produced through human effort. In normal circumstances, individuals have a responsibility to contribute what they can to this process of production, at least to the extent needed to sustain themselves and those dependent on them.

A system of liberty and rights entails a wide range of individual responsibilities, starting with, but going well beyond, the core obligation to respect the liberty and rights of all others. Each individual must also comply with the minimum conditions for the enjoyment of specific rights. For example, the commission of certain crimes implies a disrespect for law thorough-going enough to disqualify perpetrators, at least temporarily, from participating in the process by which laws are made; whence the exclusion of certain felons from otherwise universal voting rights. This is not an aberrant case: Most rights function as presumptions, with conditions of disqualification that are often tacit.

Finally, a system of liberty and rights requires that all individuals assume ownership of and responsibility for the foreseeable consequences of their actions. Individuals' efforts to shift blame for their deeds to others or to claim to be victims in situations that they themselves have produced flatly contravene the moral basis of a free society. Rather than acknowledging and even rewarding such efforts, legal systems in such societies should lean against them.

*1.3.4  Social Responsibilities.* As part of the publicly authorized system of mutual advantage, the public institutions of political communities have a range of important responsibilities. The first and most basic is to defend individual rights and liberties, using coercion if need be. No individual or subsidiary institution can legitimately deprive an individual meeting the core qualifications discussed earlier the opportunity to exercise rights, and none should be allowed to do so with impunity.

Second, there is a social responsibility to make some provision of basic goods for the helpless and vulnerable, those who are temporarily or permanently unable to make an economic contribution. (This may be seen as the collective expression of the individual moral obligation to render assistance when the costs of doing so are not excessive.) This responsibility need not be discharged through public means exclusively, but some ensemble of family, community associations, and public policy must ensure that its aim is met.

Third, there is a social responsibility to ensure that each individual's contribution is appropriately compensated. Specifically, those who perform full-time, year-round work to support themselves and their families should not be living in poverty. To be sure, their skill level may be so low that their marginal contribution to the joint economic product is not large enough to produce market-based wages sufficient to avoid poverty. That is where the social obligation to make up the difference takes effect.

Fourth, society has a responsibility to secure for all the conditions under which they have a reasonable chance to develop their talents and skills and increase their ability to contribute both to self-support and to society. This will require social assistance to compensate individuals (to the extent possible) for both physical handicaps and cultural deficits. In modern circumstances, equality of opportunity requires special attention to public education, which, rather than leaning against background disadvantages, all too often reinforces them.

As has been clear since Plato, at some point social efforts to equalize opportunity run up against the differences flowing from the socialization that occurs in families. A free society will recognize, within broad limits, the liberty of parents to raise their children in ways consistent with their understanding of what gives meaning and value to life. This respect for family integrity inevitably limits the extent to which opportunity can be equalized, a limit that society must accept.

Fifth, there is the difficult question of the nature and extent of what is called fate-sharing – that is, social responsibility for misfortunes over which individuals have no control. It makes sense that individuals devising a system of cooperation for mutual advantage would recognize the existence of such evils and provide for them through systems of social insurance. Intuitively, it seems sensible to compensate homeowners whose homes are destroyed by floods – that is, unless they have disregarded repeated warnings against building in flood-prone areas. Similarly, it seems wrong to exclude individuals from insurance pools, or to subject them to higher premiums, because of genetic vulnerability to specific diseases.

Fate control is limited by norms of self-ownership and self-direction, among others. John Rawls's effort to bring the totality of our genetic endowment into the circle of shared fate has met with almost universal rejection, and rightly so.[14] Our endowment of capacities, though unchosen and outside our control, plays a large role in defining our individuated selves. Treating our endowments as social assets comes perilously close to socializing selfhood itself, and denies individuals the opportunity for self-direction that underlines personal responsibility and constitutes the core of a free society.[15] In practice, most liberal democratic market societies allow individuals to treat their natural endowments as personal assets that they may deploy as they choose and from which they may reap market-based rewards.[16] At the same time, these societies create insurance mechanisms to address the special problems of individuals whose genetic endowments diminish their capacity to care for themselves and contribute to society.

The simple fact of common membership in a community creates some sharing of individual fates. Within broad limits, communities may decide for themselves how far they want to go down this road. But they are not free altogether to disregard this dimension of social responsibility.

Sixth, society must take responsibility for maintaining the preconditions for the effective functioning of its basic institutions, such as the market and a system of individual liberty and democratic self-government. The nature of these preconditions is a disputed empirical matter, but there is wide agreement that certain kinds of individual character and social bonds help sustain free institutions. As I observed earlier in discussing Milton Friedman, it would be unwise to the point of recklessness to assume that an invisible civic hand will infallibly supply these social goods – a point driven home by the recent round of corporate scandals in the United States. Societies must pay attention to the formative individual and social impact of broad forces such as families, schools, the media, modes of production and consumption, the distribution of resources, and the operation of the market itself. Where the impact of key trends seems adverse to the health of free institutions, there may be no alternative to intervening through collective action.

## 2 FROM MUTUALIST THEORY TO PRACTICE: A PROGRESSIVE MARKET STRATEGY

The purpose of the section just ended was to provide a theoretical template for the reciprocity-based politics of mutualism. Many strategies and policies are consistent with this template. In this section, I want briefly to sketch one of them, which I call the "progressive market" strategy. This strategy insists on the market as the principal engine of economic innovation and growth. The role of government is to bolster the preconditions for the effective functioning of the basic institutions – political, economic, and social – of a free society; to secure the rights and liberties of individuals; and to give force to the norms of fair opportunity and mutual responsibility I have just discussed. So understood, government has important responsibilities in areas such as public goods (basic research and infrastructure, for example), education, insurance against risk, and the provision of basic goods and decency to the helpless and vulnerable. It is also responsible for assuring the physical security of its citizens and for assuring the rule of law, the benefits of which must be available to every citizen.

The progressive market strategy distinguishes sharply between *what* government does and *how* it does it. Throughout much of the twentieth century, liberal and social democratic governments acted in ways that were insufficiently sensitive both to markets and to the moral preconditions of a free society. The progressive market strategy tries to remedy both these defects. At each step, it asks whether its policies are consistent with vigorous economic growth, and also with bolstering norms of individual and social responsibility.

In this regard, I want to underscore my previous distinction between market *systems* and market *mechanisms*. There are compelling reasons, I believe, to keep certain sectors of social life outside the market system of production and exchange altogether. The case for selling organs, babies, and votes is weak. At the same time, market mechanisms offer advantages that makers of public policy would be ill-advised to overlook. This is what the progressive market strategy does. There is every reason for thinkers who reject the privatization of public services to approach the public use of competition and choice in an open-minded and empirical spirit. The question of whether vouchers should be used in systems of housing, education, and health insurance is a practical issue rather than a theological dispute. That the public sector has a responsibility to ensure fair access to certain services or opportunities does not imply that there is a public responsibility to provide them directly, in kind. The responsibility may well be discharged more effectively if the public sector provides resources to individuals and ensures that individuals have access to accurate information about alternative ways of using these resources to secure the services and opportunities in question.

In the same spirit, I want to distinguish between social *intentions* and social *outcomes*. For example, the old U.S. welfare system, which originated in the 1930s during the Great Depression, was undertaken with the best of intentions. Over time, as circumstances changed, it became clear that the effects of this system were at odds with, and failed to foster, basic norms of individual responsibility and social contribution. Millions of individuals – particularly young unwed mothers – were being encouraged to see welfare as a permanent way of life, a substitute for both marriage and gainful employment, rather than as a temporary bridge to independence and self-respect. The replacement of this discredited system in 1996 with a new one based on the individual's responsibility to work whenever possible and society's responsibility to make work possible and to make work pay represents an effort to close the gap between intentions and outcomes, and to do so in a manner consistent with basic norms. The progressive market strategy is attentive at every step to sustaining the long-term preconditions for free institutions.

Many policies combine individual and social responsibilities. Consider, for example, the norm articulated in the last section: Individuals who work full-time, year-round, should be able to lift themselves and their dependents out of poverty. Rewarding work in this manner is not a new thought. Previous generations tried to do it by establishing minimum wage standards binding on most employers. There are two problems with this approach. First, when taken too far, it becomes inconsistent with economic growth and job generation. (Just how far is too far is a matter of considerable debate among applied economists.) Second, the minimum wage places the entire burden of meeting a social standard on one sector of society. This is a moral mistake. If society as a whole decides that certain market outcomes are inconsistent with basic norms, then it should give priority to measures that allow members of society to share responsibility for the remedy. (This would not be the case if a policy were designed to rectify wrongdoing, which in the first instance would be the responsibility of the wrongdoer.) In light of these considerations, contemporary strategies to combat working poverty have emphasized mechanisms such as the earned income tax credit, which bolsters the earnings of low-wage workers through the tax code rather than employers and which distributes responsibility for supplementing market wages throughout the community of taxpayers.

One more example: In recent decades, the United States has established a portfolio of student grant and loan programs designed to allow all talented and motivated students, whatever their family background and income, to attend college. In strictly educational terms, these programs have been a success (though inefficiencies abound). But unlike the GI Bill, these programs do almost nothing to foster or reward service to the community. To address this problem, President Clinton advocated, fought for, and signed into law a bill establishing a new federally funded Corporation for National and Community Service, whose principal function was to offer young people substantial college assistance in return for a year or two of service in programs addressing a range of community needs.[17] The underlying idea was that young people should have some exposure to public programs that reflect the principle of mutual responsibility rather than one-way individual entitlement to socially provided goods. As of 2004, more than 250,000 students have availed themselves of this opportunity.[18] The expectation that this experience would change students' conception of themselves as citizens is supported by anecdotal evidence but stands in need of systematic evaluation. At any rate, the point is that government may legitimately shape its policies, not just to deliver appropriate services and opportunities, but also to bolster the preconditions of free institutions.

I spoke earlier of community and its importance. It is by no means clear what form of political economy is most compatible with the maintenance of community. This question is made even more difficult by the fact that given the basic assumptions of modern life, a period of prolonged economic stagnation is itself inimical to the maintenance of community because it unleashes highly conflictual forces among individuals and groups. So the problem is that we need economic growth to diminish conflict within communities, but at the same time sustaining growth under modern circumstances makes it difficult to maintain the stability of specific forms of economic production that lie at the heart of particular forms of community. This tension represents a grave challenge for all who take seriously both community and economic dynamism.[19]

Corporations are created by, and act within, a structure of law. Questions can be raised as to whether they should make economic decisions without regard for the communities these decisions affect so deeply. If a corporation chooses to close a plant in a particular community, does it have any responsibilities to that community, or can it simply say farewell without further ado? The U.S. Congress examined that question some years ago, and responded with a law requiring corporations to give communities adequate prior notification of projected plant closings. It is not my purpose to defend that particular piece of legislation (which is not regarded as notably effective). What I am defending is the propriety of raising this question.

It cannot be raised in a void, of course. One must pay due attention to the facts of modern political economy, and to the general structure of law and regulation required for sustainable economic growth and global competitiveness in the circumstances in which we find ourselves today. Nonetheless, taking all this into account, we are not free to ignore the impact of specific economic decisions on communities that are organized around, and depend on, productive functions located in particular places.

### 3 MUTUALISM AND THE IDEA OF NATIONAL COMMUNITY

A liberal democratic polity – particularly, but not only, the United States – is an assemblage of diverse subcommunities. What, if anything, makes the broader polity a community? One answer is . . . nothing: Any nation made up of diverse subcommunities with profound social and religious differences must be understood as a Yugoslavia in the making, and as we become more conscious of the true extent of our differences, we will realize that only fragile and eroding habits are holding us together. This is the pessimist's answer; I do not subscribe to it.

In a more optimistic spirit, let me ask, "If something rather than nothing holds us together, what is it?" Three kinds of answers are typically offered. The first has been called "modus vivendi" – the Yugoslav experience with a minus sign: What holds us together is the belief that we must find a way to live together because the alternative is bloody conflict. This is the principle articulated most memorably in recent times by Rodney King, whose beating at the hands of Los Angeles police officers sparked violent and destructive riots. King appeared on television and asked plaintively, in evident shock at the conflict his imbroglio had sparked, "Can't we all just get along?" No higher principle; just the negative proposition that the conflict is intolerable and disproportionate to our differences (in spite of the fact that they are profound).

The second answer invokes some shared conception of justice. This is the point of view that John Rawls articulated for three decades. It is a view with an honorable ancestry that goes all the way back to Aristotle, and there is obviously much to it. It is what Abraham Lincoln had in mind when he declared that a house divided against itself cannot stand: If half the country believes that slavery is just and the other half that it is unjust, the basis for permanent existence as a single political community may well have vanished.

A third kind of answer, related to but distinct from the second, invokes an ensemble of shared public purposes as the basis of national community. This is the point of invoking, as I do, the Preamble to the U.S. Constitution as setting forth the public purposes that guide our interpretation of the meaning and spirit of our national public institutions; and more broadly, of advancing a constitutional faith as the most promising ground of principled political unity consistent with cultural heterogeneity.

But let us reflect a bit more deeply on the liberal pluralist community as a community of subcommunities. What are the distinctive features of a liberal national community stemming from this internal heterogeneity? First, by definition, not all the purposes and commitments of the subcommunities will be shared. That is one of the considerations that leads a liberal pluralist democracy to define a distinction between what is public and what is not. We need that legal and constitutional line in order to sustain the distinction between what the subcommunities are required to have in common and what they need not.

The metaphor of the line might suggest a neat division. The reality is less tidy, because there will be relationships of conflict as well as complementarity between public and nonpublic commitments. Consider the example of federal laws, binding on the states, concerning the prevention of "child abuse" or "neglect." What is the meaning of these terms? In particular, is it child abuse or neglect when Christian Scientist parents, acting out of sincere religious conviction, refrain from seeking orthodox medical treatment for their seriously ill child? And if it is, what rights and duties of state action are implied? This is one of a family of problems that crop up in a liberal polity that is a community of diverse subcommunities. In many instances, the effort to define a public purpose in common terms will run up against some subcommunity's conception of these same terms.

This fact raises an even broader question about the relationship between subcommunities (religious or otherwise) and the broader national community. Sociologists and neoconservative social theorists have long talked about these subcommunities as "mediating institutions." The question is – do they simply connect individuals to political institutions, or do they also function as sources of potential opposition to those institutions? In my judgment, the latter is clearly the case. In practice, this will always raise the question of when it is appropriate to accept this opposition and when it is necessary to override it. I have argued that our practical maxim ought to be "maximum feasible accommodation."[20] But that does not mean unlimited accommodation, and the precise location of any line (including mine) between accommodating and overriding group practices is bound to prove contestable.

## 4 CONCLUSION

Understood as a form of civic totalism, twentieth-century state socialism has lost, not only political power, but also intellectual respectability. Who would wish now to defend regimes that deny their citizens individual liberty and democratic self-government, impose ineffective command economies on producers and consumers, and weaken civil society through the deliberate creation of suspicion and mistrust? Who would wish to replace the consent of the governed with vanguard parties basing their claims to power on unique "scientific" knowledge? Who would deploy the spurious norm of total devotion to the collectivity as a weapon against individual rights and reasonable self-interest?

In light of all this, we must ask whether anything is left of socialism. I think there is, but it has nothing to do with its ideology or its institutional forms. What survives is a broad moral outlook: the conception of society as an association of individuals for mutual advantage and an understanding of mutual responsibility – individual and social – that flows from this conception.[21]

I have sketched the basics of this approach, among which are: political and economic institutions viewed as jointly produced goods to which all must contribute if they can; social provision for those who cannot; equality of opportunity that is more than formal but does not require equal outcomes; a limited but robust sense of shared fate; and so forth. In this approach, individualism is a central value, and society is seen as the expression of choice that is consistent with self-interest. At the same time, mutualism insists that individuals are linked through a dense network of natural duties and that societies exist in part to give force to these duties. Human beings are both separated and connected, and any viable conception of human society must give due expression to both these aspects of our existence. Socialism affirms connection to the exclusion of separation; libertarianism and market-inspired theories of politics do the reverse.

The mutualism I advocate tries to bring separation and connection together in a way that is both principled and practical. It offers an alternative, not only to socialism and laissez-faire, but also, and more subtly, to social democracy and neoliberalism. Let me put it this way, schematically. There are four basic possibilities for understanding the relationship between individuals and the political community. (1) If both the responsibility of individuals to the community and of the community to individuals are understood narrowly, we get the regime of the minimal or "night watchman" state, whose underlying principle is negative liberty. (2) If individual responsibility is understood narrowly and collective responsibility broadly, we get the social democratic welfare state, whose underlying principle is entitlement. (3) If individual responsibility is understood broadly and collective responsibility narrowly, we get the civic republic, whose principle is public-spirited devotion to the common good. And (4) If both individual and collective responsibility are understood broadly, we get a state whose guiding principle is reciprocity. This principle is the moral heart of the mutualist alternative.

While the theoretical basis of mutualism diverges from that of the welfare state, in practice it offers evolutionary rather than revolutionary change. It represents a new way of thinking about civic life and public policy in economically advanced societies rather than being a replacement for liberal democracy itself. But this is as it should be if, as I believe, we have good reasons to conclude that in societies with highly developed markets, civil societies, and legal structures, liberal pluralist democracy is preferable to other forms of political organization that are feasible under modern conditions.

## Notes

1. Lawrence M. Friedman, *The Republic of Choice: Law, Authority, and Culture* (Cambridge, MA: Harvard University Press, 1990), pp. 8–9.
2. *The Republic of Choice*, p. 23.
3. Ibid.
4. Anthony Giddens, "Introduction," in *The Global Third Way Debate*, Giddens, ed. (Cambridge: Polity Press, 2001), pp. 4–5.
5. Ralf Dahrendorf, *Life Chances: Approaches to Social and Political Theory* (Chicago: University of Chicago Press, 1979), p. 31.
6. Ibid.

7. Albert Hirschman, *Exit, Voice, and Loyalty* (Cambridge, MA: Harvard University Press, 1970).

8. Alexis de Tocqueville, *Democracy in America*, trans. George Lawrence, ed. J. P. Mayer (Garden City, NY: Doubleday 1969), p. 506.

9. This is not to say that we do not ever observe such behavior. Consider the police and fire fighters who rushed into the World Trade Center on September 11, 2001, to rescue strangers, knowing full well they were risking their lives. It is a matter of great interest and importance to determine the processes of training and group solidarity that make such extraordinary acts possible.

10. See Norman Frohlich and Joe A. Oppenheimer, *Choosing Justice: An Experimental Approach to Ethical Theory* (Berkeley: University of California, 1992).

11. Robert E. Lane, *The Market Experience* (Cambridge: Cambridge University Press, 1991), p. 421.

12. William A. Galston, "Value Pluralism and Liberal Political Theory," *American Political Science Review* 93 (4) (December 1999): 769–778; see also Galston, *Liberal Pluralism: The Implications of Value Pluralism for Political Theory and Practice* (New York: Cambridge University Press, 2002).

13. I believe that contributing to national defense (at least against aggression) falls in the former category rather than the latter, but this raises broader questions that I cannot consider here.

14. See Brian Barry, *Political Argument: A Reissue with a New Introduction* (Berkeley: University of California, 1990), pp. lvii–lviii, for a summary of the grounds on which most theorists have rejected Rawls's position on this matter.

15. See Robert Nozick, *Anarchy, State, and Utopia* (New York: Basic Books, 1974), p. 228.

16. See Friedman, *Republic of Choice*, p. 225, n1.

17. The legislation authorizing these activities is the *National and Community Service Trust Act of 1993*. Pub L. No. 103–82, 107 Stat. 785 (codified at 42 U.S.C.A 12501 et seq. [1995 and supp. 2000]).

18. Corporation for National and Community Service: "Americorps: Who We Are," available online (2004) at http: www.americorps.org/whoweare.html

19. For the best recent effort to grapple with this issue, see Thad Williamson, David Imbroscio, and Gar Alperovitz, *Making a Place for Community: Local Democracy in a Global Era* (New York: Routledge, 2002).

20. See Galston, *Liberal Pluralism*, chapters 8 and 9.

21. See Raymond Plant, "Is There a Third Way?" paper presented at the VIII Encontro Internacional de Teoria e Cienca Politica, Sintra, Portugal, October 16–19, 2000, p. 38.

# PART IV

# DEFENDING LIBERAL PLURALISM

# Liberal Pluralism and Liberal Egalitarianism

The politics of liberal pluralism has been questioned from a number of standpoints, liberal egalitarianism prominent among them. In this chapter, I examine and respond to three of liberal pluralism's most important egalitarian critics – Ronald Dworkin, Brian Barry, and Susan Okin.

### 1 RONALD DWORKIN

Let me begin by contrasting Ronald Dworkin's latest approach to political philosophy[1] with that of two well-known competitors. (1) In contrast to John Rawls, Dworkin does not treat political philosophy as free-standing, but sees it as grounded in general ethical values, such the structure of good lives and the principles of personal responsibility. (In Rawls's terminology, Dworkin's theory is comprehensive rather than "political.") The direct appeal to ethical foundations means that Dworkin makes no use of social contract devices. (2) As we have already seen, Dworkin is an ethical monist rather than a pluralist. While theorists working in the tradition of Isaiah Berlin contend that basic goods and values are heterogeneous, incommensurable, and conflicting, Dworkin seeks to dissipate these conflicts and integrate key political values into a harmonized whole. In particular, Dworkin sees no conflict between liberty and equality, rightly understood. If there were such a conflict, liberty would have to give way to equality, which Dworkin understands as the master-value of liberalism, as "sovereign."

Each of these contrasts raises questions. In one important respect, Dworkin's claim to offer a "comprehensive" as opposed to Rawls-style "political" theory is puzzling. Early on in *Sovereign Virtue*, he suggests that his thesis concerning equality rests on "more general ethical values" – including the "structure of a good life described in chapter 6."[2] But when we reach Chapter 6, we find him disclaiming this intention. Although he proposes to defend a "challenge" model of a good life – that a life is successful insofar as it is an appropriate response to the distinct circumstances in which it is lived – he "do[es] not mean to rest the case for liberal equality on that model."[3] Indeed, he believes that his account of the nature of good lives is bound to be more controversial than his account of equality. His argument is thus poised uneasily between comprehensive foundations and the political appeal to shared moral intuitions.

Dworkin's antipluralism is equally puzzling. He argues that rightly understood, liberty and equality cannot conflict because they are interdependent dimensions of a more general moral concept that is expressed principally (though not fully) in the distributive principle that he calls "equality of resources." Liberty is intrinsic to equality, so understood, because individuals who lack the freedom to form, revise, argue for, and act on their conception of the good cannot "authentically" participate in the auction process through which the concrete meaning of equality of resources is spelled out. In ideal societies in which equality of resources prevails, individuals would enjoy full liberty to use their share as they wish. But in real-world situations in which the principle of equality of resources is not honored, the liberty claims of those with disproportionate shares of resources are not dispositive, if some restriction of their liberty could bring about a result that more closely approximates what equality of resources requires.

Three kinds of objections may be raised against Dworkin's proposed reconciliation of liberty and equality. In the first place, not everybody will be persuaded by his account of distributive justice. For example, some will reject his contention that a just distribution of resources will reflect differences of ambition and endeavor but not differences of natural talents or endowments. (Robert Nozick argues that both may legitimately shape distributive outcomes. John Rawls, that neither may.) Second, while Dworkin acknowledges that an adequate conception of liberty will pick out some specific liberties as more important than others, his effort to do this within the framework of equality of resources is forced and unpersuasive. Third, his thesis leads to practical conclusions that many would reject and that seem far from compelling. For example, he has no doubt that in nations characterized by indefensible inequalities of resources, government may prohibit the practice of private medicine if that would reduce inequality in the delivery of medical services. Perhaps so; but surely the fact that the abolition of private medicine would in effect draft all doctors and commandeer their talents for state-defined purposes on state-dictated terms is worthy of discussion. It is suggestive that even in Britain, with its long-established National Health Service, most of the public rejects the abolition of private medicine on the ground that it would violate freedom of choice in medical care.

Let us now turn from the tension between liberty and equality to the ethical issue that Dworkin regards as most fundamental – the meaning of equality itself. He offers two principles of "ethical individualism" that frame and support his account of equality. The first is the principle of "equal importance": From an objective moral point of view, not only does it matter that human lives be successful rather than wasted, but also the success or failure of each human life is of equal moral importance. The second is the principle of "special responsibility": In the end, one person has final responsibility for the success or failure of his life – "the person whose life it is."[4] Responsibility, which involves choice, and therefore liberty, is in Dworkin's account a part of equality rather than at odds with it. What obligations does the principle of equal importance impose on society? What obligations does the principle of special responsibility impose on individuals? Dworkin's theory of equality is framed by answers to these two questions.

The principle of equal importance, he argues, requires equality of re-sources (as opposed to equality of welfare), when "resources" are under-stood to include not only transferable material means but also natural endowments and negative endowments, and "equality" means that all individuals are satisfied with their shares.[5] Individuals must be compen-sated for deficiencies of natural endowments over which they have no control. In addition, a just system of distribution will seek to distinguish, and correct for, the effects of differences of talent and ability. Conversely, the principle of special responsibility requires individuals to accept the consequences of how they choose to use their abilities and lead their lives. There is no breach of justice if someone of (say) average abilities achieves success through ambition and hard work, while another indi-vidual with roughly the same natural endowments lacks ambition and as a result achieves less. Every individual is responsible for choices flowing from his own convictions, preferences, and personality.[6]

It is illuminating to contrast Dworkin's position with traditional welfare state liberalism, on the one hand, and advocates of "equality of opportu-nity," on the other. Many welfare state liberals (John Rawls, for example) see not only natural talents, but also preferences and character, as the product of forces over which individuals have no control and for which they should not be held responsible. From their perspective, systems of

distribution should not be (in Dworkin's terms) "ambition-sensitive," because ambition is the result of brute luck – for example, growing up with
loving and competent parents (or with inspiring mentors and role mod-
els) in circumstances in which there is reason to believe that hard work
will be rewarded. Conversely, while equality of opportunity requires fair
opportunities for individuals to develop and exercise their talents (for
example, education of equal quality for all and jobs open to all without discriminatory restrictions), it does not require society to nullify the
distributional effects of natural endowments.

It is not altogether clear how Dworkin can justify the disparate treatment of talent and ambition. He explicitly does not assume that individuals are responsible for their character any more than they are responsible for their endowment. But he does presuppose an ethical outlook in
which we are responsible for the choices we make when our acts reflect
our character.[7] But life-plans and actions flow from unchosen talents in
much the same way. Why should society intervene in the latter sequence
of events but not the former? At one juncture, Dworkin contends that his
distinction "tracks ordinary people's ethical experience. Ordinary people, in their ordinary lives, take consequential responsibility for their own
personalities."[8] Fair enough, except in cases where psychological distortion or illness warrants a judgment of diminished competence. But in
the same way, ordinary people (most U.S. citizens, anyway) take consequential responsibility for their own endowments, except when individuals are so under-endowed or handicapped as to warrant compensatory
treatment. The average American is not inclined to begrudge a heart
surgeon his $500,000 annual earnings on the grounds that he was born
with above-average fine motor dexterity, visual imagination, and capacity
for sustained concentration. (One can endorse a progressive income tax,
as many do, without endorsing a moral imperative to nullify the effects
of natural endowments.) As far as I can tell, Dworkin nowhere provides
a compelling theoretical justification for a distinction between talent
and personality that ordinary moral consciousness fails to ratify. In this
important respect, Dworkin's elegant and elaborate edifice rests on a
shaky foundation.

## 2 BRIAN BARRY

Ever since the publication of *Political Argument*[9] in 1965, Brian Barry has
been regarded as one of the most insightful political philosophers working in the Anglo-American tradition. His approach is broadly liberal, in

both the philosophical and political senses of the term. In the tradition of philosophical liberalism, he seeks principles to which persons he regards as reasonable could give their willing assent. In keeping with contemporary political liberals, he emphasizes equality, suitably understood, as the guiding value of decent politics. In his recent books, *Theories of Justice*[10] and *Justice as Impartiality*,[11] he has offered both a critique of John Rawls's theory of liberal constitutional democracy and an alternative theory leading to similar conclusions about the role of the activist state in securing the conditions of fair equality. While he has changed his mind on some important matters during the past thirty years (more on that later), he has never wavered in his belief that reason is capable of arriving at general principles of politics applicable to all human beings.

Barry is affronted by the challenge to universal principles posed by contemporary theories of group rights, cultural nationalism, and special privileges and exemptions from generally valid laws. He views these theories, which he lumps together under the aegis of "multiculturalism," as a return to the errors of the nineteenth-century Romantic-irrationalist revolt against the Enlightenment, a stance that if put into practice could exacerbate both ethno-cultural conflict and the oppression of individuals. His purpose in *Culture and Equality*[12] is to delegitimize multiculturalism, theoretical root and practical branch. His strategy takes the form, if not the content, of a nineteenth-century Catholic Syllabus of Errors, arraying and refuting all manner of what he regards as dangerous foolishness.

We encounter a difficulty at the threshold: In his drive to bring multiculturalists to justice, Barry rounds up a heterogeneous group of suspects and charges them all with the same crime. He suggests that what he calls multiculturalism is of a piece, and that internal differences are quantitative rather than qualitative – doses of different strength, as he puts it. But that is not the case; many of the principles and policies Barry lumps together are distinguishable both in theory and in practice.

As I have made clear, I believe that a strong case can be made, on liberal grounds, for exempting members of religious groups from many (not all) laws that have the effect of restricting religious free exercise. Barry disagrees. I believe that absent compelling reasons to the contrary, principled liberals must defer to individuals' own sense of what gives life meaning and purpose, and ensure that the intrusion of state institutions on individual lives is restricted to what is needed to secure the minimum conditions of civic unity and social justice. Barry views this as an unreasonable regard for "diversity" at the expense of other important values. But whatever the truth of these matters, a person who believes in religious exemptions, or in maximum feasible deference to individual understandings of the good life, is not thereby committed to endorsing Iris Marion Young's group-centered conception of political decision-making, or Will Kymlicka's linkage between culture and nationality, or Chandran Kukathas's defense of group immunity from the most basic liberal norms, all of which positions I question for reasons not unlike Barry's. So let me engage Barry on the terrain I wish to defend; others will have to speak for themselves.

As I made clear in Chapter 4, I endorse the following view: The free exercise of religion and conscience is one of the most basic rights human beings possess. (It would not be a huge exaggeration to suggest that this freedom is the grain of sand in the oyster of politics around which the pearl of liberalism gradually formed.) It is so fundamental, as James Madison argued in the "Memorial and Remonstrance," as to constitute a reservation against the authority of the state.

This is not to say that the public order has no authority over religion and conscience. There are some basic interests that the state has a right, and sometimes a duty, to defend – if need be, with coercive power.

In order for state intervention to be legitimate, two conditions must be satisfied. First, the state interest defended through intervention must be urgent and important – in the language of American jurisprudence, "compelling." Second, the state must employ the least intrusive means needed to achieve its purpose; the remedy must be "narrowly tailored." Put otherwise (but still in the language of jurisprudence), there is a presumption in favor of the religious and conscientious liberty of the individual, and the state bears a substantial burden of proof when it seeks to overcome this presumption.

In his controversial *Smith* decision, Justice Antonin Scalia rejects this entire way of thinking. If a law is neutral on its face, of general application, and directed to matters within the state's competence, the mere fact that it has the effect of selectively burdening the free exercise of religion is neither here nor there. The state has no burden of proof to discharge. Quite the reverse: Any society adopting a presumption in favor of religious free exercise would be "courting anarchy." The greater the religious diversity within a polity, the greater the risk. So even fundamental rights must be subjected to the democratic political process. If that means that minority views are systematically disadvantaged, tough luck: "That unavoidable consequence of democratic government must be preferred to a system in which each conscience is a law unto itself."[13] It is this majoritarian Hobbism that Barry so vigorously applauds.

Barry seems to think that religiously based claims for exemption from general laws are urged on grounds of justice, that the faithful are unequally or disproportionately burdened. Not so; the objection is qualitative, not quantitative. The argument is that the centrality of religion to conscience, and of conscience to personal integrity, generates claims of special significance. To subject these claims without further ado to ordinary majoritarian processes is to deny that conscience is special, and that its exercise, with due limits, is a right worthy of protection against government. Barry is free to affirm this as an interpretation of liberalism, but he is wrong to suggest, as he does repeatedly, that those who take the Madisonian rather than the Hobbesian view of individual conscience have forfeited their right to be considered liberals.

Judged from the standpoint of American law and jurisprudence, Barry goes to extraordinary lengths to curtail religious liberty. For example, he argues that state authority should extend to the content of religious doctrines taught in private school: For example, "the educational authorities of a state can quite properly take the view that creationism is too intellectually corrupting to be taught in any school, whether public or private."[14] And he expresses the hope that Scalia's *Smith* opinion, suitably enlarged in scope, may someday persuade a majority of the U.S. Supreme Court to grant states the right to exercise such authority.[15] Fortunately, the current Court is wiser than that, and seems as disinclined as were its predecessors to tamper with, let alone reverse, its decisions in *Meyer v. Nebraska* and *Pierce v. Society of Sisters*, which interpreted the liberties guaranteed in the Bill of Rights as ruling out the powers Barry wants the states to exercise. The principle underlying Barry's position, the Court observes in *Pierce*, is contrary to the "fundamental theory of liberty upon which all governments in this Union repose." Barry's principle, says the *Meyer* Court, amounts to the theory of the plenipotentiary state asserting its authority based on superior rationality. It is, the Court concludes, nothing other than the theory of Plato's *Republic*.

I come, finally, to the philosophical issue: What principles must one endorse in order to be a liberal, and what are the reasons for believing them to be true? In posing the question this way, I express my agreement with three fundamental points Barry urges: that liberalism asserts truths and is therefore incompatible with postmodernism; that the truths liberalism asserts are intended to be of universal, not merely local, application; and therefore that liberalism cannot be derived from, and is not compatible with, strong forms of moral or cultural relativism.

Here our agreement ends. In a 1995 article that Barry calls a "canonical statement" of the thesis he rejects, I argued that there are two quite different ways of thinking about liberalism, one with its roots in Enlightenment rationalism, the other in the post-Reformation struggle to deal with the political consequences of religious diversity. I suggested that while the Enlightenment approach, with its emphasis on the value and cultivation of rational autonomy, has many attractions (especially to secularized intellectuals), it tends to marginalize religious belief and constitutes an unlikely basis for a public order that endeavors to deal fairly with believers as well as unbelievers. I offered an approach to liberalism that refuses to give pride of place to either side, acknowledges the fact of deep irresolvable differences (not just between belief and unbelief, but generally), and seeks a principled basis for respectful mutual coexistence. And I argued that this diversity-based approach is superior both in practice, by accommodating more ways of life of genuine value, and in theory, by reflecting more accurately the limits of reason to resolve disputes among ways of life.[16]

Barry rejects this entire way of thinking. Although he insists that the Enlightenment did not and does not constitute a unified approach or "project," he tacitly retracts this strenuously urged claim, in part by conceding that "there were some things the Enlightenment was against, so that the Enlightenment can be defined negatively," and then by endorsing the "faith of the Enlightenment" (an affirmative, not merely negative, characterization) that "we can, by cooperative effort, approach the truth ever more closely."[17] He also insists that while liberalism, rightly understood, has much in common with what many theorists mean by autonomy, liberalism neither embraces autonomy as an ideal nor establishes the promotion of autonomy as a right or duty of the state. But consider the following statement by a leading political philosopher:

A liberal must take his stand on the proposition that some ways of life, some types of character, are more admirable than others, whatever may be the majority opinion in any society. He must hold that societies ought to be organized in such a way as to produce the largest possible proportion of people with an admirable type of character and the best possible chance to act in accordance with it . . . Liberalism rests on a vision of life: a Faustian vision. It exalts self-expression, self-mastery and the control over the environment, natural and social; the active pursuit of knowledge and the clash of ideas; the acceptance of personal responsibility for the decisions that shape one's life.[18]

As the discerning reader will have inferred from the stylistic verve and certitude of this passage, its author is none other than Brian Barry, albeit in a younger mode. At one time, Barry believed that philosophical liberals must embrace rational autonomy as the moral core of liberal society; now, without ever quite saying so, he has changed his mind.

Or has he? Despite the wedge Barry tries to drive between liberalism and a privileged position for rational autonomy, his preferred brand of liberalism continues tacitly to rely on the presumed superiority of secular rationalism. *Culture and Equality* is suffused with a commitment to rational autonomy as an ideal of living (which I share with Barry) and with a thinly veiled contempt for a wide range of religious beliefs and practices (which I do not). Let me offer one characteristic quotation as evidence. After mocking the claims of a religious sect that makes ritual use of cannabis, Barry remarks that "it might perhaps be said of many other religious truths that they too would be more easy to believe in under the influence of mind-altering drugs."[19]

The younger Brian Barry was more than willing to acknowledge the existence of plural and conflicting (but nonetheless legitimate) goods, principles, and outlooks. The later Barry more closely resembles Ronald Dworkin in his confidence that sound principles plus strenuous reasoning are equal to the Herculean task of finding singular right answers to most of life's problems. For my part, as I have argued throughout this book, I believe that Isaiah Berlin had it about right: The distinction between good and evil is objective, but the good things of life are heterogeneous, are not neatly rank-ordered, and cannot be combined into a single harmonious package. To live well is to choose a good life, which inevitably means excluding other good possibilities. The philosophical justification for social pluralism is the diversity of legitimate human goods. This same diversity undergirds what I am not alone in regarding as the liberal stance toward life – namely, a generous receptivity to ways of life other than one's own, and a deep commitment to making the effort to understand why others come to embrace outlooks that one regards as peculiar, even repellant. It is this enlarged imaginative sympathy that characterized Berlin's work. Would that egalitarian liberals shared it.

Barry claims that liberalism, rightly understood, gives individuals universally valid claims against various forms of oppression; I agree. The real work is to make out the content of these claims: too narrow, and individuals are left exposed to unconscionable evils; too broad, and both states and groups are debarred from pursuing legitimate courses of action. Barry claims that liberalism, rightly understood, offers a robust endorsement of freedom of association; again, I agree. Within broad limits, the state may not impose public norms on the internal life of groups so long as membership in these groups is voluntary and groups refrain from forbidden forms of coercion. The challenge is to determine when group practices constitute an affront to basic public goods that the state is obliged to defend with coercive power, and to define the conditions under which membership in a group should be construed as voluntary.

## 3 SUSAN OKIN

Susan Okin offered a critique of liberal pluralism from the standpoint of egalitarian feminism. In her last work, she focused on exit rights, which, as we have seen, are vital safeguards against oppression in a liberal pluralist order. She argued that pluralists – Joseph Raz, Chandran Kukathas, myself, and others – downplay the vital fact that women in many cultural and religious subgroups are less likely than men to be able to effectively exercise the right of exit. Because they cannot exit easily, they have a less than fair chance of influencing the internal practices of their group. Besides, they should not have to leave in search of fairness; they should have the right of fair treatment within their group of origin. Specifically, Okin accused me of inconsistency – because I allegedly treat race and gender differently – and indifference to women's diminished life chances.[20]

Let me begin by clearing away some underbrush. Okin was not the first to observe a tension between my defense of robust, substantive exit rights designed to ensure genuine individual choice, one the one hand, and my critique of autonomy-based liberalism on the other. Now is the time to resolve this by acknowledging an error of emphasis in *Liberal Pluralism*. In the course of arguing against placing a Socratic/Millian ideal of autonomy, understood as rational reflection and self-creation, at the center of liberal philosophy, I appeared to deny a place for a more modest conception of autonomy as freedom of choice, secured by internal as well as external conditions. This was never my intention, and I regret that my exuberant prose gave rise to a misunderstanding.

Jacob Levy offers a more balanced formulation, which I heartily endorse. There is an enduring division within the liberal tradition, he writes, that is once again becoming prominent:

On one side of this divide lies a pluralist liberalism, hostile to the central state and friendly toward local, customary, voluntary, or intermediate bodies and communities and associations. On the other we see a rationalist liberalism, committed to intellectual and equality before a unified law, opposed to arbitrary and irrational distinctions and inequalities, and determined to disrupt local tyrannies in religious and ethnic groups, the family, the plantation, feudal institutions, and the provincial countryside. Today the tension between these two plays out in debates among liberals about multiculturalism, freedom of association, federalism, and the family.

Levy goes on to make a crucial, and deeply pluralist, observation about this debate:

> It is not the case that a correct understanding of one of the key concepts – toleration, autonomy, diversity, freedom of association – will dissolve the conflict. There are genuine moral and liberal goods defended by each of the two streams of thought, and those goods are genuinely in tension with each other.[21]

This is what I have always believed. The real question is how to achieve a balance, defensible in theory and sustainable in practice, between these two dimensions of liberalism. My real quarrel is with liberals, such as Barry and Okin, who appear to assign a moral weight of near-zero to the pluralist dimension.

I turn now to the real disagreements. Citing my discussion of two Supreme Court cases, Okin charged that I treat racial discrimination as a more serious matter than gender discrimination. She failed to acknowledge that the two cases present different legal issues. In *Bob Jones University v. United States*,[22] the question before the Court was whether the Internal Revenue Service could revoke the University's tax exempt status on the grounds that it prohibited interracial dating. The Court held that the IRS could do so: Tax exemption is a privilege, not a right, and may be withdrawn when an organization's conduct is manifestly inimical to public policy. As the Court said, "The Government has a fundamental, over-riding interest in eradicating racial discrimination [that] substantially outweighs whatever burden denial of tax benefits places on petitioners' exercise of their religious beliefs."[23] I endorse both the Court's holding and its reasoning.

Note that the question was *not* whether some instrumentality of the state had the right to order a private, denominational university to abandon its internal policy, on pain of civil or criminal sanction. That step would have implicated basic rights of freedom of association and free exercise of religion that the Court has long defined and protected, and it would have called for an entirely different legal analysis. Even employing the line of reasoning it used to settle *Bob Jones*, the Court would almost certainly have found that unlike the mere revocation of tax exemption, a direct order to change the discriminatory policy would have failed the balancing test by imposing an "undue burden" on petitioners' free exercise.

I have reviewed this matter at some length to underscore my contention that the second case I discussed, *Ohio Civil Rights Commission v. Dayton Christian Schools, Inc.*,[24] raised an issue quite distinct from the first. The latter case revolved around a private fundamentalist school that had decided not to renew the contract of a pregnant married teacher because of its religiously based belief that mothers with young children should not work outside the home. After receiving a complaint from the teacher, the Ohio Civil Rights Commission found probable cause to conclude that the school had discriminated against an employee on the basis of religion, and proposed a consent order including full reinstatement with back pay. Here, unlike *Bob Jones*, the issue was not revocation of a state-conferred privilege but rather the state-imposed alteration of the school's internal, faith-based practice. What I said nearly a decade ago, and continue to assert today, is that there is, or ought to be, a powerful presumption against the state's taking this additional step.

Okin disagreed, and claimed that the Supreme Court was on her side, contrary to my assertion that the Court's decision did not resolve the substance of the controversy. In fact, it did not. The issue before the Court was jurisdictional, not substantive, and its holding merely remanded the case to lower courts for consideration of the merits of the issue.[25] So my position is hardly inconsistent with the Court's. Indeed, in an important decision handed down the very next year, the Court not only upheld the statutory exemption of religious organizations from the anti-employment discrimination provisions of Title VII of the Civil Rights Act, but extended its reach to a wide range of nonritual activities conducted under the aegis of such organizations.[26] It is Okin who disagreed with the Court, not me.

It is of course possible that the Court's holding is wrong, from a moral if not constitutional point of view. That is the issue on which Okin and I disagreed. I continue to defend the position that the Court has taken, on the theoretical grounds that Dayton Christian Schools offered a clear case that meets the conditions for robust exit rights. No evidence was presented that the teacher's original choice to submit to faith-based employment rules (and by the way, to resolve employment disputes through private negotiation rather than the judicial system) was anything other than free and uncoerced. No was there evidence that the teacher lacked meaningful opportunities to pursue her chosen career in other venues. Okin may have disliked the school's employment rules (as do I), but she could hardly have based an argument for forcibly changing them on the denial of meaningful exit rights. I am perfectly willing to entertain the possibility, which Okin stressed, that other fact patterns may constitute a systematic abrogation, warranting state intervention, of women's exit rights. But the Dayton case, for which she criticized me so severely, does not present such a pattern.

As far as I can tell, Okin's elaborate discussion of exit rights was a proxy for the deepest issue between us. She implicitly affirmed, and I explicitly deny, that a genuinely liberal state has an unlimited right to enforce general public principles (however meritorious) on all aspects of the social life within its jurisdiction. The state, she seemed to believe, may move to abolish discrimination in all its forms, wherever it may appear. If I am right about this, then Okin in effect embraced the doctrine of civic totalism, which I criticized at length in Chapter 3.

Perhaps I have misinterpreted Okin's position. Perhaps she did, after all, accept some restrictions on the state's power to enforce public principles throughout society. If so, it was incumbent on her to state where she would have drawn the line between permissible and impermissible exercises of state authority or (if I may be allowed antique terminology) between public and nonpublic matters. I have drawn and defended my line. To the best of my knowledge, Okin never did.

### Notes

1. Ronald Dworkin, *Sovereign Virtue: The Theory and Practice of Equality* (Cambridge, Mass: Harvard University Press, 2000). The following is drawn in part from my review, which appeared in *The Review of Politics* 63 (3) (2001): 607–611.
2. Dworkin, *Sovereign Virtue*, p. 5.
3. Dworkin, *Sovereign Virtue*, pp. 240–1.
4. Dworkin, *Sovereign Virtue*, p. 5.
5. For the so-called "envy test," see *Sovereign Virtue*, p. 67
6. Dworkin, *Sovereign Virtue*, p. 7.
7. Ibid.
8. Dworkin, *Sovereign Virtue*, pp. 290–1.
9. Brian Barry, *Political Argument: A Reissue with a New Introduction* (Berkeley, CA: University of California Press, 1990).
10. Brian Barry, *Theories of Justice* (Berkeley, CA: University of California Press, 1989).
11. Brian Barry, *Justice as Impartiality* (Oxford: Clarendon Press, 1995).
12. Brian Barry, *Culture and Equality: An Egalitarian Critique of Multiculturalism* (Cambridge, MA: Harvard University Press, 2001). The following remarks are drawn in part from my review, which appeared in *The Public Interest* 144 (Summer 2001): 100–108.
13. *Employment Division v. Smith*, 110 S. Ct 1595 (1990), at 1605.

14. Barry, *Culture and Equality*, p. 248.
15. Barry, *Culture and Equality*, p. 249.
16. William A. Galston, "Two Concepts of Liberalism," *Ethics* 105(3) (1995): 516–34.
17. Barry, *Culture and Equality*, pp. 16, 237.
18. Brian Barry, *The Liberal Theory of Justice* (Oxford: Clarendon Press, 1973), p. 126.
19. Barry, *Culture and Equality*, p. 39.
20. Susan Moller Okin, "Mistresses of Their Own Destiny": Group Rights, Gender, and Realistic Rights of Exit," *Ethics* 112 (2) (2002): 205–30.
21. Jacob T. Levy, "Liberalism's Divide, After Socialism and Before," *Social Philosophy and Policy* 20(1) (2003): 279, 281.
22. 461 U.S. 574 (1983).
23. 461 U.S. 574 (1983), at 604.
24. 477 U.S. 619 (1986).
25. 477 U.S. 619 (1986), at 629.
26. *Corporation of the Presiding Bishop v. Amos*, 483 U.S. 327.

# 11

# Liberal Pluralism Between Monism and Diversity

In this chapter, I continue to examine the major challenges to my account of liberal pluralism that have thus far emerged. These include claims, first, that my conception of liberal pluralism is inferior to rival understandings of liberalism that also rest, as mine does, on value pluralism; second, that value pluralism makes impossible any foundational or "comprehensive" liberal theory; third, that liberal pluralism is incompatible with democracy; and, finally, that value pluralism arbitrarily rules out the central claims of monotheism.

## 1 RIVAL CONCEPTIONS OF VALUE-PLURALIST LIBERALISM

As I have insisted throughout this book (and previously), my conception of liberal pluralism draws strength from the account of morality known as value pluralism. Still, fellow value pluralists offer accounts of politics that diverge sharply from mine. John Gray argues, in effect, that my politics is excessively prescriptive, so much so that it becomes inconsistent with value pluralism. By contrast, George Crowder argues that the political implications of value pluralism extend well beyond what I am prepared to affirm.

Gray's core thesis is that the morality of value pluralism leads to a politics of *modus vivendi.* The quest for "peaceful coexistence" is what is living in the liberal tradition today, *not* any particular specification of liberal rights, freedoms, or institutions. Isaiah Berlin was wrong to believe that value pluralism leads to, or is even consistent with, the endorsement of negative liberty (or for that matter any form of liberty) as a dominant human good, or to the vindication of liberty-protecting regimes as superior forms of political organization. Indeed, Gray insists, the range of good lives that human beings may lead is too wide to be contained in any one kind of political regime. A political theory of *modus vivendi* "is not the search for an ideal regime, liberal or otherwise."[1] The preamble to the constitution of a regime oriented to *modus vivendi* would speak of the blessings of coexistence rather than of liberty. It is from Hobbes that we have the most to learn today.[2]

Gray works mightily to distinguish his focus on peaceful coexistence from an antipluralist elevation of peace to the status of highest value. In the end, he fails. Consider, for example, the following proposition: "If one of the core projects of liberalism is a form of peaceful coexistence that is not held together by common beliefs, Hobbes is a liberal thinker *au fond*."[3] Au contraire: Hobbes's political philosophy rests squarely on shared belief. Recall this famous passage: "So long as a man is in the condition of mere nature, which is a condition of war, as private appetite is the measure of good, and evil; and consequently all men agree on this, that peace is good, and therefore also the way, or means of peace."[4] It is no exaggeration to say (indeed, Hobbes says it) that his entire account of the laws of nature and of politics represents "conclusions, or theorems" from this core proposition.[5]

Gray is ultimately led to acknowledge that to the extent that peaceful coexistence is, as Hobbes suggests, a substantive proposal about a human good that trumps others, then value pluralism does not logically entail *modus vivendi*. "If value pluralism tends to undermine . . . universalist claims, it cannot at the same time show peaceful coexistence to be a universal imperative."[6] What then lifts Gray's form of liberalism above the arbitrariness that he so severely criticizes in other forms? His answer: "The case for *modus vivendi* is not that it is some kind of transcendent value which all ways of life are bound to honor. It is that all or nearly all ways of life have interests that make peaceful coexistence worth pursuing."[7]

There are two important objections to this line of argument. First, Gray slides too quickly over the ways of life that do not and need not see peaceful coexistence as central. These modes of life are not confined to Nietzschean odes or some analytical philosopher's hypothetical example; they are the subject of front-page articles in today's newspapers. For many, it seems, peace itself is a contestable ideal.

Second, if peace is justified as generically conducive to a wide range of good lives, then we are forced to wonder whether it is the only political condition that plays this role. This reopens the question of the status of liberty within liberal thought. I have argued that to have a conception of the good life is to have an interest in living one's life in a manner that acts out, or expresses, that conception, and it is to have an interest in institutions that create a space for, and protect, each individual's ability to do so. This is the core meaning of "expressive liberty," which I have advanced as one of the three pillars of liberal pluralism. I fail to see why liberty, so understood, is more arbitrarily related to liberalism (or for that matter, to any conception of a minimally decent common life) than is peace.

It seems to me that Gray does not follow the logic of his own commitment to value pluralism to the end. What I mean is this: Value pluralism as Gray and I understand it suggests that above the line that separates human goods from the great evils of the human condition, there is a wide range within which various individual and communal ways of life are rationally defensible. Because there is no single, uniquely rational ordering or combination of values, no one can provide a valid reason, binding on all individuals, for a particular ranking or combination. There is therefore no basis for restrictive state policies whose justification rests uneliminably on the assertion that there is such a uniquely valuable ordering. As Steven Lukes puts it, "For the state to impose any single solution on some of its citizens is thus (not only from their standpoint) unreasonable."[8] Put in legal terms: Taken seriously, value pluralism generates a principle of estoppal that denies the admissibility of the sorts of claims that the bearers of state power have used throughout human history to justify restrictions on individuals' ability to live in accordance with diverse but defensible conceptions of what gives life meaning and worth. This principle of estoppal lends support to an understanding of liberal pluralism that incorporates a conception of liberty. I do not see how Gray can expel expressive liberty from liberalism, rightly understood, without at the same time (or for the same reasons) rejecting peaceful coexistence.[9] And if he does that, he is left with no definable political theory whatever.

By contrast, George Crowder believes that value pluralism leads to a strong form of liberalism whose central value is autonomy, understood as a form of positive rather than negative liberty. Crowder's argument is that in a moral world of plural values, it is choice that defines our lives. Not just any choice – *rational* choice. And in order to choose rationally among contending values, Crowder insists, "one needs to be autonomous." Autonomy requires not only the capacity to reflect critically on one's first-order desires, but also the understanding to do so from an explicitly pluralist standpoint that critically interrogates all priority rules among desires.[10]

While this line of argument certainly advances one permissible and attractive orientation within a pluralist society, I do not believe that it succeeds in showing that autonomy is a virtue that all individuals must possess.

In the first place, pluralism may actually circumscribe the role of rational choice: In a given choice situation, there may well be a range of legitimate alternatives that reason does not permit us to rank-order. When we incline toward an option, we may do so on the basis of background features of our lives and circumstances that we need not submit to further critical examination.

Second, while pluralism protects choice, it does not insist that all valid ways of life must reflect choice. From a pluralist point of view, many lives based on habit, tradition, or faith fall within the wide range of legitimacy. Value pluralism distinguishes between permitted and forbidden ways of life based mainly on the content of the lives themselves, not on the manner in which individuals come to espouse those lives.[11]

Third, value pluralism does not insist that all individuals live their lives as consciously aware and committed value pluralists. The reason is straightforward. It is one thing to say that X is true, another to say that truth is good, yet another to insist that truth is the highest good, or some sort of deontological side-constraint on legitimate ways of life. Many forms of what value pluralists must regard as illusions will embody other kinds of goodness. It is no part of value pluralism to equate illusion with badness *simpliciter.*

A concern at work here is that absent the conscious endorsement of value pluralism and the virtue of autonomy, individuals will have neither the habit of tolerance nor reasons for it.[12] This worry is misplaced. There are many roads to tolerance. Some run through value pluralism, others through ways of life that do not explicitly endorse value pluralism, still others through lives organized around one or another versions of antipluralism. Many religious faiths, for example, are led to the practice of tolerance through the logic of their own beliefs.

## 2 CAN VALUE PLURALISTS BE "COMPREHENSIVE LIBERALS"?

Robert Talisse has offered the most searching critique of the philosophical path that, I claim, leads from value pluralism to a species of liberalism.[13] He argues that there are three kinds of coherent relationships between value pluralism and liberal political theory. One can (1) affirm value pluralism and deny liberalism understood as a foundational, universalist thesis (roughly, Gray's position); (2) affirm liberalism while grounding it on nonpluralist premises, as Dworkin, Barry, and others do; or (3) reject the idea of comprehensive liberalism altogether and follow Rawls in constructing some form of "political" liberal theory.

By contrast, Talisse contends, my proposal for a comprehensive liberalism built on value pluralism is hopelessly incoherent. He offers three main arguments for his contention. First, he criticizes my negative argument for this connection. To argue, as I do, that value pluralism and liberalism are linked because no illiberal regime can justify its practices in a manner consistent with value pluralism is to engage in a suspect "burden-shifting." Otherwise put, it presupposes that liberal negative liberty is the "default position." Second, he denies that value pluralism in fact renders illiberal arrangements unreasonable: "There is nothing inconsistent in the idea of a state imposing a single way of life on its citizens without thereby making *any* claim about the worth of other ways of life." Third, he criticizes my claim that the "pervasive human desire to go our own way" means *ipso facto* that coercion stands in need of justification, on the grounds that the inference from the fact of desire to the badness of repressing it requires the premise of autonomy as an overriding value, a premise that no value pluralist can consistently endorse. Otherwise put, my presumption against coercion leaves me, against my intentions, in the camp of political liberals who appeal to basic ideas and principles implicit in liberal polities.

Concerning Talisse's first argument: I do not think my position that illiberal arrangements must discharge a burden of proof is idiosyncratic. Western political theory virtually begins with the question of why certain individuals or groups are entitled to rule others. Theorists divide on what counts as an acceptable answer. If value pluralism is the philosophically preferred account of the structure of the moral universe, then many traditional answers are ruled out. It seems uncontroversial to say that if X is true of domain A and has some bearing on what can be affirmed within domain B, then we cannot affirm as true any element of B that is inconsistent with X. My contention is that while illiberal associations with full exit rights are consistent with value pluralism, illiberal polities that impose a way of life on some subset of their citizens are not.

With regard to Talisse's second argument: Once again, imagine a dialogue between rulers and ruled. The rulers say, in effect, we will "establish" (secular or religious) way of life T as binding on all citizens. Some of the ruled object and ask why. *Ex hypothesi*, the rulers cannot respond by saying that T is preferable to (U, V, W, . . . n) for all citizens. Presumably, Talissian rulers will say instead that if T exceeds the value-pluralist threshold for goodness, they need no further justification. But the ruled can respond that the fact that they endorse (U, V, W, ... N) instead makes these ways of life preferable, not *simpliciter*, but for them. So it is not good enough to say that in the abstract, there is nothing to choose between T and its alternatives, because the fact that some members of the society endorse the alternatives means that there is something to choose between them. The rulers must then offer a sufficiently compelling reason to overcome the weight of endorsement.

It is not my view that no such reason ever exists. It may be the case that the costs to society, measured along another dimension, of not imposing a single way of life on all are so compelling as to override citizens' endorsement of competing alternatives. My point, once again, is that the authorities are obligated to make that case. Simply saying "We choose to establish A" is not good enough.

Nor, finally, does this commit me against my intentions to endorsing autonomy as a trumping value. My defense of expressive liberty rests on other grounds entirely. To prefer, for oneself, a particular way of life is not (only) to embrace some conception of what is good or true; it is to have the desire to live in accordance with that conception. Assuming that one's conception crosses the threshold of pluralist acceptability, social arrangements that needlessly restrict my ability to translate my convictions into the structure of my life deprive me of a great human good. A life lived with the requisite symmetry between the inner and the outer is a life of integrity. To live otherwise is to "live a lie," a point appreciated by groups ranging from Marranos to closeted gays. This idea of integrity has little to do with liberal autonomy, which is at most one way in which the value of integrity may be made real.

### 3 DOES LIBERAL PLURALISM UNDERMINE DEMOCRACY?

Stephen Macedo worries that liberal pluralism as I understand it is in tension with democracy. Indeed, he argues, "Galston's 'maximum feasible accommodation of diversity' ... is a dangerous assault on the democratic authority to make public policy."[14]

Let me begin by restating the obvious. Any account of liberal democracy imposes principled limits on the scope of democratic authority. So unless we are prepared to embrace what I have criticized as "civic totalism," the charge that a particular specification of principled limits restricts democratic authority misses the mark; any specification would do so.

The question then becomes whether my proposed principle is arbitrary and (worse) "dangerous." It is not arbitrary because it is the translation of the core concept of expressive liberty into the language of law and jurisprudence. It is not dangerous because its consequences are not what Macedo fears. A policy of accommodation does not mean that a democratic government cannot enact laws of broad application. It means only that certain considerations are enough to rebut the presumption that these laws will apply to particular groups. Consider the much-discussed case of *Employment Division v. Smith,* where the issue was whether, notwithstanding the state of Oregon's drug control statutes, Native Americans would be allowed to continue to use peyote in their religious rituals. Suppose the Court had returned an affirmative answer, citing the Free Exercise clause. This holding would not have nullified Oregon's drug laws. In the same way, permitting certain individuals to be "conscientious objectors" never came close to undermining the military draft.

Macedo also worries that "maximum feasible accommodation" somehow undermines liberalism's "traditional egalitarian impulses." It depends on what one means by egalitarianism. There is nothing about the principle that calls into question vigorous enforcement of civil rights laws, or a much more vigorous use of government's fiscal and economic powers to attack poverty and promote equal opportunity. (I favor both, and see no tension between them and my philosophical stance.)

On the other hand, if one thinks that egalitarianism requires every subunit of the community to organize itself in accordance with the polity's public principles, then Macedo has a point, but it is not particularly telling. In my version of liberal pluralism, the Catholic Church may choose to continue excluding women from its priesthood, while Episcopalians may choose to admit openly gay men and women into theirs. And the Boy Scouts may go in a different direction. This is certainly a restriction on the scope of democratic authority. But is it dangerous? On the contrary: It is far less dangerous than a democratic government that recognizes no limits on its power to reorganize expressive and intimate associations or to exercise jurisdiction over religious institutions.

Nicholas Meriwether seeks to turn the tables on me by arguing that a political theory based on value pluralism is more likely to invade the liberties of differing ways of life than are those guided by some forms of monism. He points out, quite correctly, that both secular and religious monists can arrive at principled defenses of expressive liberty. But he takes an additional step, charging that to use value pluralism as the public foundation for liberty would be "*every bit as emphatic and invasive as any theologically-based political regime.*"[15]

Here I must disagree, on grounds that apply to Rawls's political liberalism as well. My argument is not that liberal citizens must pledge allegiance to value pluralism as the community's official public creed. It is rather that as a philosophical matter, pluralism gives a more accurate account of our moral universe than do its competitors. Yes, an overlapping consensus may exist in the realm of public opinion, and it may be more politically prudent to rely on that consensus that on any single religious, metaphysical, or moral doctrine. But that does not imply that these foundational doctrines are irrelevant to political philosophy. There is no guarantee that what is philosophically defensible will coincide with what is publicly and politically desirable. To read the practical requirements of consensus back into the practice of philosophy is to distort and disfigure the process of rational inquiry.

## 4 VALUE PLURALISM AND THE THEOLOGICAL *SUMMUM BONUM*

Can value pluralism make room for religion? Many persons of faith believe, or fear, that it cannot, and they reject it for that reason. Consider the views of Nicholas Wolterstorff, one of the most philosophically sophisticated theologians of our time:

A dominant strand in Judaism, Christianity, and Islam alike holds that there is in fact a highest good for all human beings in all circumstances, that highest good consisting in being related rightly to God. Those within these three religions who hold this thesis specify somewhat differently what exactly that right relationship is; but that there is a highest good for everyone in all circumstances, and that that consists in being related to God in a certain way, is, as I say, the conviction of a dominant strand in each of these Abrahamic religions. Now I assume that . . . the value pluralist means to deny this claim. Accordingly, those who hold this theistic view concerning the highest good will not accept the premise of Galston's argument. In our present day American society, that's a large number of people; it might well be the majority.[16]

Let me respond, first politically, then theologically. When Americans are asked to choose between two propositions, "My religion is the one true faith leading to eternal life" and "Many religions lead to eternal life," 75 percent endorse the latter proposition and only 18 percent the former. Remarkably, commitment to this ecumenicism is seen across all faiths and backgrounds.[17] In light of this, the prevailing sentiment among America's faithful might be described roughly as follows: While one mountain in the range of human goods is the highest, there are many ways (perhaps an indefinitely large number) of scaling that peak, and there is no compelling reason to prefer one of these paths to the others, let alone to prevent others from following their preferred paths.[18]

Now to theology. While Wolterstorff is obviously right that the Abrahamic faiths endorse the general *concept* of the highest good as right relation to God, they disagree, not only among one another, but also internally, as to the specific *conception* of that right relation. A transcendent God is not only inexhaustibly infinite, beyond the capacity of finite speech to describe (let alone circumscribe), but also substantially hidden. Not surprisingly, as the Abrahamic faiths have developed over time, each has undergone a process of internal pluralization. Depending on how a specific religious community specifies and orders God's attributes and interprets God's word, there may be an endless variety of orientations – toward faith as opposed to works, the heart as opposed to the law, inner spirituality as opposed to external observance, self-improvement as opposed to social reform, retreat from the world as opposed to immersion in the world, contemplation as opposed to action, political innocence as opposed to worldliness, and so forth.

My point, briefly, is this: For the Abrahamic faiths, the unknowable inexhaustibility of God's nature recapitulates, at the level of theology, the diversity that value pluralists observe on the plane of the mundane. So to endorse the concept of right relation to God as the highest good is to leave room for much the same variation in conceptions of that right relation, and in corresponding ways of life, that we observe in secular thought. To be sure, those who believe that God has been fully, finally, and unequivocally revealed through a specific act must reject this theological pluralism as well as philosophical value pluralism. But this is hardly a majority of the faithful, and is certainly not required by faith in the Abrahamic God. (If anything, the reverse is true.) So value pluralism is consistent after all with the principal thrust of monotheism, and with the self-understanding of most of the communities that orient themselves monotheistically.

## Notes

1. John Gray, *Two Faces of Liberalism* (New York: New Press, 2000), pp. 5–6, 32, 94–6.
2. Gray, *Two Faces of Liberalism*, pp. 133–5.
3. Gray, *Two Faces of Liberalism*, p. 28.

4. Thomas Hobbes, *Leviathan* (Oxford: Oxford University Press, 1986), chapter 15.
5. Ibid.
6. Gray, *Two Faces of Liberalism*, p. 135.
7. Ibid.
8. Steven Lukes, *Moral Conflict and Politics* (Oxford: Clarendon Press, 1990), p. 20. For a fuller discussion of this and related points, see my *Liberal Pluralism: The Implications of Value Pluralism for Political Theory and Practice* (New York: Cambridge University Press, 2002), chapter 5.
9. Robert B. Talisse makes a similar point in his "Two-faced Liberalism: John Gray's Pluralist Politics and the Reinstatement of Enlightenment Liberalism," *Critical Review* 14 (4) (2000): 454–5. Also relevant on this point is Jonathan Riley, "Interpreting Berlin's Liberalism," *American Political Science Review* 95 (2) (June 2001): 283–95.
10. George Crowder, *Liberalism and Value Pluralism* (London: Continuum, 2002), pp. 207–9.
11. To be sure, as I noted in chapter 10, there are some minimal conditions for real as opposed to spurious choice, but they fall far short of the conditions for autonomy as Crowder defines it.
12. See Crowder, *Liberalism and Value Pluralism*, pp. 256–7, n8.
13. Robert B. Talisse, "Can Value Pluralists be Comprehensive Liberals?" forthcoming in *Contemporary Political Theory*. Available online at http://people.vanderbilt.edu/~robert.talisse/RBT_pluralist_liberals.pdf
14. Stephen Macedo, "The Perils of Diversity," *The American Prospect*, December 30, 2002, pp. 36–9.
15. Nicholas Meriwether, "The Irrelevance of Value Pluralism for Political Theory," speech given at the Eastern Regional Meeting of the Society of Christian Philosophers (Grantham, PA: November 15, 2002), *ms.* on file with the author, p. 13; Meriwether's emphasis.
16. Nicholas Wolterstorff, "Comments on William A. Galston's *Liberal Pluralism*," prepared for delivery at The Pew Forum on Religion and Public Life (Washington, DC: June 20, 2002), pp. 8–9.
17. "American Views on Religion, Politics, and Public Policy," The Pew Forum on Religion and Public Life and the Pew Research Center for the People and the Press, Washington DC, April 2002, pp. 11–12, 60.
18. For much more evidence along these lines, see Alan Wolfe, *One Nation, After All* (New York: Viking, 1998), chapter 2.

## 12

## Conclusion

### *Liberal Pluralism at Home and Abroad*

In an intellectual and political context reshaped by the events of September 11, 2001, it is necessary to state, as far as possible, the implications of liberal pluralism for the conduct of international as well as domestic affairs. As I have argued elsewhere, liberal pluralism stands opposed to the liberal triumphalism that enjoyed a vogue in the immediate wake of the fall of the Berlin Wall and the collapse of the Soviet Union. John Gray and other critics of liberal excess are right to emphasize the need for political flexibility and to suggest that differences of national history, culture, and circumstances should shape judgments about what specific political communities should do, here and now. Value pluralism distinguishes between the multiplicity of goods, on the one hand, and the great, undoubted evils of the human condition, on the other. To the extent that the international politics of liberal pluralism has a common core, it consists in the effort to ameliorate these evils and to work for their eventual eradication. Liberal pluralist internationalism overlaps with the international human rights movement and with some (though not all) of the specific measures set forth in the International Covenants on Civil and Political Rights and on Economic, Social, and Cultural Rights.[1]

Even in this domain, pluralism affects political judgments and strategies by sensitizing us to the possibility that in dire circumstances, even the most basic constituents of decent human lives may come into conflict. We may not be able to move against all the great evils of the human condition at the same time or with equal vigor. If political authorities have used repression to keep the lid on ethnic and political tensions, a pell-mell move to liberal institutions may unleash communal strife. Increasing the role of markets may prove counterproductive in the absence of transparency, a social safety net, and the appropriate framework of laws and regulatory institutions. Without elementary order and security, no progress is possible, but the means needed to maintain order in badly damaged societies may violate otherwise desirable public norms.

The conclusions of liberal pluralist "ideal theory" (whatever they may be) are manifestly inadequate for practical policymaking here and now. In some circumstances, the best response to ethnic strife may be constitution-making that emphasizes federalism and communal guarantees rather than political equality understood in individualist terms. In other circumstances, it may be necessary to undertake the division of dysfunctional multi-ethnic societies into a multiplicity of more homogeneous independent states. In still other circumstances, where diverse groups are geographically intermingled and cannot be disentangled without bloody strife, strong central institutions capable of wielding the threat of coercion to keep the peace may be the best anyone can do. And the kinds of institutions and policies needed to restrain the activities of international terrorists may require sacrifices of other important political goods.

Liberal pluralists can accept all the requisites of political prudence operating in highly imperfect and challenging circumstances. They can even accept that democracy as the United States and the parliamentary democracies variously understand it is not the only legitimate mode of government, especially if there is reason to believe that specific non-democratic governments enjoy a high level of public authorization and support. But liberal pluralists cannot accept the adequacy of political orders oriented toward peace and stability at the expense of other human goods such as basic liberty.

Liberal pluralists readily acknowledge that not all societies are, or need be, well disposed toward the preference of individual choice characteristic of advanced industrial societies. But they nonetheless believe that human beings everywhere bridle at repressive policies and rightly resist them when they can. While liberal pluralists celebrate legitimate diversity among cultures, they suspect that diversity will typically exist within cultures as well, and that a smoothly homogeneous official face reflects the covert operation of state power.

For those reasons, among others, liberal pluralists think it necessary and proper to advocate international institutions and policies that thwart oppression wherever it may occur, and to encourage their respective governments to support these institutions and policies. But we cannot leave individuals groaning under oppression while we wait for international pressure to induce domestic reform. At the very least, the same exit rights that restrain oppression within domestic societies should be available internationally as well. This means that no state has the right to prevent individuals from emigrating. And it implies a corresponding duty, binding on the international community as a whole, to ensure that these dissenting emigrants have someplace to go. The fair allocation among individual nation-states of the burdens flowing from this broad duty is an urgent moral imperative.[2]

While the guarantee of exit rights is necessary for international decency, it is unlikely to prove sufficient. Whatever independent moral value may be attached to national sovereignty, no pluralist can believe that it is the *summum bonum* of international relations, to be respected under all circumstances. The pluralist account of what I have called the great evils of the human condition – genocide, tyranny and oppression, wanton cruelty, malnutrition and starvation – offers the best starting point for understanding the circumstances in which humanitarian intervention in the affairs of other nations is, at the least, justified, and perhaps even required.[3] The development of such an understanding, and its incorporation into the basic structure of international law and conduct, is among the most urgent tasks facing the international community today.

### Notes

1. For interesting, if preliminary, efforts to think through the relationship between value pluralism, political pluralism, and international law, see Surya Prakash Sinha, *Legal Polycentricity and International Law* (Durham, NC: Carolina Academic Press, 1996) and Hanne Petersen and Henrik Zahle, *Legal Polycentricity: Consequences of Pluralism in Law* (Aldershot, UK: Dartmouth, 1995). In *Moral Conflict and Legal Reasoning* (Oxford: Hart Press, 1999), Scott Veitch offers a careful analysis of the relationship between value pluralism and legal structures, the implications of which for international law are potentially significant.
2. The remarks in this section represent an expansion and adaptation of arguments I first offered in *Liberal Pluralism*, chapter 5.
3. It is hard to read Samantha Power's *"A Problem from Hell": America and the Age of Genocide* (New York: Basic, 2002) without reaching the conclusion that the United States' failure to intervene in Rwanda was morally culpable.

# Index

## CONCEPTS

altruism, 100–3
  and impersonal values, 98–100
  and value pluralism, 111–12
  different capacities for, 97–8
  possibility of, 96

civic totalism, 23–4
  contemporary advocates of, 26–40,
    185
  historical roots of, 24–5
  state socialism as a form of, 167
  *See also* democracy, liberal; political
    pluralism
civil society, 122–3
community, 156
  and economic growth, 164
  as modus vivendi, 165
  as shared conceptions of justice, 166
  as shared purposes, 166–7
  as social cooperation, 156–8
conscience, freedom of, 45–6, 64–5,
    66–8
  and citizenship, 50–2
  and education, 50
  and pacifism, 49
  as defense against compulsion,
    60–2
  as free exercise of religion, 59–60

Barry on, 178–9
Frankfurter on, 52–5, 56–8, 62–4
Madison on, 46–9
Stone on, 55–6
*See also* expressive liberty
constitutionalism, 3–5, 117–18, 158

democracy, liberal, 1, 23, 25–6, 125–6
  *See also* civic totalism

economy, 121–2
expressive liberty, 2–3, 177–8
  *See also* conscience, freedom of

governance, 123–4
government, limits on, 1–5, 65–6,
    68–9
  *See also* liberal pluralism; political
    pluralism

individualism, 148–51
  relation of modern markets to,
    133–6

liberal pluralism, 3–5, 173, 179–81
  and democracy, 192–3
  and feminism, 182–5
  and international relations, 197–9

markets, 128–9, 162
  and civic virtue, 126, 143–4
  and the collapse of socialism, 124–5
  as condition of liberal democracy,
    125–6, 128
  corporations in, 164–5
  distributive outcomes of, 126
  effects on civic life of, 130–3,
    136–44
  versus politics, 144

philosophy
  moral, 7–8, 21, 97
  political, 7, 155
  public, 118–20
political pluralism, 1–2, 40–2
  contrasted with civic totalism, 24–5
  roots of, 23–4
  *See also* civic totalism

religion, 25, 40
responsibility
  and reciprocity, 168
  individual, 159, 163, 175–6
  mutual, 163–4, 167–8
  social, 160–1, 176
rights, 1

theory
  comprehensive, 4–5, 42
  political, 4, 42
tolerance, 4, 190

value pluralism 2, 6, 11–12, 154–5
  and comprehensive liberalism,
    190–2
  and moral motivation, 95
  and modus vivendi, 187–9
  and personal autonomy, 189–90
  and theology, 193–5
  commensurability in, 12–16, 19–20
  decisions guided by, 19–20
  value conflict in, 16–19
  versus monism, 174–5, 180–1
  versus pure egalitarianism, 177
virtue
  Aristotelian, 76–7, 82, 103–8
  as limit on self-interest, 152–4
  instrumental, 76–8, 80–1
  intrinsic, 76–8, 80–1
  Kantian, 76, 82
  political, 75–6, 78–80, 81–3, 88–90
    as limit on purposive action, 90–2
    as mean, 87–8
    in democracies, 83–6, 151–2

## NAMES

Abraham, 17
Allen, Woody, 158
Anderson, John, 84
Anderson, William F., 57
Arendt, Hannah, 87
Argentina, 126
Aristotle, 16, 18, 21, 24–5, 77, 78, 80,
    103–5, 106–8, 155, 156, 165
  approaches influenced by, 76, 77,
    80, 82, 87, 95
Army (U.S.), 135

Badhwar, Neera Kapur, 98, 114 n19
Barry, Brian, 176–82, 183, 191
Barry, Norman, 143
Becker, Gary, 127 n8

Berger, Peter, 128
Berlin, Isaiah, 2, 6, 11, 16, 21, 29, 109,
    173, 181, 187
Biden, Joseph, 88
Black, Hugo (Justice), 60, 61–2
Bodin, Jean, 25
Boy Scouts, 113
Brandeis, Louis D. (Justice), 49, 141
Bush, George H. W., 84, 86

Calvinism, 23, 25
Carney, Frederick, 25
Carson, Sonny, 90
Catholic Church, 37, 193
Chang, Ruth, 13, 14–15, 19–20
China, Peoples's Republic of, 127 n3

Christianity, 25, 34, 95, 108, 194
Christian Scientists, 166
Civil and Political Rights,
    International Covenant on, 197
Civil Rights Act (U.S.), 184
Combes, Emile, 24–5
Clinton, William J., 164
Crowder, George, 187, 189–90
Congress (U.S.), 164
    House of Representatives, 48–9
Constitution (U.S.), 5, 151–2, 158, 166
    Bill of Rights, 48–9, 61
    First Amendment, 66, 193
    Fourteenth Amendment, 49, 66
Croly, Herbert, 141
Cushman, Robert E., 57

Dahl, Robert, 26–7
Dahrendorf, Ralf, 149–50
de Tocqueville, Alexis, 133–4, 135,
    150–1
Declaration of Independence (U.S.),
    1, 5
Dewey, John, 27–9, 35
Dickens, Charles, 137
Douglas, William O. (Justice), 60,
    61–2
Dukakis, Michael, 84–5, 89
Dworkin, Ronald, 16–17, 173–6, 181,
    191

Economic, Social, and Cultural Rights,
    International Covenant on, 197
Eisgruber, Christopher, 66, 67
Enlightenment, 177, 180
Episcopalians, 193

Fennell, William, 56–7
Fishkin, James, 77
Foot, Philippa, 77
Frankfurter, Felix (Justice), 52–5,
    56–8, 62–4, 68, 70 n33
Friedman, Lawrence, 148–9
Friedman, Milton, 126, 161
Foley, Thomas, 91
Frost, Robert, 4
Fullinwider, Robert, 94 n14

Gandhi, Indira, 79
Genovese, Kitty, 107, 113 n12
GI Bill, 164
Giddens, Anthony, 149
Gray, John, 187–9, 197
Green, John Raeburn, 60
Gutmann, Amy, 33–5

Habermas, Jürgen, 26
Hampshire, Stuart, 75–6, 77, 92
Hampton, Jean, 98, 113 n5
Harlan, John Marshall (Justice), 67
Hayek, Friedrich, 124–5, 143
Hegel, G. W. F., 28
Helms, Jesse, 91–2
Hirschman, Albert, 150
Hobbes, Thomas, 24–5, 41, 178, 179,
    188
Hooker, Brad, 7
Hughes, Charles Evans (Chief
    Justice), 51–2
Hume, David, 12
Hunt, James, 91–2
Hutcheson, Francis, 5

Islam, 194

Jackson, Robert (Justice), 46, 60–1,
    65, 66
James, William, 29
Jefferson, Thomas, 47, 63, 141
Jehovah's Witnesses, 46, 53, 57,
    59
Jesus, 108
Johnson, Lyndon B., 82
Judaism, 34, 100, 110, 194

Kant, Immanuel, 28, 76, 82
Kateb, George, 29
Kelly, Walt, 86
Korsgaard, Christine M., 99–100
Kukathas, Chandran, 178, 182
Kennedy, Robert F., 142
Keynesian economics, 140, 141
King, Martin Luther, Jr., 91
King, Rodney, 165
Kinnock, Neil, 88

Kymlicka, Will, 178
Korea, South, 125

Lane, Robert, 138, 153
Larmore, Charles, 11
Levy, Jacob, 182–3
Lincoln, Abraham, 140, 165
  Gettysburg Address of, 118
Locke, John, 5
Lord's Prayer, 34
Lukes, Steven, 189

Macedo, Stephen, 24, 27–8, 192–4
Machiavelli, Niccolo, 75–6, 79, 88, 89
MacIntyre, Alasdair, 77
McReynolds, James (Justice), 50
Madison, James, 46–9, 65, 66, 151–2,
  178, 179
Marranos, 192
Mason, Jackie, 90
Meir, Golda, 79
"Memorial and Remonstrance," 47–8,
  178
Meriwether, Nicholas, 193–4
Michelangelo, 16
Mill, John Stuart, 182
Monroe, Kristen, 96, 100, 102, 107,
  109–10
Montesquieu, Baron de
  (Charles-Louis de Secondat), 137
Moore, G. E., 13
Moses, 67
Murphy, Frank (Justice), 59–60, 62

Nagel, Thomas, 75, 93 n1, 93 n7, 94
  n15, 98–9, 109, 113 n6
National and Community Service,
  Corporation for, 164
National Health Service (U.K.),
  175
Native Americans, 193
New Deal, 120, 123
New Democrats, 129
New Labour, 129
Newey, Glen, 12, 16, 18
Nicholls, David, 41–2
Nietzsche, Friedrich, 96, 188

Novak, Michael, 143–4
Nozick, Robert, 174
Nussbaum, Martha, 5, 76–7

Okin, Susan, 182–5
Olson, Mancur, 79

Pinochet, Augusto, 125, 126
Plato, 80, 117, 160, 179
Pledge of Allegiance (U.S.), 85
Powell, Thomas Reed, 57–8
Power, Samantha, 199 n3
Progressives, 120, 123, 140–1
Prudential Insurance, 135
Putin, Vladimir, 125
Putnam, Robert, 130–4

Rawls, John, 4, 7, 33, 34, 38–40, 42, 44
  n47, 117, 138, 157, 161, 165, 173,
  174, 175–6, 191, 194
Raz, Joseph, 19, 20, 182
Reagan, Ronald, 82
Reed, Stanley (Justice), 59
Reformation, the, 180
Regan, Donald, 13–14, 15–16, 20
Revolution, the Cultural (China), 97
Revolution, French, 97
Richards, Ann, 86
Roman law, 25
Roosevelt, Franklin D., 82, 118,
  158
Roosevelt, Theodore, 141
Ross, W. D., 7
Rousseau, Jean-Jacques, 24, 41, 117

Sacks, Jonathan, 143–4
Sager, Lawrence, 66, 67
Sandel, Michael, 140–2
Sasso, John, 88–9
Scalia, Antonin (Justice), 178–9
Scanlon, T. M., 33, 99
Sennett, Richard, 138–9
Shapiro, Ian, 35–8, 44 n40
Shaw, George Bernard, 19, 86
Shklar, Judith, 77
Smith, Rogers, 68
Socrates, 16, 182

Soviet Union, the, 126, 127 n3, 197
Stocker, Michael, 18
Stone, Harlan Fiske (Justice), 55–6, 59
Supreme Court (U.S.), 3, 45, 47, 49, 179, 193
Sutherland, George (Justice), 51

Talisse, Robert, 190–2
Taylor, Charles, 17
Thatcher, Margaret, 79
Thomas, Norman, 84
Thompson, Dennis, 33–5
Tribe, Laurence, 66, 67, 85

Unger, Roberto, 30–2, 35
United Kingdom, 145

Waldron, Jeremy, 27
Walzer, Michael, 75, 82–3, 136
Watson, James D., 106
Weber, Max, 75, 80, 81, 82, 92–3, 127 n3
Williams, Bernard, 75, 77, 81, 83, 87
Wolf, Susan, 109
Wolterstorff, Nicholas, 194–5

Yad Vashem, 96
Yugoslavia, 165
Young, Iris Marion, 178

## CASES

*Bob Jones University v. United States,* 183
*Boy Scouts of America v. Dale,* 23
*Cantwell v. Connecticut,* 47, 53, 58
*Employment Division v. Smith,* 69 n6, 178–9, 193
*Gilbert v. Minnesota,* 49
*Jones v. Opelika,* 59–60
*Lochner v. New York,* 49, 54
*Meyer v. Nebraska,* 50, 179

*Minersville v. Gobitis,* 46, 52–8, 62, 64, 65, 68
*Murdock v. Pennsylvania,* 60
*Ohio Civil Rights Commission v. Dayton Christian Schools, Inc.,* 184–5
*Pierce v. Society of Sisters,* 50, 54, 56–7, 179
*United States v. Macintosh,* 50–2
*United States v. Seeger,* 66
*Welsh v. United States,* 66–7
*West Virginia v. Barnette,* 46, 60–4, 65